DEADLY
TRIANGLE

DEADLY TRIANGLE

The Famous Architect, His Wife, Their Chauffeur, and Murder Most Foul

SUSAN GOLDENBERG

DUNDURN PRESS

Publisher: Kwame Scott Fraser | Acquiring editor: Kathryn Lane | Editor: Michael Carroll
Cover and interior designer: Karen Alexiou
Cover image: Background: Annie Spratt on Unsplash; mallet: Erik McLean on Unsplash; blood spatter: shutterstock.com/akepong srichaichana; Image of Francis Rattenbury: City of Victoria Archives, M10334; Image of Alma Rattenbury: City of Victoria Archives, M00846

Library and Archives Canada Cataloguing in Publication

Title: Deadly triangle : the famous architect, his wife, their chauffeur, and murder most foul / Susan Goldenberg.
Names: Goldenberg, Susan, author.
Description: Includes bibliographical references and index.
Identifiers: Canadiana (print) 20220252580 | Canadiana (ebook) 20220252947 | ISBN 9781459750302 (softcover) | ISBN 9781459750319 (PDF) | ISBN 9781459750326 (EPUB)
Subjects: LCSH: Rattenbury, Francis Mawson, 1867-1935—Death and burial. | LCSH: Murder—England—Bournemouth. | LCSH: Trials (Murder)—England.
Classification: LCC HV6535.G6 B68 2022 | DDC 364.152/30942338—dc23

We acknowledge the support of the Canada Council for the Arts and the Ontario Arts Council for our publishing program. We also acknowledge the financial support of the Government of Ontario, through the Ontario Book Publishing Tax Credit and Ontario Creates, and the Government of Canada.

Dundurn Press
1382 Queen Street East
Toronto, Ontario, Canada M4L 1C9
dundurn.com, @dundurnpress 𝕏 f ⊙

To my parents

Be careful what you wish for, lest it come true.
— *Aesop's Fables*, circa 260 BCE

CONTENTS

MAIN CHARACTERS

The Rattenburys

Francis Mawson Rattenbury, architect

Florence ("Florrie") Eleanor Nunn Rattenbury, Francis's first wife

Frank Rattenbury, Francis and Florence's son

Mary Rattenbury, Francis and Florence's daughter

Alma Victoria Clarke Dolling Pakenham Rattenbury, Francis's second wife

Christopher Pakenham Rattenbury, Alma's son with her second husband

John Rattenbury, Alma's son with Francis

Alma's Previous Husbands

Caledon Robert Radclyffe Dolling, Alma's first husband

Thomas Compton Pakenham, Alma's second husband

Alma's Parents and Other Relatives

Frances Wolff Clarke, Alma's mother

Walter Clarke, Alma's father

Ernest Wolff, Alma's uncle

People in Victoria

Margaret Catherine ("Daisy") Maclure, society and cultural leader

Samuel Maclure, Margaret's husband, an architect

Miss S.F. Smith, Alma's childhood music teacher

Frederick Adams, contractor, British Columbia Parliament Buildings

Ellen Howard, Florence's childhood guardian

People in Toronto
F.H. Torrington, director, Toronto College of Music

People in Bournemouth and Vicinity
Irene Riggs, Alma's companion-maid
Louise Maud Price, landlady
Dr. William O'Donnell, Alma's doctor
George Percy Stoner, the Rattenburys' chauffeur-handyman
George Reuben Russell Stoner, George Percy's father
Olive Stoner, George Percy's mother
Richard Stevens, Olive's brother and George Percy's uncle
Samuel and Elizabeth Stevens, George Percy's grandparents
D.A. Wood, Francis's friend
Shirley Hatton Jenks, Francis's friend and legal adviser
Alfred Rooke, a surgeon
Frederick Clements, a retired police officer

People in London
John Hall Morton, governor and chief medical officer of Holloway Prison
Keith Miller-Jones, Francis Rattenbury's nephew and John Rattenbury's
    godfather
Katherine Miller-Jones, Keith's sister
Daphne ("Pinkie") Kingham, Christopher Pakenham Rattenbury's aunt
Dr. Bathurst, a Harley Street doctor
Reginald Tabuteau, governor of Pentonville Prison

People in Christchurch
William Mitchell, a cowman

Alma's London Music Acquaintances
Simon Van Lier, head of Keith Prowse Company talent agency
Edward Frederick Lockton, a lyricist
Frank Titterton, a singer
Beatrice Esmond, Frank's accompanist/secretary

Bournemouth Police

Constable Arthur Ernest Bagwell
Inspector William James Mills
Detective Inspector William Goldsworthy Carter
Detective Constable Sidney George Bright

Lawyers/Judge

Robert Lewis-Manning, Alma's solicitor
E.W. Marshall Harvey, George Percy Stoner's solicitor
Terence James ("T.J.") O'Connor, Alma's lead counsel
Joshua Casswell, George Percy Stoner's counsel
Reginald Croom-Johnson, Crown prosecutor
Edward Anthony ("Tony") Hawke, junior Crown prosecutor
Justice Richard Somers Travers Humphreys, trial judge

PROLOGUE

Bournemouth, England, March 24, 1935, Near Midnight

A n elderly man slumps in his armchair, blood pouring from his head. His false teeth have flown out of his mouth. A heavy wood mallet dripping with blood is on the floor nearby. His young wife runs about barefoot, gulping whisky and crying out, "Look at him! Look at the blood! Someone has finished him!"

"One of the most dramatic 'triangle' cases," the Canadian Press news wire service wrote about the three main deadly triangle characters: victim Francis Mawson Rattenbury, a very famous architect, and the two people charged with his murder — his second wife, Alma, and her lover, the family chauffeur.

Francis's 1935 killing is in Wikipedia's list of "notable" murders in the U.K. since 1800, one of five singled out for the period 1931–40. Google calls his and Alma's premarital affair British Columbia's all-time most famous sex scandal.

Love, hate, abuse, squandered talent and wealth, lust, adultery, lies, deception, cocktails, whisky, cocaine, conventional versus uninhibited, class divisions, massive press coverage, riveted public, false confessions, hypocrisy, misogyny, biased trial, disputed verdict, shocking aftermath. This murder, this deadly triangle, had it all!

It sparked widespread debate over social mores and social strata distinctions, issues that remain today, making it of current significance, too.

No wonder it continues to fascinate.

FRANCIS

During his lifetime, admirers praised Francis Mawson Rattenbury as "a visionary, a genius." Critics called him "unscrupulous, a thief, fraudster, cheating husband and drunk."[1] All these descriptions were accurate.

Victoria, the capital of British Columbia, Canada's westernmost province, looks great largely due to him. He also changed the appearance of many other places in the province, as well as in the neighbouring province of Alberta, for the better.

However, Francis made many enemies along the way because he didn't handle success nicely. Rather, he was egotistical, rude, fiery-tempered, and frequently unprincipled, which led to sensational investigations that he managed to squirm out of. He overspent, overcharged, and overdrank.

Francis was born October 11, 1867, in Leeds, England, a large industrial city in West Yorkshire in northern England, the second son of John Owen Rattenbury and Mary Ann Mawson, whose relatives were prosperous textile merchants. At the time of Francis's birth, John was working for them but chafed under their supervision. In 1877, when Francis was 10, he quit to become a professional artist. He wasn't very good and didn't earn much. The family had to downgrade to a much smaller house.

Francis apprenticed in architecture at a practice owned by his mother's brothers. He was gifted, winning a national competition organized by the Royal Institute of British Architects when he was just 23. He was handsome and dashing as a young man, tall, slim, with red hair and moustache.

He didn't want to wait patiently to be promoted gradually through the ranks at his uncles' firm. He decided to start his own practice, not in England but in Vancouver, British Columbia's business centre. The province at the time was promoting itself as "a land of hope, promise, and opportunity." Francis arrived in May 1892 at age 24 and set up shop.

Unfolding events in British Columbia were in his favour. Provincial officials wanted Victoria to be regarded as a world-class city. They believed the best way to convey this was to replace the existing humble and squat wooden Parliament Building with a new imposing one that would give the capital status and prestige. They launched a design contest open to candidates across Canada and the United States. Francis is said to have learned about it because a notice for the competition coincidentally happened to be on the same page as the placement of an advertisement of his in Vancouver's *Daily World* on July 5, 1892. He had many rivals; all told, there were 67 submissions.

To prevent charges of bias, the judges instructed the contestants to submit their ideas under a descriptive pseudonym. Francis astutely appealed to local pride by calling himself "A British Columbia architect," saying his design was "to the glory of Our Queen."

He wasn't afraid to think big and had a flare for showmanship. Francis knew first impressions were important. For this reason, he said the Parliament should be at Victoria's Inner Harbour, the entrance to the city for most visitors. He proposed a complex of three multi-domed majestic buildings, a big centre one in which the legislative chamber would be and two smaller ones on either side for government offices. The newcomer to Canada promised to use B.C. sandstone and granite for the exterior, B.C. copper for the domes, and marble in the interior. He had a passion for marble.

When the five finalists were selected, Francis was the only one from Canada, giving him an advantage. Declared the winner on March 16, 1893, he had been in British Columbia only 10 months and was just 25. It was a remarkable achievement. "The buildings will afford a striking example of what Canadian materials, combined with Canadian skill, can effect," Victoria's *Daily Colonist* wrote enthusiastically and proudly the next day in an editorial. It heaped praise on Francis: "The competition for the Government buildings afforded him an opportunity of showing the knowledge and skill which he had acquired, particularly in this class of building, and against great odds. Success has crowned his endeavours and made for him a name, not only here but on the whole west coast."

Francis closed his Vancouver office and relocated to Victoria to oversee construction. It was problem-plagued, mainly due to him. He gained a reputation for unsavoury business practices, obtaining materials and funds through means that bordered on dishonesty.[2] He treated anyone who questioned him with contempt and had no respect for their experience. They regarded him as a rude, arrogant young pup. Frederick Adams, the building contractor, accused Francis of shortchanging him in payments and overspending on materials. They constantly quarrelled.

Adams desperately wanted to no longer deal with Francis. That led to his acting imprudently. On March 22, 1895, two years into the construction, he insisted that the *Velos*, a steamboat he had hired to take him to a marble stone quarry in the north on Haddington Island, proceed despite the captain warning it was extremely risky because of gale-force winds. Just 30 minutes into the trip, the fierce winds slammed the boat into rocks. It quickly sank, and most of those on board died, including Adams. Francis's detractors maintained he was partly to blame.

Francis had negotiated that he would be paid based on a percentage of the buildings' *final* cost. Apparently, the government foresaw no possibility that he would go overbudget; it soon realized it had made a big mistake. The original budget was $500,000; the final cost was $923,000, close to double, and equivalent to $21 million today. Thus, the payout to Francis would be much bigger than the government had anticipated. Naturally, officials were very displeased. They pored over work orders, memos, and accounts to ensure that he wouldn't profit from increased expenditures caused by his own mistakes or by extras he had included without government approval. The very public feud went on for two years.

Francis *had* made sloppy mistakes of the kind that even a rank amateur wouldn't. He had ignored the obvious — his pride and joy, the high-vaulted ceiling in the legislative chamber he designed, would swallow up sound. Politicians like to be heard. They were very annoyed at Francis, whose habit was to walk away from problems he created and let others clean up the mess. Finally, somebody, not him, came up with the bright idea to hang a huge salmon fishing net from the ceiling to improve the acoustics. (British Columbia has a large salmon fishing industry.)

Why in the world didn't he include a washroom in the suite of the lieutenant governor, the Crown's senior representative in the province? Was he trying to antagonize all VIPs, or did he simply pay no attention to detail? By the time the lieutenant governor and his guests had hiked to the faraway nearest washroom, it was filled. There was a lot of griping. Furthermore, Francis neglected to include a press gallery. It's not a good thing to irritate the press plus legislators who want their every word recorded by reporters. Francis made amends, sort of. He turned a high loft into a makeshift press gallery, but adding insult to insult, he made the only access a narrow, steep staircase. By the time they reached the top, reporters were huffing and puffing.[3] Francis didn't care whom he offended. But when he needed friends as he ran into difficulties in the future, he would find that he had alienated everyone, and nobody wanted to help.

Francis's Parliament Buildings win had thrust him into the limelight, and he quickly built up a clientele of the rich and powerful, which gave him entry into high society, his goal. He always pursued big assignments that would enhance his glory and his bank account; he was never interested in small-scale, lower-income projects. His other prestigious commissions during the 1890s included new courthouses (Vancouver, Chilliwack, Nanaimo); renovation of Victoria's courthouse; bank branches for the Bank of Montreal in Victoria, Rossland, New Westminster, and Nelson; upscale homes in Victoria; and office blocks in Vancouver and New Westminster. He designed a castle-style mansion for Calgary meatpacker tycoon Pat Burns, one of Canada's wealthiest businessmen, with 10 bedrooms and the previously unheard-of luxury of four bathrooms. It cost $32,000 (equivalent to $1 million today), $7,000 more than Francis had quoted, in keeping with his disdain for remaining within budget.

It took five years, until 1898, for the massive Parliament Buildings complex to be completed. The opening ceremonies were held on February 10, 1898, on a grand scale befitting this splendid, tangible expression of civic pride, the focal point of the city. Thousands lined up to see the "Marble Palace," the public's nickname for the marble-filled buildings. The day was declared a school holiday, and every student was given a picture of the buildings. Nearly 4,000 people asked to be included in the official reception in the legislative chamber, but there was only room for 650.

Francis was conspicuously absent. He was in England lining up investors for a paddlewheel steamer line that would operate from lakes in northern British Columbia to the Klondike River gold rush in Canada's adjacent Yukon Territory. Francis anticipated huge success as tens of thousands of people from around the world flocked to the site, hoping to strike it rich.[4]

He got the money and placed an order for three paddlewheel steamers. At this point, his business life intersected with his love life. He named the boats *Ora*, *Flora*, and *Nora*, after his lover, Florence ("Florrie") Eleanor Nunn, four years his junior. He had met her when visiting a friend who temporarily had his office in the boarding house where she lived. Her father, who had menial jobs on B.C. coastal steamships, died when she was young, and her mother deserted her and her brother, Charles, placing them in the care of an acquaintance, Eleanor Howard, the owner of the boarding house.

When Florrie became pregnant, Francis did what was then considered the proper thing to do — he married her. Victoria high society, unaware of the reason, was baffled. As Victoria's most eligible bachelor, he could easily have married into high circles. Their wedding was on June 18, 1898, at Victoria's Anglican Christ Church Cathedral, the church of choice for Victoria's upper tier. Only a handful of guests were invited.

In that era, the standard procedure was for well-to-do newlyweds to spend their honeymoon at a luxury resort. Not Francis. He saw his and Florrie's honeymoon as an ideal opportunity to reconnoitre the Chilkoot

Florrie Eleanor Nunn, Francis Rattenbury's first wife.

Trail, the overland route up through British Columbia to the lakes that his steamers would ply toward the Klondike. The trail is 33 miles long and rugged, and Florrie was in what was then euphemistically called "a delicate condition." She was lucky not to suffer a miscarriage.

Francis was also involved in the development of Oak Bay, a new luxury home subdivision on the east side of Victoria alongside the Strait of Georgia, which separates Victoria from mainland British Columbia. He designed a large gabled home for himself and his family, located on five waterfront acres. "The name Rattenbury chose for his home — *Iechinihl* — is unusual in that it doesn't reference an estate in the Old Country, but rather is a B.C. aboriginal term meaning 'a place of good things,'" *The Oak Bay Encyclopedia* says. "A second interpretation of the term is that speech was delivered to the tribes on that very spot. *Iechinihl* is situated near the mouth of Bowker Creek — a place with thousands of years of aboriginal history."

The five-mile-long main channel of Bowker Creek flows through sections of the Greater Victoria area, discharging at Oak Bay, on the east side, into the Georgia Strait. Oak Bay is part of the historical territory of the Coast Salish people of the Songhees First Nation. Evidence of their ancient settlements has been found along local shores.

In a letter written to his English family on May 30, 1900, Francis wrote about his choice of name:

> We have at last found a name for the house, Iechinihl, pronounced softly, Eye-a-chineel. It is an Indian name, and has a story connected with it. In one part of our garden I have often noticed a good many clam shells, and there is also a spring of fresh water. Mentioning this to an old timer, he told me that for centuries our particular garden had been an Indian camping ground and that they had a legend that formerly all men were dumb and looked at each other like owls. But one day on this very spot the good spirit conferred on them the gift of speech. The name means "The place where a good thing happened." (I. is "good" in Indian.)

In general usage, the estate became known as Icheneel. It is now the junior campus, kindergarten to Grade 5, of Glenlyon Norfolk School, a co-ed university preparatory institution.

Francis and Florrie planted flower beds, and he built a greenhouse. There was also a "coach house," a garage with living quarters above for the chauffeur, and a boathouse. Concerned that his view of nearby mountains would be blocked if the vacant island a few hundred yards offshore from Iechinihl

Iechinihl, Francis and Florrie Rattenbury's home in Victoria, British Columbia. The name is a Coast Salish term for "the place where a good thing happened." It wasn't.

were built on, he bought it. He gave the island tender, loving care, growing gorse in his greenhouse to plant on barren spots.

The baby, a boy born on January 1, 1899, was named Francis after his dad but was called "Frank." People who did the math realized that his birth was only seven months after the wedding. They now believed they knew the answer to why Francis married Florrie. Baby Frank was born with a clubfoot for which he had to have eight operations during childhood. It was never fully corrected.

Francis lavished gifts on Florrie of beautiful, costly jewellery and expensive furniture. He hired servants so that she wouldn't have to lift a finger — a cook, gardeners, uniformed chauffeur, maids, and a governess.

Their second child, a daughter, was born on May 11, 1904, and named Mary in honour of Francis's mother. He paid for the construction of a new school and home for the headmaster of St. Michael's School, which Frank attended, and declined to accept payment for plans he drew up for a new building for St. Margaret's School where Mary was enrolled.

The family lived the kind of life that wealthy people can afford. They were part of Oak Bay's nouveau riche social set and had their own tennis court. Florrie spent hours arranging flowers from their garden in baskets to be hung as decorations on trees at their frequent garden parties. Tea and birthday parties were held on the vast lawn, with guests sitting at white linen-covered tables under huge, protective umbrellas to shield them from the sun. Croquet was played on the lawn, too. There were annual Easter egg hunts for the children. Francis and Mary went horseback riding in formal equestrian habit. There was a family dog, Moses, that Francis doted on, and a family cat, Herman. Francis kept a collection of parrots. To all appearances, it was a happy family and Francis was an indulgent lord of the manor. He was also active in local politics, first as a councillor, then as reeve (mayor), working hard for Oak Bay to get good roads and a sewage system.

All this was Francis at his best, totally opposite to his ruthlessness in business — a real-life Dr. Jekyll and Mr. Hyde.

His hopes that he would make a fortune from his steamers were dashed when the Klondike gold rush petered out, but luckily his architectural practice continued to thrive. Just seven years after his arrival in British Columbia, he was the province's most prominent architect. His name was well known across Canada and internationally. He was still very young, only in his early thirties. He was so in demand that in one year alone he made $100,000, equivalent to well over a million dollars today. It was a sensationally quick rise to the top. As the 1900s approached, it looked as if he was secure at the pinnacle, supreme over everyone else.

On May 18, 1899, Government House, the official residence of the province's highest-ranking official, the lieutenant governor, was destroyed by a fire. A replacement, of course, was necessary. The government decided to hold a design contest as it had for the Parliament Buildings. Success had swelled Francis's ego. He felt the job should automatically go to him and refused to participate in the contest.

The government went ahead with the competition and selected a Vancouver firm. That was when Francis showed how unscrupulous and unethical he could be. He told all and sundry that the design was unworthy for a lieutenant governor and that the Vancouverites had only won because they lowballed the cost. His scheming worked. The government replaced the Vancouverites with him. Other firms that had followed the rules and entered the contest were furious.

Some decided to retaliate. They accused Francis of fraud — ordering materials in his own name rather than the government's as he should have and pocketing the commissions. His opponents also said he stole pieces of marble plus an ornate fireplace grate for his own house, pointing out that his kitchen had marble walls, countertops, and pantry shelves and that much of the servants' hallway to the kitchen was marble, all places where ordinarily it was very unusual to have marble. The grate was in his dining-room fireplace.

The government set up a members' investigative committee. Francis's opponents rubbed their hands in glee; finally, they thought, the full weight of the law would descend upon him and he would no longer be a menace. They rejoiced too soon. Francis was wily. He depicted himself as the victim of a smear campaign, insisting that he had consulted the government about expenditures. Yes, the dining-room fireplace grate was from Government House, but he hadn't stolen it. Rather, he had sent it to his house when he discovered it was too small for its intended placement in the residence's smoking room. (He could have, of course, instead returned it to the supplier.) Yes, the supplier had billed the government for the grate, but he had instructed that the error be corrected. As for the marble, he said he had ordered it for his own home, but it was mistakenly delivered to Government House. When he learned this, he said, he redirected the marble to his home. No, he had no supporting documents. "I am poor at record-keeping," he said. "I don't have a filing system. My desk is always piled high with unsorted paperwork."

The committee cleared Francis but said its decision might have been different had they been allowed more time.

Despite the controversy, the Canadian Pacific Railway (CPR), which was building luxury hotels along its cross-country train network, commissioned him to design one for Victoria. They called it the Empress but left unclear whether the name was in honour of reigning Queen Victoria who also had the title Empress of India or because of its "Empress" ocean line.[5]

The Empress Hotel and Parliament Buildings in Victoria, British Columbia.

Francis thought the best location was at the Inner Harbour, despite the poor condition of the site, which consisted of swampy tidal mud flats. He said the solution was land reclamation. Francis overrode people's concerns that the hotel would be in danger of sinking through the ground by saying there would be layers of supportive land. It would be a prestigious location because the Parliament Buildings were nearby. It was a winning argument; he was given the go-ahead. After the reclamation of the flats, a causeway was built to establish the frame behind which the hotel would stand on 10 acres of land. Victoria has always been grateful that Francis had this idea. The panorama stretching from the Empress to Parliament remains the city's signature image.

He dutifully adhered to the CPR's standard style for its hotels, an adaptation of the French château that CPR executives, many of whom had Scottish roots, called "Scottish Baronial," but added flourishes: gables, domed turrets, elaborately carved cornices, pointed arches, and a steep green slate roof. As he had with the Parliament Buildings, he used local materials — B.C. brick for the facade and copper for the roof. The facade was covered with ivy, a distinctive touch. The grounds were landscaped with flowers. The overall effect was Old World glamour and elegance.

Legislative Chamber (from the Bar of the House), Parliament Buildings, Victoria, British Columbia. The vaulted ceiling caused acoustical problems.

Upper Rotunda, Parliament Buildings, Victoria, British Columbia. British Columbia's motto *Splendor Sine Occasu* is Latin for "Splendour Without Diminishment."

When possible, Francis believed in natural lighting via transparent glass roofs that transmitted sunshine, and decided to go this route with the hotel's Palm Court on the ground floor. He made the room into a showpiece with a lofty stained-glass dome, a kaleidoscope of colours that shifted with the weather, entrancing people and bringing them back time after time. The dome collapsed during a New Year's Eve snowstorm in 1968 and was subsequently covered over and forgotten for two decades. During an overall restoration of the hotel in 1988, it was uncovered and faithfully reconstructed using old photographs and an original piece of glass found in a nearby shop as guides.

Once again, Francis had had a brilliant concept. And once more he was his own worst enemy. Still a hothead, he clashed frequently with the CPR's head architect, Walter S. Painter, over the hotel's interior layout. "I can see no reason, or at the very best a very inadequate reason, for the sweeping changes suggested by Mr. Painter," he complained, then refused a request from management that he come to its Montreal headquarters to discuss the situation, preferring to resign instead.

Francis's rupture with the CPR was the beginning of a series of misfortunes. He lost out in a competition design for the Saskatchewan legislature. The commission went instead to a Montreal firm, and his design for a Victoria high school was ridiculed as "barnlike."

The First World War caused a downturn in British Columbia's economy. Projects Francis had designed and counted on for income were cancelled. After the war, he got little work as people, tired of his arrogance and tantrums, turned to architects who weren't temperamental. Samuel Maclure, Francis's chief rival, particularly benefited.

Francis had spent almost all the money he had earned to purchase a large amount of land along the planned right-of-way of the Grand Trunk Railway expansion in British Columbia and was under contract to design hotels for the line, a direct competitor to the CPR. The railway, however, went bankrupt in 1918. He had gambled both his career and his savings on the Grand Trunk and lost.[6]

No private investor was interested in buying his land. The B.C. government purchased some on which to build housing for war veterans but at a lower price than he had paid, which greatly annoyed him. He was infuriated further when the government said he had to pay taxes on previously exempt land that he still owned. Francis appealed all the way to the Supreme Court of Canada with no success and had to liquidate.

Concurrent with his financial difficulties, his marriage was crumbling. He and Florrie had nothing in common outside their love for their children and for Iechinihl. Florrie was wonderful at flower arranging but otherwise boring. He was a social butterfly, fun-loving, hard-drinking, a talented pianist happy to play at parties, and therefore much in demand as a guest. He was at ease with Victoria's Old Money high society. Florrie, however, was snubbed because she lacked a blueblood pedigree and polish, and her brother, Charles, was a waiter. Another divisive issue was the move into Iechinihl, at Florrie's invitation, of Eleanor Howard, whom Florrie thought of as her mother. Francis hated the constant clacking of Eleanor's, "Grannie's," knitting needles.

The marriage became so strained that Francis and Florrie stopped speaking to each other. They communicated through their daughter, Mary, who still lived in the house.

Neither wanted to move out of Iechinihl, so they lived far apart in the house. Florrie spent her time in bed. She suffered from heart strain, probably due to the constant tension plus her substantial increase in weight. Unhappiness can prompt overeating. For his part, Francis consumed a bottle of whisky each night in his separate quarters, trying to dull his misery.

He perked up in 1921 when the Victoria Chamber of Commerce invited him to design a building to house an indoor heated sea-water public swimming pool that would be the largest of its type in the entire British Empire. His response was that a pool of that magnitude should be the centrepiece of another landmark that would distinguish Victoria — a transparent Crystal Garden, a glass-roofed building that would also contain a dance floor, tea garden, art gallery, shops, Turkish baths, and a fountain that would shoot water 40 feet into the air.

The estimated price tag was $200,000, then a very big sum, equivalent to $3 million today. The CPR offered to pay the bill if the city in return allowed it a number of tax write-offs. It was a shrewd manoeuvre since it would turn out that the write-offs amounted to more than its contribution. A city-wide referendum on the deal was scheduled.

A massive promotional campaign in favour of the project was launched by the Chamber of Commerce starring Francis. He loved being back in the limelight and addressed groups throughout the city — the Music Society, the Rotarians, the Alpine Garden Society, etc. His sketches were reproduced on thousands of handbills, shown on movie theatre screens, and displayed in shop windows.

The upshot was that the referendum, held on December 29, 1923, approved the deal. That evening, by chance, Francis met a beautiful young woman named Alma.

Francis Mawson Rattenbury at the time he met Alma Victoria Clarke Dolling Pakenham.

ALMA

M en were attracted to Alma like moths to a flame. She was entrancingly beautiful, with dark blond hair, mesmerizing grey eyes, a low, seductive voice, a shapely figure, and an engaging personality. She looked somewhat like beautiful blond 1930s movie screen siren Madeleine Carroll, described by the press as having "looks and allure in abundance."

Alma was born on June 9, 1892, in Victoria,[1] but in adulthood shaved several years off her age, which led to the press giving various birth years later than the actual one. Her middle name at first was Belle, later changed to Victoria.

Her mother (Mary) Frances (née Wolff) came from a family of music hall performers and had played minor roles in Gilbert and Sullivan operettas put on by the famous D'Oyly Carte Opera Company of London, England. Her father, Walter William Clarke, was a printing typesetter. They had emigrated from London the year before Alma's birth because Britain's economy had slumped and they thought they could do better in Canada, which was regarded as a land of opportunity, of a new start in life. They had had a child

MRS. RATTENBURY

Alma had been married twice already.

before Alma, a girl, who died in infancy, but had no further children after Alma. Frances's parents and siblings also moved to Victoria.

Walter got a job as a printer, first at Victoria's *Daily Times*, then at the B.C. government printing office. Frances recited poetry in shows her family did and opened a music school with a couple of them, where she taught elocution and deportment.

In 1897, the Clarkes, along with Frances's brother, Ernest, a pianist and violinist, moved to Kamloops in British Columbia's interior because it was enjoying an economic boom. Walter purchased a partnership in the *Kamloops Standard*, a weekly newspaper, doing everything — manager, editor, reporter, typesetter, and printer — out of his home, where he installed a printing press. Frances and Ernest opened a music school.

For the first 25 years of her life, Alma was a model of good behaviour. Nobody could have guessed that she would go on to become one of the world's most notorious women. Little Alma inherited musical talent from the Wolff side of her family, quickly learning how to play the piano and violin from Uncle Ernest at a very young age.

Her proud parents enrolled her at Kamloops's Zetland House, a private girls' day and boarding school where "pupils prepared for high-school matriculation and music examinations."[2]

Two years after the Clarkes settled in Kamloops, Walter unexpectedly inherited £10,000 from a relative in England.[3] According to the Bank of England inflation calculator, £10,000 in 1899 is equivalent to £1,294,659 today. In Canadian dollars, that's $2,212,041.

The Clarkes could now afford to do whatever they wanted. Walter sold his interest in the *Kamloops Standard* and became a roaming freelance journalist throughout Canada, moving around so much that he was nicknamed "The Rambler." His financial windfall made it possible to enroll Alma in Havergal College in Toronto, an expensive private boarding and day school for girls from kindergarten to Grade 12.[4] The family was also able to afford piano lessons for Alma under prominent Victoria music teacher Miss S.F. Smith, who advertised herself in Victoria's *Colonist* as teaching "pianoforte playing, theory of music, history and harmony."

Luckily for Alma, Miss Smith knew F.H. (Frederick Herbert) Torrington, head of the prestigious Toronto College of Music. She persuaded Torrington to come from Toronto to judge an examination of her students on July 7, 1906. Alma placed first, receiving both the Torrington Medal for Excellence and a scholarship to his school. It was a remarkable achievement. She had just turned 14. Alma was that rare type of musician — a child prodigy. Alma could transpose into 18 tonal keys, playing in any of them requested. In her entire career, she never received a bad review, extraordinary for a performer. Torrington called her "a musical wonder."

The awards made her a celebrity. Her name was so well known that the *Colonist* reported that she was "near death" from appendicitis in May 1907 and her parents were "in despair."[5] In those days, appendicitis was regarded as "a death sentence, like pneumonia." In August, the paper followed up with good news: "She is out of danger. All fears are dispersed. Miss Clarke is out of the hospital and making rapid progress towards complete convalescence."[6]

When she returned to the concert stage, the music and drama critic of Toronto's *Globe*, E.R. (Edwin Rodie) Parkhurst, lavished praise on her: "Brilliant; her execution is admirable and all with perfect ease, not the slightest extravagant movement."[7] A February 1910 article by Mary Lomas in *Westward Ho!*, a monthly B.C. periodical that called itself "The Magazine of the West," hailed her as "Western Canada's Musical Prodigy."[8]

In addition to being talented, Alma was very pretty. At performances she wore her long hair in ringlets with a big bow at the top. Her debut as a professional concert pianist on April 28, 1911, in Victoria, six weeks before her 18th birthday, received a rave review (no byline) from the *Daily Colonist*: "Musical genius, wonderful young virtuoso, mastery of tone, tune and touch, her playing seemed in tune with the Infinite."[9]

Around this time, Alma's father, who had given up journalism and gone into real estate in Vancouver, introduced her to Caledon Robert John Radclyffe Dolling, a handsome realtor in that city then in his early twenties. Distantly related to Irish aristocracy, he had emigrated from Ireland because his hopes of a British Army career had been dashed due to his poor eyesight. Alma and he fell head over heels in love with each other.

They married on July 23, 1913, in St. Mark's Church in Seattle where a sister of her mother lived. Her parents had separated. Her father was in England, so her mother escorted her down the aisle. Alma wore a "travelling suit" with a hat and carried a bouquet of lilies of the valley. Dolling's brother, Harry, later recalled that when they returned from their honeymoon car trip throughout British Columbia, he saw them coming out of Dolling's office: "She was dressed in a white suit and looked absolutely radiant, superb."[10]

A little over one year later, on August 4, 1914, Britain declared war on Germany because the latter had ignored Britain's ultimatum to end its invasion of Belgium. Canada was a self-governing dominion of the British Empire, but foreign affairs remained under British control. Thus, legally, Britain's declaration of war automatically brought Canada into the conflict.

Most Canadians then were of English, Scottish, Irish, and Welsh descent and believed that Canadians had a duty to fight on behalf of the British

Empire. But Canada had only a tiny standing army of 3,110 men, a two-ship navy, and no air force. Posters quickly went up calling for volunteers.

By the war's end, 619,000 Canadians had enlisted in the Canadian Expeditionary Force of whom 424,000 served overseas. Of these, 51,748 were killed in action.[11] In 1914, Canada's population was a little under eight million. Approximately 7 percent of the total population was in uniform at some point during the war, and hundreds of thousands of additional Canadians worked on the home front in support of the war effort.

Three days after war was declared, Dolling, whose eyesight had improved, applied for army service. He was accepted, and likely because of his Irish background, was assigned to the Royal Irish Fusiliers of Canada, which was stationed at Prince Rupert in northern British Columbia. Dolling was appointed second-in-command, and Alma went with him and gave piano performances for the soldiers. His commanding officer had high praise for Dolling: "A splendid officer, a magnificent character, and a fine man in every sense of the word."

Dolling, however, wanted to serve on the warfront. He got his wish after a year. In August 1915, he was dispatched to the Royal Welsh Fusiliers, who were fighting in France. Alma got a job at the British War Office in London so she could share his leaves in England. Her husband was awarded the Military Cross for gallantry and was made a captain. On August 10, 1916, he turned 30.

Tragically, 10 days later, on August 20, he was blown up by an enemy exploding shell. His commanding officer wrote, "I have lost a brilliant Company Commander and a friend." Dolling's few personal possessions were sent to Alma wrapped in his sleeping bag. Harry, Dolling's brother, helped her unroll it. The first items she saw were broken pieces of Dolling's glasses. "That was a terrible sight to her," Harry later recalled.[12]

Dolling is "Remembered with Honour" at Flatiron Copse Cemetery, Mametz, a Commonwealth cemetery for soldiers killed in the war, located in northern France.[13] Britain had a strict policy that fallen soldiers be buried in situ.

Alma was a widow at the age of only 24. She had loved Dolling deeply and was devasted by his death. Six months later, seeking to honour his service, she courageously signed up as a volunteer orderly with the highly respected Scottish Women's Hospital Organization.[14] Founded in 1914 by Elsie Inglis (1864–1917), a Scottish surgeon and suffragette, the organization was funded by the Scottish Federation of the National Union of Women's Suffragette Societies. It provided doctors, nurses, ambulance drivers, and orderlies — all women. The British War Office refused its offer of two fully equipped hospitals because its medical staff was all female. The French government, however, gratefully accepted them, placing them under the direction of the French Red Cross.

The new widow hoped that being in France would enable her to visit Dolling's gravesite at Flatiron Copse Cemetery. She was assigned to a 400-bed hospital that Scottish Women's Hospital had set up in the nearly 700-year-old Royaumont Abbey in northern France where intense fighting was occurring, resulting in many soldiers needing medical help.

Up to then, Alma had led a comfy, cocooned life. Now she was seeing the horrors of war first-hand. As a stretcher bearer, she carried the wounded under shellfire. It was her duty to support a soldier's leg on her shoulder as it was amputated and to wash away blood after surgeries. "The first time I had to hold a leg on my shoulder while it was being sawn off, the smell of blood and anaesthetic sickened me to the point that I thought I would faint, but I bore up because it frightened me to think I might drop the leg and possibly kill the patient," she wrote to an aunt. "Sleep??? I hardly know what I'm doing for naturally one does not *sleep* solidly during the few hours off. Am *supposed* to be asleep now; the noise is dreadful. There is a French push on now and one can hardly think straight for noise."[15]

Alma volunteered to help set up a battlefield hospital 50 miles to the east at the village of Villers-Cotterêts where there was fierce fighting. Conditions were primitive; staff slept on the ground, fending off mice by throwing a shoe at them. Alma was both a field orderly and battlefield ambulance driver. She was wounded twice but never considered quitting.

The French government expressed gratitude, awarding her the Croix de Guerre with star and palm for bravery.[16] "Precious little protection; *c'est la guerre*," she would tell her children when showing them the medal. Her tour of duty ended on January 6, 1918. Whether she managed to get to Dolling's gravesite is unknown.

In its coverage of Francis Rattenbury's murder, the press made no mention of Alma's valiant war service, choosing to depict her as totally despicable, but it shows there was good in her.

Maybe Alma became addicted to cocaine during the war as many soldiers and medical helpers on the front lines did to boost their energy, combat fatigue, and reduce anxiety, carrying on the habit when they returned to civilian life. Or maybe she didn't. Opinion was divided. Francis's children by his first marriage, the police who arrested Alma for Francis's murder, and her and Francis's son, John, all thought she was. But Dr. William O'Donnell, her doctor for several years, and her maid-companion, Irene Riggs, insisted she wasn't.

After her warfront service, Alma returned to London. War widows received only modest pension amounts from the government. Most, like Alma, had to spend considerable time dealing with bureaucracy to get the money. She asked British Columbia's agent-general in London, Sir Richard McBride, to help, which worked.

Her war experience had a profound impact on her psyche. Like many in her age group, she was traumatized and disillusioned. She became an entirely different person, going from responsible to aimless, part of what was called "The Lost Generation," which had no purposeful goals, was focused only on having uninhibited fun and instant gratification, and rebelled against conventional sexual mores. A one-person faithful relationship was regarded as outdated, replaced by "free love."

As part of the Lost Generation, Alma saw nothing wrong in embarking on an affair with a married man with a young daughter — Thomas Compton Pakenham, "Compy" to family and friends. As was common in these hedonistic times, Compy didn't believe in fidelity. He had been born in 1893, one year after Alma. Alma might have become enamoured because he reminded her somewhat of Dolling, in that he was about the same age and had also served in the war and received a Military Cross. Like Dolling, he was distantly related to Irish aristocracy. Alma probably was fascinated that he had been born and spent his early childhood in Japan, where his father was a naval attaché and was fluent in Japanese. He was charming.

Before the war, divorce was rare in most countries, including England (and Canada). It was considered scandalous, confined by expense to the rich and by legal restrictions requiring proof of adultery. People hired strangers for a staged adulterous assignation. It was a ridiculous situation. As Member of Parliament and law reform activist A.P. Herbert sardonically put it, "We are not here, Mr. Adam, to secure your happiness but to preserve the institution of marriage and the purity of the home. And therefore, one of you must commit adultery — someone has to behave impurely to uphold the Christian idea of purity."

In the first decade of the 20th century, it was far easier for men to get a divorce than women. Men could sue on the grounds of a single act of adultery; wives had to cite an additional reason such as desertion or cruelty. This double standard reflected the long-standing view that adultery was far more serious when committed by a wife than a husband because as the child bearer she could pass off a love affair child as her husband's.

Following the war, marriage breakdowns soared in England as returning soldiers and their spouses found they no longer loved each other. The disintegration of Pakenham's marriage was typical. He told his wife, Phyllis, he wanted a divorce, planning then to marry Alma. Phyllis filed for divorce in January 1919, naming Alma as the reason.

Alma and Compy decided to relocate to the United States. They sailed to New York City in September 1919, pretending they were married, although his divorce wasn't finalized yet. That occurred in January 1920, but Alma and Compy waited until July. A year later, on July 8, 1921, they had a son whom they named Compton Christopher, "Toffy" for short when he was a tot, "Christopher" when he was older. Pakenham wrote for newspapers and magazines and gave lectures on Japan under the assumed lofty title "Dr. Pakenham." Alma gave piano lessons; her concert career had dried up. Interest in concerts had declined, and in the prevailing chauvinism it was thought concert performances were solely a male purview while female pianists should be confined to teaching.

The Lost Generation morphed into the frenetic Roaring Twenties, a declaration of freedom from long-followed, inhibited conventions. *Roaring* because of the roaring (booming) economy, "loud/roaring music," and blatant/roaring rejection of tradition. Its chief aspects were the "Jazz Age," a term popularized by the title of a 1922 F. Scott Fitzgerald book, *Tales of the Jazz*

Age; "speakeasies" — nightclubs that ignored government Prohibition law; the sexy Charleston, Black Bottom, and Shimmy dance crazes; and "flappers" — uninhibited young women. The 1920s had their own vernacular, words and terms such as *cat's meow* and *bee's knees* ("that's great"); *baloney, bunk, applesauce, nerts, all wet,* and *hokum* ("nonsense"); *big cheese* ("important person"); *gams* ("sexy legs"); *bootlegger; gin mill* ("speakeasy"); *ritzy; heebie-jeebies* ("scared"); and *scram*.

The flapper was the symbol of the Roaring Twenties. The term is thought to have been inspired by behaviour similar to colourful butterflies flapping their wings. Symbolically speaking, they were "flapping their wings" to escape what they regarded as outdated. The byword of the flappers was to shatter old taboos. What traditionalists regarded as "scandalous" conduct, they thought of as "freedom." In defiance of much-entrenched social taboos, they drank; smoked with long, elegant cigarette holders; plucked their eyebrows; wore bright red lipstick, hitherto only something a "hussy" did; used eye makeup; cut their hair short ("bobbed it" with bangs); pursued men; danced solo if they wished; drove rather than being driven; and slept around, employing a new type of contraceptive, the latex diaphragm.

The freewheeling Charleston ("twist your feet, kick your legs, swing your arms in unison"), Black Bottom ("mooch to the left, then mooch to the right, hands on the hips, and do the mess around"), and Shimmy ("move the chest and shoulders rapidly back and forth, keep the rest of the body still") led to a new way of dressing.

In the past, the epitome of feminine beauty was the "hourglass" figure. Women wore a close-fitting boned and laces-tied undergarment that extended from below the chest to the hips called a corset, which thrust out bosoms and clinched in the waist to as narrow as 10 inches. Corsets weren't just uncomfortable; over time, they could misalign the spine. Arms and legs were covered. The clothing was representative of how constricted women's lives were.

Flappers wanted clothing designed to assist their liberation. Those who arrived at a dance hall wearing a corset removed it and put it in the "Corset Check Room" before going onto the dance floor. Flappers used a brassiere or went braless, taping their bosoms flat, and wore loose-fitting, sleeveless dresses, silk or satin beaded with sequins or rhinestones with fringed hemlines above the knees that jiggled provocatively, and bare legs or sheer silk stockings. An ornamental headband kept hair in place. They wore T-strap shoes, so called because a vertical strap from the pointed toe connected with a horizontal strap at the ankle, ensuring the shoe wouldn't fly off when kicking legs and swinging feet. At the top of their thighs, they wore alluring garters, a come-on signal and to tuck liquor flasks to circumvent Prohibition.

Alma dressed and behaved like a flapper. Pictures show her wearing bright red lipstick and eye makeup, hair bobbed with a narrow, jewelled hairband around her forehead. She chain-smoked cigarettes in an elegant holder, drank cocktails, and perhaps did the Charleston.

Compy and Alma's marriage quickly crumbled. Alma realized Pakenham was only superficially like Dolling. In character he was far different. Dolling had been faithful; Pakenham continued to have a roving eye. Alma divorced him in March 1923.[17] She got custody of Christopher, and they moved into her mother's apartment in Vancouver.

With the help of Margaret "Daisy" Maclure, the doyenne of Victoria high society and a leading patron of the arts along with her prominent architect husband, Samuel, Alma resumed her musical career with a series of recitals in Vancouver and Victoria. Since she had been away for many years and was performing under the name Mrs. Compton Pakenham, she was thought by Victoria's *Daily Colonist* to be a newcomer. The newspaper gave her a rave review on December 6, 1923: "Brilliant pianist, big concert style and polished technique combined with much individuality; assurance, authority and ease."[18]

Francis Mawson Rattenbury, a talented amateur pianist, was in the audience.

A few weeks later, on December 29, following an evening recital she had given in Victoria, Alma was relaxing over cocktails with a girlfriend, Kay, in the lounge of the city's premier hotel, the Empress, a Francis Mawson Rattenbury creation. It was six months after she had divorced Pakenham. In the adjacent dining room, a banquet was being held in celebration of the approval of the Crystal Garden project Francis had conceived. Francis, at the head table, was the guest of honour.

Alma and Kay heard the enthusiastic singing of "For He's a Jolly Good Fellow" coming from the room. "From the banqueting hall came the sounds of revelry and singing," Alma later wrote another friend. "These men whoever they were put some real enthusiasm into 'For He's a Jolly Good Fellow.' You know how raucous this can sound. This was quite different. So much so that we guessed every word was meant."

Curious, the two women peeked in. They saw that the singing was directed at a distinguished-looking, middle-aged, broadly smiling man sitting at the centre of the head table. "That's Francis Rattenbury, the famous architect," Kay said. "I know him slightly. If you want, I'll try to introduce you to him."

When the banquet ended, Francis strolled out to the lounge, and Kay seized the opportunity to say, "Good evening, Mr. Rattenbury."

"Good evening," he replied courteously.

"Of course," said Kay, "you won't remember me." She explained where she had been introduced to him.

Francis gallantly replied that he "remembered her very well." Then, turning to Alma, he said, "And I know who you are. I had the great pleasure to attend one of your concerts and was enthralled by your wonderful talent."

Alma beamed. Francis, indicating an empty chair at the table, asked whether he might sit with them for a moment.

"And so it was that I first met my Ratz," Alma gushingly wrote in her letter about the encounter to her friend. "The memory of that singing had gone to my head, and though I had resolved, as you know, never to marry again, but to devote myself to my music, that song seemed to make all the difference. Well, my dear, if I don't love him, I simply don't know what love is."

ALMA AND FRANCIS

Soon afterward, Alma and Francis ran into each other again at a ball at the big new home of W.F. Bullen, president of the British Columbia Marine Railway Company, and his wife.

Francis requested her to be his dance partner. As they danced, Alma flatteringly asked, "Do you know you have a lovely face?"

"Great Scott," Francis responded. "Have I? I'm going right home to have a look at it. I've never thought it worth looking at."

"I'm not joking," she said. "You have the kindest face I've ever seen."

Few men could resist such a come-on; Francis was enchanted. Alma was everything Florrie wasn't — young, glamorous, slim, sexy, scintillating, sophisticated, a woman of the world, at ease in society, talented, well known. By contrast, Florrie was plain and now stout. The mean-spirited compared her protruding eyes to the bulging eyes of a frog. She was a homebody with limited interests and wasn't much of a conversationalist.

For her part, Alma was attracted to Rattenbury, largely because he was rich and famous. His success made her discount that he was twice her age and on the verge of becoming an old man. She was a quintessential man-hunter, defined by the *Oxford English Dictionary* as "a woman who seeks to become acquainted with men especially for sexual purposes or with a view to marriage." She had already shown in her affair with the married Pakenham that she had no scruples in stealing a husband from his wife and child.

They quickly became lovers. He was 56, she, 31, although she said she was 26. Alma said the age difference between them didn't matter.

Ratz set her up in a nice house on upscale, quiet, tree-lined Niagara Street in southwest Victoria in the lovely James Bay district near Beacon Hill Park, the crown jewel of Victoria's parks. Its meandering footpaths past moss-covered oaks and woodland flowers, including violets, buttercups, and lilies, are perfect for a romantic stroll. Oak Bay, where Iechinihl, Francis and Florrie's home, was located, was across town on the southeast side.

At first it was a discreet back-street affair. Alma conveyed the impression that she valiantly was supporting herself and little Christopher, then two years old, by giving piano lessons that brought in enough money for her to afford the very nice house.

Some people were skeptical, but Daisy Maclure remained loyal. To underscore her support, she graciously invited Alma to bring Christopher with her for afternoon tea. Christopher, nicknamed "Toffy" by Alma, was going through the disruptive "terrible twos." He wreaked havoc, beginning with dragging chair cushions one by one to the centre of the floor and piling them atop one another. He proceeded to place precious ornaments at the pinnacle. Daisy held her breath; there was a strong chance the ornaments would topple off and break.

"Mummy doesn't want you to do that, Toffy," Alma admonished. However, she didn't try to stop him. Toffy ignored her. He climbed upon a now-cushion-less chair and tried to pull down pictures from the walls.

Daisy decided to intervene. "Don't let him get at the pictures," she said. "They might fall and hurt him." Amazingly, she invited Alma to bring Christopher again, which shows how much she was on Alma's side.

Daisy was a mother hen to Alma. When she heard that Alma wasn't feeling well, she generously took her hampers of food.

At this point, a brief digression is necessary to note that Daisy and Sam Maclure themselves didn't have a 100 percent squeaky-clean record. Years earlier, in August 1889, they had scandalized society when they eloped from Victoria to Vancouver to get married.[1]

But by 1924, 35 years later, this was ancient history. The Maclures were pillars of Victoria society. Besides, in terms of moral standards, a back-street affair like Alma and Francis's was far worse.

Victoria's upper echelon was a small circle with a very active grapevine. Efforts to keep secrets were doomed to failure, since somebody always found out and rapidly spread the news. Someone in the group was bound to catch proof of Francis and Alma's liaison, and someone soon did.

One day a friend of Daisy, who lived across the street from Alma, spotted Alma and Francis as they left Alma's house together, headed for nearby Beacon Hill Park with Daisy's latest food hamper. She reported her sighting to Daisy.

Victoria was a very uptight city. Its bywords were *respectability*, *probity*, *marital fidelity*, *gentility*, *decorum*, *refinement*, and *virtue*. Francis and Alma had broken all the rules. Even worse for them, they had deceived Daisy. She regarded that as unforgivable. Daisy might have been especially incensed that the lovers, unbeknownst to her, had been fuelling their romance with her food.

No matter what the era is, people hate being duped. Furious, Daisy telephoned Alma. "People have been saying things about you," she sputtered in fury, "and now I can see that they were right."

Alma didn't care what people thought. "Those same people will be begging to come to my house one day," she retorted. Alma failed to consider that Daisy, as the grand doyenne of Victoria, could break as well as make people. Daisy was now her enemy.

To show that they didn't care what Victoria's upper echelon thought, Alma and Francis merrily flaunted their relationship, beginning with a sensational entrance at a theatre performance. To be sure of attention, Francis wore a dramatic, swirling, floor-length velvet cape he had bought for the occasion. Alma was expensively begowned and bejewelled. Francis had booked a box where they would be in full view. Haut Victoria was aghast at their brazenness. Sam Maclure, who had known Francis for almost 30 years, summed up the horrified reaction. "The man's bewitched," he said, shaking his head in dismay.

Francis's children, Frank, then 25, and Mary, 20, told people they were certain Alma had bewitched him through hooking him on cocaine.

He sought a divorce from Florrie so he could marry Alma. Although he was an utter cad, she refused because divorce was frowned on both by religious strictures and by the social mores of the time. Canada prided itself on having one of the Western world's lowest divorce rates, only 543 all told in 1924. The largest number — 150 — was in British Columbia where Francis lived.[2]

Francis and Alma embarked on a fiendish harassment campaign to make Florrie's life so miserable that she would give in. He began by hiring movers to haul away the best furniture from Iechinihl. Florrie and her Chinese maid, Wee, grabbed the most valuable and locked them in Wee's room for which Francis had no key. In addition, Florrie held on to his treasured stock of imported champagne, which had been a priority on his removal list. There is some dark humour in this tug-of-war.

When Florrie didn't budge, Francis decided to take time out. He and Alma retreated from Victoria for two months. It was rumoured they were on a Mediterranean cruise.

On their return, according to Mary, who was also at Iechinihl, Francis brought Alma regularly to the house where she banged on the downstairs parlour piano night after night, deliberately tormenting Florrie who was bedridden, because of heart strain, overhead. "I came downstairs and pleaded for her to stop, but she and my father ignored me," Mary said.

One night, Mary told people, Alma even went as far as to thunderously pound Frédéric Chopin's famous, lugubrious "Funeral March." The powerful chords — *dum dum da dum* — echoed through the house and filled the ailing Florrie's room as she huddled in bed.

Francis ordered the electric light, heat, water, and telephone companies to cut off Florrie. The electric light company refused. Daisy Maclure, who lived nearby, brought food to Florrie, making clear whose side she was on.

When his measures didn't work, Francis had Florrie's bed hauled away. "Go to a boarding house," he sneered, a jab at Florrie's boarding-house past.[3]

Florrie had an iron will. She stayed put, got a sleeping cot, and used an apple crate as a chair.

The sensational story circulated around Victoria. Francis and Alma were regarded as deplorables.

Finally, Florrie filed for divorce, naming Alma as co-respondent, the second time in the space of just four years that she had been named as the other woman in a divorce suit. Florrie wanted revenge. She demanded that Francis give her money for a house of her own and hired Samuel Maclure, Daisy's husband, and Francis's number one foe professionally and personally, to design her a spacious hillside home at 1513 Prospect Place in Oak Bay perched above Iechinihl, down below at 1701 Beach Drive. As the well-known expression says, "Hell hath no fury like a woman scorned."

Even today, close to a century later, the story continues to be regarded as the most sensational sex scandal in British Columbia's history.

The divorce was granted on January 28, 1925, and Florrie and Mary departed Iechinihl. Just a little over two months later, on April 8, 1925, Francis and Alma were married in Bellingham, Washington, 50 miles south of Vancouver, an easy driving distance.[4] The location indicates that they realized that a B.C. ceremony would be boycotted.

Shortly after Alma moved into Iechinihl, Francis blissfully wrote his sister, Kate, in England: "We are very happy. Alma is a brick and a wonderfully bright and loveable companion. I can't imagine life without her and fortunately she seems as contented with me. With the disparity in years, it seems astonishing to me. We seem to enter everything together, as if we were the same age."

Alma had plenty of chutzpah — she telephoned Daisy. If she had hoped for a reconciliation, she went about it the wrong way. It was a disaster. "Mrs. Rattenbury speaking," she chirped.

"I know only one Mrs. Rattenbury — *the* Mrs. Rattenbury of Prospect Place," Daisy said glacially, and hung up.

Word of Daisy's ostracism rapidly spread. As always, Victoria society copied its behaviour on hers. Both Francis and Alma were blacklisted professionally and socially. Exacerbating the situation was Francis having alienated over many years fellow architects, clients, businesspeople, politicians, and many others. Now they had an opportunity to retaliate with impunity. The lieutenant governor made it clear they were persona non grata when he commissioned Sam Maclure, not Francis, to build him a luxury vacation retreat. People crossed the street rather than speak to them. Francis's children cut him out of their lives. Their loyalty was solidly to their mother. Also, Frank blamed Alma for Francis's refusal to give him $10,000 (equivalent today to CDN$157,935), no strings attached, to start a business. However, the reason might have been that Frank never stayed in a job long and was profligate with money.

To show whose side they were on, Victoria's upper echelon, which originally had snubbed Florrie, now warmly welcomed her into its circle. Her name began to appear in the social events column in Victoria's *Daily Colonist*. Her presence at teas and garden shows was regularly noted such as this June 12, 1926, item about a "fashionable wedding": "In the living room hung a magnificent floral bell, composed entirely of roses and maidenhair fern, the charming arrangement being the handiwork of Mrs. Florence Rattenbury."[5] Florrie was a leading figure in the Oak Bay Rose Society, which held its annual show and competition, in a twist of irony, at the Crystal Garden, a creation of her ex-husband. As was the practice with divorcées, now that she was divorced, Florrie called herself "Mrs. Florence Rattenbury": before, she had gone by "Mrs. F.M. Rattenbury."

On July 19, 1926, Alma's mother, Frances, married Russell Melville Smith, an agent with Union Steamships, a B.C. company, in Bellingham, Washington. He listed himself as single and 45, which was true. She listed herself as 50 and a widow, both falsehoods.[6] Having been born in 1864, her real age was 62. (In shaving years off her age, Alma was copying her mother.) Frances had started calling herself a widow in 1917 after her still-alive husband, Walter, moved permanently to Birmingham, England. They never formally divorced; divorces were difficult to obtain then, and the pretence of being widowed was a popular ploy. Walter was still living when she married Smith and remained so for the next three years. He died in May 1929 in Birmingham, according to a brief story in the *Province* (Vancouver) on May 17, 1929. Whether anyone outside of Alma knew Frances was committing bigamy is a question mark.

On December 27, 1928, Alma and Francis had a son whom they named John.

Florrie died on October 13, 1929. Shortly after her funeral, Mary answered the front door at Prospect Place to find to her great displeasure that the caller was Alma, who said she wished to extend her condolences. Mary suspected Alma's real motive wasn't sympathy but rather to wriggle back into society via her, and it also seemed to her that Alma was "high on drugs," so she ordered Alma to leave. When Alma reported the incident to Francis, he was furious. Already fed up with Mary's and Frank's disapproval of his marriage to Alma, he regarded Mary's snub of Alma as the final straw. In retaliation, he wrote a new will, dated December 18, 1929, disinheriting them and making Alma his sole heir.

The same day, Francis and Alma, along with John, then one, his nurse, Mrs. Almond, and Christopher, eight, departed on what the *Colonist* reported was an "indefinite length trip to Europe." But they had no intention of ever returning. They were pariahs, and there was no future for them in Victoria. In effect, they were being run out of town. Christopher later recalled that the family gardener, a Chinese man named Foy, "cried as we departed." Frank was also there to see them off, likely unaware that he had been disinherited. "Alma was in a stupor, booze, I suppose, or something else," he told people. "My father looked pretty blue, realizing what a frightful mistake he had made." Maybe Frank was telling the truth, or perhaps he was fabricating because of his hatred for them.

The couple began by travelling through the Panama Canal to Havana, Cuba. On the next leg, Havana to New York City, Francis lost a lot of money in poker games with players he hadn't realized were card sharps. He didn't want to fork over the money, so he decided to pull a fast one on them. While the ship was docked in New York, he and his family sneaked off in the middle of the night, took a train to Montreal, and sailed from there to Europe.[7]

They visited Venice, stayed in northern France for several months, and arrived in England on June 28, 1930, with a Fiat car Francis had bought in France. The circuitous journey from Victoria had taken six months. Francis and Alma had John baptized at Okehampton, a town in the southwest county of Devon, where Rattenbury roots dated back to the late 15th century when

Johannes von Ratenburg, a well-to-do burgher from southern Germany, settled in Okehampton and anglicized his name to John Rattenbury. When a later John Rattenbury was mayor of Okehampton in 1644, King Charles I stayed at his home during a visit to Devon. The first name "John" seems to have been passed on through generations of Rattenburys, indicated by Francis's father and son both being called "John."

Rattenbury and Alma, however, didn't want to live in Okehampton. It is inland, 25 miles from the nearest beach. Their choice was the southwest English Channel resort and retirement community of Bournemouth. There, George Percy Stoner, the third part of the deadly triangle, entered the story.

VILLA MADEIRA

ournemouth is on a low cliff overlooking the English Channel. Funiculars connect it to the beach below, it has seven miles of what it calls "golden" sandy beaches, and it is regarded as one of England's top holiday resorts. Like Victoria, British Columbia, it has a year-round pleasant climate, seaside location, genteel ambience, and unrushed pace. Its population was nearly three times that of Victoria. According to *Historical Population of Britain, A Vision of Britain Through Time*, November 29, 2014, Bournemouth's population in 1931 was 113,557. According to *Statistics Canada, Canada Year Book*, 1937, Victoria's population in 1931 was 39,082. The city was such a popular mecca for retirees that people joked, "Dover for the Continent, Bournemouth for the incontinent."

The word *bourne*, meaning "small stream," is a derivative of *burna*, Old English for "brook." The River Bourne flows nearby, its mouth at the English Channel, hence the name "Bournemouth."

In earlier days, the area was a deserted heathland occasionally visited by fishermen and smugglers. It was turned into a settlement by Lewis

Tregonwell (1758–1832), a local squire. As the story goes, his second wife, Henrietta, sank into melancholia after the death of their second child, Grosvenor, from an accidental double dose of medication. Tregonwell thought a holiday on the English Channel in Devon would lift her spirits.

During the holiday, the family visited a place known as "Bourne," which they found so delightful that they bought land in 1810 and built a house. More people moved in, the community was given the name "Bournemouth," it was marketed as a health resort, and received a boost when it was included in an 1841 book entitled *The Spas of England.* The village's growth accelerated with the introduction of railway service, and in 1870 it became a town.

In 1880, the town had a population of 17,000; by 1900, when railway connections to Bournemouth were fully developed, the population had risen to 60,000, and the community became a favourite location for retirees, vacationers, tourists, artists, and writers. As Bournemouth's growth increased in the early 20th century, cafés, theatres, cinemas, and hotels were opened in the town centre. Other structures included a war memorial in 1921 and the Bournemouth Pavilion in 1925, with a concert hall and grand theatre.

The Rattenburys lived on Bournemouth's East Cliff above the English Channel.

Villa Madeira in Bournemouth was much smaller than Iechinihl in Victoria.

The French windows of the drawing room at Villa Madeira led to the backyard.

All these attractions appealed to Francis and Alma, but the main reason they settled in Bournemouth was that it was cheaper than other coastal retirement/resort communities. Francis had to stretch out his finances, since his earning years were over and he had lost money in the 1929 stock market crash.

Francis rented Villa Madeira, the pretentious name of a detached house at Five Manor Road, from Louise Maud Price, the owner with her husband of a local tobacco shop. It cost £6.6 per week, equivalent to £475/CDN$820 today. Lined with pine trees, Manor Road is at the forefront of Bournemouth's East Cliff, providing a splendid view of the beach and channel below. The East Cliff and the beach had been connected since 1908 by a short funicular railway.

A low stone wall separated Villa Madeira from the street. The wooden gate in the middle led into a short walkway through a postage-stamp-size lawn to a small porch with a trellis and the stained-glass-panelled front door. Painted white, the house was two storeys with a balcony across the entire back of the second floor. There were five bedrooms, a dining room, drawing room (British term for "living room"), kitchen, two bathrooms, and an attached garage. In the nice-sized backyard, Alma planted lots of flowers, which she and Francis loved.

The house felt damp because there was no central heating. In those days, few homes in England had such an unaffordable luxury. Central heating didn't become commonplace until the 1970s.

◈　◈　◈

Alma and Francis had stopped sleeping together after John's birth, since Francis had become impotent. He converted the room at the end of the long ground-floor hallway into his bedroom. Alma's bedroom was upstairs. French doors led to the balcony.

The only telephone was in Francis's room. That the Rattenburys had a telephone was a sign they were comfortably off. A residential telephone then symbolized affluence in England. Fewer than 10 percent of the population were telephone subscribers. The majority used local pay phone boxes, which continued until the 1960s when improvements in home-phone technology brought down the price.

An adjoining door connected Francis's room and the drawing room, which would be the focal point of what the press would call "Murder at the Villa Madeira," the main set in the sensational drama. Twenty feet long and six feet wide, the room had French windows at the back that led into the garden. The wallpaper, carpet, and furniture upholstery were all floral-patterned, in keeping with Alma and Francis's love of flowers. They hung "Victorian prints" — romanticized pictures of the Victoria Era, such as pastoral scenes, festive family dinners, and demure maidens in virginal long white dresses.

The room's centrepiece was Alma's beloved grand piano, which she had shipped over from Iechinihl. There was a fireplace with a damask upholstered armchair on each side. The one on the right was always used by Francis. An autographed framed photo from well-known English tenor Frank Titterton who recorded songs Alma wrote hung above the fireplace. Close by were two mounted crossed swords and a pistol with a heavy butt.

Also in the room was a damask upholstered settee and a combination radio and record player machine. Alma danced around the room at all hours to hit records. She was a fan of singer Bing Crosby, and it was thought that she named the family's little terrier Dinah after the title of one of his many hits. The last thing Alma did each night before going upstairs to her room was to let the dog out through the drawing room's French windows into the backyard to do "her duty."

Christopher was enrolled as "Christopher Rattenbury" — although he wasn't officially adopted by Francis — at Cliff House School, a "pre-prep" private institution for boys seven to thirteen in Southbourne, a suburb of Bournemouth. Francis drove Christopher to Cliff House on Monday mornings in his Fiat and picked him up on Saturday to spend the weekend at Villa Madeira.

So much bad was said about Alma that it was ignored that she loved her children very much and that they loved her very much.

John was too young to attend Cliff House, so he spent the day with Alma. She woke him at dawn to go in the sea, with John riding on her back. The rest of the morning he played on the beach while she watched. Francis

Alma, John, and Francis, with John's nursemaid in the background, on Bournemouth Beach.

sometimes joined them. Afternoons were spent in Villa Madeira's backyard where Alma taught John how to garden. When it was time for his afternoon nap, she had a sun shelter canopy stored in the garage brought out to protect him from the strong sun. She taught him reading and dancing. Evenings were spent in the drawing room with Francis. Alma played the piano while John danced to the music, delighting Francis.

"One of my strongest memories of my early years was time I spent in the drawing room," John said in an interview he gave in 2007 to York Membrey of the *Times* of London. "My mother played the piano. Next to the piano was a low easel with a drawing of a building that Father had designed: clean, straight lines drawn on crisp white paper. An entrance door and steps. Trees on either side. Some hand lettering." This probably was the genesis of John following in his father's footsteps by becoming an architect, too. "I was thrilled with a wood toy house that Father made for me. I felt some awe for my father and a great sense of love for my mother."[1]

Alma always wore the latest fashions. She especially liked lounging pyjamas, which were in vogue in the 1930s.

On the weekends when Christopher was home, Alma took the two boys on picnics in nearby New Forest, a big park with the River Bourne flowing through. After the boys had a swim, they picnicked, and Alma played the violin. Christopher loved to draw, and his drawings were all over the house.

Alma not only had the looks of a movie star, she also had the mannerisms, flourishing her cigarette holder theatrically and speaking seductively. Like 1930s Hollywood sex symbol Jean Harlow, "the blonde bombshell," she didn't wear a brassiere. Harlow iced her breasts to keep them firm; perhaps Alma did, too. "Men like me because I don't wear a brassiere," Harlow famously said about her movie roles. "Women like me because I don't look like a girl who would steal a husband. At least not for long."

Most of the time, day and night, Alma wore slinky, elegant, silk "lounging pyjamas" popularized in the 1930s by Hollywood's sensuous beauties. The clinging trousers flared gracefully at the bottom. The hip-length jacket, long-sleeved or sleeveless over a blouse, was often lavishly embroidered.

High heels and sometimes a jewelled headband were the finishing touches. Lounging pyjamas were for women who had the money to recline idly on a sofa for hours, smoking.

Late at night, Alma danced barefoot in the garden to records she put on the drawing room record machine, with the French windows open so she could hear the music. She then lay in bed until midday, chain-smoking and drinking coffee brought by her maid.

Word of her bohemian behaviour spread throughout Bournemouth, scandalizing the conventional, sedate community. Bournemouth matrons wore sensible tweed skirts, wool cardigans, flat tied shoes, or low pumps, thought smoking was unladylike, and didn't inconsiderately blare music late at night, disturbing neighbours. They snubbed her. It was the same situation as in Victoria. The only frequent female visitor was landlady Mrs. Price whom Alma regarded as a busybody.

Lonely, Alma placed an ad in the *Bournemouth Daily Echo* for a "companion-help." The ad was answered by Irene Riggs, a local girl, 22, the daughter of a gravedigger, who had been in domestic service since the age of 14.

Irene and Alma were complete opposites. Alma was beautiful and extroverted, Irene rather plain and shy. Despite or perhaps because of their differences, they became friends. Alma wasn't a class-conscious snob, in stark contrast to the social barriers prevalent in England. "I regard everyone as equals," she liked to say. She called Irene by her first name rather than the usual snooty practice of addressing servants by their surnames and told Irene to call her "darling" instead of Mrs. Rattenbury.

"We were two great friends rather than mistress and maid," Irene later said. "She was the most kind-hearted woman in the world and equally as generous. She often gave me clothes and money. She helped anyone in need that she came across, friend or stranger, with money and gave away her belongings to anyone who admired them. She frequently asked me to accompany her on trips away, to restaurants and to the theatre."[2]

Alma suffered from chronic mastoiditis. Immediately on coming to Bournemouth, she turned to local society doctor William O'Donnell for help. In his early sixties, O'Donnell had arrived in Bournemouth a few years before the Rattenburys, following practising in several communities throughout Britain. In addition to seeing patients at his Richmond Chambers office near Bournemouth's town square, O'Donnell made house calls. Balding, he wore dapper, expensive suits and dark-rimmed glasses. He chain-smoked, as did Alma.

There were no antibiotics then to treat mastoiditis. O'Donnell cleaned Alma's ears from time to time and referred her to local surgeon Alfred Rooke when the mastoid needed draining. Since there was no government regulation yet of medical fees, O'Donnell was able to charge exorbitant rates. Alma was a very lucrative patient. Between March 20, 1934, and February 1935 alone, he went to see her at Villa Madeira 70 times for which he charged "50 guineas total, maybe more," equivalent to £4,260/CDN$7,250 today.

Over time he and Alma became good friends; exactly how good was something people speculated about. She frequently asked him to stay on after a house call and join her and Francis for dinner.

Going to phrenologists was a fad in the 1930s. They claimed they could determine personality and intelligence through examination with their fingertips and palms of a person's skull. Alma took Christopher to Bournemouth phrenologist W.G. Clarke for diagnosis because she was concerned about the "weird dark pictures" he was drawing. Pleased that Clarke's conclusions "were exactly what Christopher was like," she paid him an extra £5 in gratitude, which was substantial then, equal to £335/ CDN$590 today. She asked him to analyze her, too. Rattenbury accompanied her to the appointment, and Clarke told her to "guard against emotional excitement."

Alma began to compose romantic tunes with the aim of getting them published even though the times weren't propitious. The Great Depression was at its worst. Sheet music was considered a wasteful luxury. Music publishers were publishing and selling little. Public taste had largely shifted to bouncy "swing." Nevertheless, Alma forged ahead with Francis's enthusiastic support. Years in business had instilled in him the importance of good connections. To gain interviews for Alma, he obtained letters of introductions from Sir Daniel Godfrey, conductor of the Bournemouth Symphony Orchestra, and British Columbia's then agent-general to London, Frederick Parker Burden.

The letters worked. Simon Van Lier, the head of Keith Prowse Company, said by Godfrey to be "*the* people" for Alma's style of music, agreed to see her. Van Lier at first listened indifferently to Alma, but within minutes said, "I am greatly impressed. I'll publish them." Van Lier later recalled, "Rattenbury danced for joy and clasped his young wife affectionately."

The music publisher took Alma and Francis to the elegant Mayfair Hotel for a celebratory dinner, declaring throughout that Alma possessed "one of the scarcest gifts of humanity — a mind teeming with exquisite tunes."[3]

Alma adopted the professional name "Lozanne," likely after the Lozanne district in southeastern France. Van Lier teamed her with Edward Frederick Lockton (1876–1940), a prolific English writer of sentimental song lyrics.[4]

Alma believed a tenor singer would do the most justice to her songs. She bought a selection of records by British tenors to pick her choice. As soon as she heard the first notes sung by Frank Titterton, a well-known and respected solo tenor recitalist and recording artist, she declared, "That is the voice for my songs." She asked Francis, in his role as her agent and manager, to write to Titterton, requesting a lunch meeting at a London hotel of his choice. Titterton brought along his accompanist/secretary Beatrice Esmond. He later recalled,

> We found Mr. and Mrs. Rattenbury to be a striking-looking couple. Mrs. Rattenbury was very smartly dressed, and her conversation was that of a well-travelled, cultured woman with keen powers of observation. Her intense emotionalism, which since has impressed itself on me over and over again, was apparent at that first meeting. At one moment she would be wildly gay, and would fling her arms in the air to emphasize her voluble flow of words. The next moment she would be silent and subdued. Her eyes, so grey and magnetic, compelled attention to everything she said. I noticed particularly — as I have since noticed often — they very intense way in which she looks into one's face and her eyes become large with emotion or excitement.[5]

Titterton thought Francis to be "a man of the most genial personality who told a good story as well as he sang a romantic ballad." They met frequently from then on — lunch, dinner, sometimes at Titterton's estate, Shelmerdene, outside London, dancing, and the theatre. Titterton found that Alma "liked festivity but didn't drink. She never took anything stronger than orange juice, except on one occasion when she had a little champagne to celebrate the broadcasting of some of her music."

The British Library in London has recordings and scores of Alma's music catalogued under "Lozanne." The biggest Alma/Lockton/Titterton hit was "Dark-Haired Marie," which can be heard in a YouTube video that shows Alma, in a formal gown, accompanying Titterton, formally dressed in tails, on piano.[6]

> Are you waiting in your garden
> By the deep wide azure sea?
> Are you waiting for your loveship,
> Dark-haired Marie?
>
> Through the flowery golden springtime,
> Where the summer winds blow free,
> Through the lovely days of autumn,
> Dark-haired Marie.
>
> I am far across the waters,
> But I hear you call to me,
> In my dreams your eyes are shining,
> Dark-haired Marie!
>
> I shall come to claim you someday,
> In my arms at last you'll be,
> I shall kiss your lips and love you,
> Dark-haired Marie.

The public wasn't interested in her old-fashioned songs, so Van Lier dropped her and Titterton drifted away. Concurrently, Francis was unable to get anyone to back construction of a row of flats he designed on speculation.

The 30-year age difference that Francis and Alma had dismissed as inconsequential when they began their relationship a decade earlier became a big problem. Nearing 70, he was, for that era, considered an old man. He was no longer handsome. His once red hair had turned grey and was thinning. His face was mottled from decades of heavy drinking. Francis no longer had his own teeth and now wore a full set of dentures. He had almost totally lost his hearing and couldn't move swiftly. Alma, on the other hand, was in peak condition.

Constant over-drinking, such as Francis had always engaged in, might have caused his impotence. The resultant depression can lead to heavy drinking to dull the misery.[7] It's a vicious circle.

Francis might also have been going through male menopause, a decrease in testosterone related to aging that causes a decline in sexual potency. "I didn't love him," Alma said at her trial. "I was more of a companion than anything."

He consumed a bottle of whisky every night, drinking himself into a stupor downstairs in the drawing room after she went upstairs to bed. Alma had been an occasional social drinker when they married. But she found life with Francis "so monotonous" that she took, as she put it at her trial, "too many cocktails and too much wine." She went on days-long binges with brief periods in between of abstinence.

"Give it up," Dr. O'Donnell urged.

"Not drink at all?" she replied, aghast.

"No," he reiterated.

She ignored him.

"She always was very excited, unstable, when in drink and when she didn't get her own way," O'Donnell later testified. "She didn't habitually drink. She went on drinking bouts." Was she perhaps using cocaine and/ or heroin, both popular in that era among upper-class society, including women? Did that explain why she had a hypodermic needle in her medicine cabinet? O'Donnell said, "She was averse to any treatment which she considered dope."

Irene Riggs also insisted that Alma didn't use illegal drugs. She said the hypodermic syringe was for injections that Christopher's doctor had told her to give him for glandular problems in his legs.

"By now it was not a happy house," John said when York Membrey of the *Times* interviewed him in 2007. "My father was reclusive and wasn't a happy man. The age gap between my parents was a problem. He was fast becoming an old man; she was a vibrant, beautiful woman and wasn't only getting into drink, I think she might have been getting into drugs, too."[8]

Or, to speculate, were Alma's mood swings due to bipolar disorder, not understood then? It's aggravated by drinking.[9]

Francis and Alma quarrelled bitterly over money. They lived entirely on his savings. He gave her an allowance of £1,000 a year for personal and household expenses, equivalent to £70,000/CDN$120,000 today. He thought he was generous; she thought him "very close, not very generous," as she said at her trial, because not much was left for her after she paid food, maintenance, and repair bills. She was often overdrawn at the bank. "He lost his temper on several occasions. People said he was kind and gentle. He wasn't in private." In Victoria, he had displayed his temper in public with government officials, clients, and anyone else he disliked.

Francis complained, "You're wasteful, extravagant, and reckless."

"He was always talking as if he was running out of money," Alma said at her trial.[10] "It was a case of the lamb calling wolf. If it was so, we would not have believed him. All his life he talked like that so that no one ever took him seriously on the point of money. I always kept him pacified so as not to rouse his temper."

She told him lies to get more money. "That way there were no rows," she said. He always accepted her invented stories: "I always agreed to everything with a smile. All he saw was a smile, all he heard was 'yes, darling,' 'no, darling,' a mask that agreed with his every mood. And heaven help one if they did otherwise." She took to asking him for more money when he'd had several whiskies and was feeling mellow. "I don't think I ever spoke one word of truth to Ratz," she said at her trial. "He knew as much about me as I know about Timbuktu."

Upset that he couldn't get anyone interested in his flats proposal, Francis frequently said he wished to kill himself. "I'll stick my head in the oven," he said over and over. British ovens ran on gas, not electricity, as most do in Canada.

Alma pleaded that he not and did her best to be sympathetic about what she called "his blues." But over time she got annoyed at his constant harping on the subject. Late at night on July 9, 1934, drunk, he declared yet again, "I'm going to kill myself. I'll stick my head in the oven."

"Why not do it for a change?" Alma retorted.

Enraged, he slugged her in the eye. To stop him from attacking her further, she bit his arm. He stormed out of the house, shouting as he left, "You'll see if I'm such a coward. I'll go over the East Cliff. That'll teach you a lesson."

Irene, an onlooker to the violent scene, was stunned because she had always found Rattenbury to be "a quiet, old gentleman." She urged Alma to lie down and try to calm herself. But Alma was too agitated. She ran around the house, screaming, crying, and swearing. Irene telephoned Dr. O'Donnell and asked him to come. He arrived around midnight. Later, he recalled that he was "surprised" when Alma told him Francis had hit her; he had always found Francis "very charming and quiet. Also, there had been no signs of any violent disruptions before."

O'Donnell treated Alma's eye and a cut above the eyebrow, injected a quarter grain of morphia to calm her and help her sleep, and instructed her to go to bed. After Alma was settled, the doctor and Irene went out looking for Francis. Failing to find him, they called the police at 1:30 a.m., requesting a search party. But before it was organized, Francis returned home on his own at 2:00 a.m.

For the next three days, Alma shunned Francis, staying in her room. When she emerged, her eye black, he apologized and gave her a cheque for £100, a large sum of money then equivalent to £7,615/CDN$12,696, as an expression of his remorse.

Suppose Alma had wanted to divorce Francis. It wouldn't have been possible. As of 1923, women in Britain were permitted to file for divorce based on their husband's adultery; previously, only a husband could sue for divorce. Francis hadn't committed adultery. Moreover, despite the change in rules, divorce continued to be regarded as shameful, and therefore, continued to be uncommon until after the Second World War when attitudes changed. The term *domestic violence* at the time meant "domestic terrorism." It wasn't until the 1970s that domestic violence was redefined in Britain as violence against wives by their husbands and made a crime.

Alma wouldn't have walked away from the marriage because that would have taken her from her children, whom she deeply loved, and left her penniless.

Francis never struck her again. They might have continued to muddle along for years if the need hadn't arisen shortly afterward for a chauffeur. Francis rarely drove anymore, and John, now six, was going to be a weekday boarder at Cliff House school, coming home on weekends. Alma didn't want John at his young age going to and from school on the public tram. She didn't know how to drive. Theoretically, she could have accompanied him, but upper-class women felt that going on a public tram with the masses was beneath their status in life.

She asked Francis if they could hire a chauffeur, primarily to drive John. Although Francis expressed concern that it would be an additional drain on his shrinking savings, he agreed, saying he wanted someone who could also help around the house as a handyman.

In the 1930s in England, only the well-to-do could afford to have a car. Chauffeurs with mechanical experience were especially in demand because operating a car required much more mechanical work than today. Tires were much thinner, wearing out rapidly. Punctures were frequent. Oil had to be constantly cleaned from the spark plugs; radiators tended to boil over on steep hills; before each journey, the distributor, fan belt, oil filter, valves, plugs, and carburetor all had to be checked. Cars were hard to steer, requiring a muscular driver.

And so George Percy Stoner came into the story.

GEORGE

On Wednesday, September 26, 1934, the classified section on page two of the *Bournemouth Daily Echo* contained a small help-wanted ad that would unexpectedly lead to one of the most sensational murders of the 20th century.[1] Placed by Alma, the ad read: "Daily willing lad, 14–18, for housework. Scout-trained preferred. Apply between 11–12, 8–9, 5 Manor Road, Bournemouth."

The first applicant was a local youth named Bert Parsons. Alma was in silk lounging pyjamas and smoking a cigarette in a long holder. Like all men, he was awestruck by her beauty.

Alma's first question was, "Can you drive a car?" The ad, though, had said nothing on that subject.

"No, I'm afraid I can't," he replied.

She brushed this away. "We'll soon teach you. The job's yours if you want it."

Instead of grabbing it, Parsons asked if he could think it over. He consulted his sister. "It sounds a little bit dicey," she advised him. He declined the offer.[2]

Another applicant appeared shortly afterward, arriving by bicycle. He said his name was George Percy Stoner.

George Percy was born on November 19, 1916, to George Reuben Russell Stoner, a bricklayer, and his mistress, Olive Stevens. At the time, George Reuben had a wife with whom he'd had three children. Divorces were hard to get because of the high cost and red tape, so George and his wife resorted to the common ploy of her declaring she was a widow, a sham that enabled him to marry Olive and her to remarry, too. As mentioned in chapter 3, Alma's mother, Frances, did the same thing.

George's second name, Percy, was in honour of George Reuben's brother, Percival, who had died at age six of measles, then frequently a killer disease because there was no immunization vaccine yet.

George Reuben and Olive had no further children. The family lived in the Bournemouth suburb of Ensbury Park at 104 Redhill Drive, a one-storey bungalow built by George Reuben. Olive's brother, Richard, lived two doors away at 108 Redhill, and their parents, Samuel and Elizabeth Stevens, around the corner at 109 Pine Valley Crescent. George Percy called his grandparents Mother and Dad because he spent much of his early childhood with them while his father travelled around the country in search of work. Later, George Reuben and the Stevenses established a small housing construction business.

George Percy left school at 14, common in that era, and went to work for the family business unpaid. His father regarded him as "very backward"; his teachers said, "He wasn't above average intelligence, but he wasn't very backward." His Uncle Richard thought he was "a very good boy at his work."

A loner, George Percy spent his spare time tinkering on his bicycle. He had few male friends, was a virgin, never had a girlfriend, and never drank. His family thought he was "a very good lad, an extraordinarily good lad."

Alma believed George when he said he was 22, five years older than he was. "He looked it," she later said. He told her that he was an only child. "So am I," she told him. "We already have something in common."

Alma outlined the job. "You'll drive my little boy, John, to Cliff House school on Mondays. John will board there through the week until Saturday morning when you're to pick him up and drive him home for the weekend. You can sleep at home but must arrive every morning at 7:45 a.m. During the week, you'll do errands, drive me to the shops, and help in the house and garden. I'll pay you £1 a week." That was the average weekly salary in England, which was in the throes of the Great Depression. It was just a smidgeon less than Irene's £1.50 salary.

George instantly accepted the job offer, his first paying position. He wasn't matinee-idol handsome, but he was pleasant-looking. The teenager was of medium height, five foot six, and had well-brushed blond hair, blue eyes, long fair eyelashes, clean-cut features, and a nice smile. However, he

George Percy Stoner was a teenager half Alma's age.

wasn't Alma's equal socially, culturally, intellectually, or professionally. Nevertheless, they hit it off. "We loved each other from the moment we met," she said later. "We just came together because it was fate."

Francis took a liking to the young man. "Mr. Rattenbury was kindly disposed toward Stoner," Francis's friend, D.A. Wood, a frequent visitor to Villa Madeira during this time, told investigators later. "He regarded Stoner more as an object of sympathetic charity than as a servant. Stoner wasn't of bright intellect, and he had difficulty in obtaining employment. Mr. Rattenbury was asked to do something for him, and therefore took him into his house and treated him in the most considerate way." George spoke fondly of Francis to his parents.

Irene and George, however, took an instant dislike to each other, rivals for Alma's affection, but were outwardly civil.

George had been working for the Rattenburys for one and a half months when he had his birthday on November 19. He decided to confess to Alma that his real age was 18, not 22, as he had said when she interviewed him for the job. She was "shocked because that meant he was just a few years older than Christopher," but she didn't fire him for lying.

Shortly afterward, she asked him to drive her and Irene on an overnight excursion to Leeds in northern England where Francis was born, 267 miles from Bournemouth. When they arrived at Oxford, a little under a quarter of the distance, it was evening. Alma decided they would spend the night there. She had expensive tastes, so she selected the elegant Randolph Hotel, located in the city's centre.

Alma requested three adjacent rooms. There was an intercommunicating door between her room and Irene's but not between hers and George's. Alma later testified that she didn't have sex with George that night, and Irene backed her up, saying she was "quite sure" that Alma and George "didn't sleep together on that night."

Upon their return, Alma invited George to move into Villa Madeira rather than go to his parents' home overnight. She gave him the hitherto rarely used guest bedroom on the second floor, located near hers. At her trial, she said they first had sex on November 22, which would have been right after the Oxford trip, around the time he moved in.

The two had sex every night in her bedroom except when Christopher came home for holidays, since the boy's room was adjacent to hers. On these occasions, she tiptoed over to George's room. Six-year-old "Little John," as Alma called him, had always slept in a separate bed on the other side of her room when he came home on weekends. She continued to have him do this while keeping up her nightly routine of sex with George in her bed. It wasn't a large room. She maintained that John didn't know because "he was a sound sleeper."

Alma invited George to call her Lozanne, her exotic professional name. The teetotalling George disapproved of her drinking, so she stopped, which she hadn't done when Dr. O'Donnell had urged her.

"Never have I known anyone with so much determination and strength of opinion and character," she said to him.

"I feel I haven't earned this love. It's dropped into my hands too easily and I must surely have to pay the price for it someday, somehow," he told her.

"The one word I'll never say to you is 'goodbye,'" George promised.

Since his wristwatch was unreliable, she loaned him indefinitely her father's expensive gold pocket watch, which she told him, "I've kept as a reminder of my dad."

"Write a song for us," George requested.

"I could never write such a song," she replied. "How could I write a love song while I'm living one?"

She didn't buy him anything lavish that would make people wonder if there was more to their relationship than employer and servant. All she did was give him a few cigarette holders from "the dozens I had in the house. That's nothing for me. If anyone sees a cigarette holder and they like it, I always say, 'Take that.' It's my disposition."

George visited his family almost every day, always politely asking for permission to use Francis's car. They observed a marked change in him. "After he had gone to the Rattenburys, I noticed that he was very pale," his grandmother, Elizabeth Stevens, recalled. "I said so to his mother. I put it down to them giving him too much work driving the car about."

Her son, Richard, George's uncle, commented, "There was a big change in the colour of his face. He looked very, very white."

"My wife and I spoke about the difference in his appearance and demeanour frequently," George's father related. "He became pale. I put it down to the fact that perhaps he might have been indoors too much, but after looking at him as he lay in the chair and sometimes went to sleep, we used to say that he was sunken in the eyes and rather drawn. I noticed that on more than one occasion."

Villa Madeira landlady Mrs. Price thought George was "very pale, sleepy and peculiar" when he dropped in at her tobacco store.

At Christmas, Alma gave George £10, then a large sum equal to £720/CDN$1,240 today, to buy Christmas presents for Christopher and John and told him to use any leftover money to purchase something for himself. Instead, he bought a child's set of garden tools for John.

Alma and George were carrying on double lives — employer and employee when around Francis, lovers behind his back in his own home. As part of the deception, Alma always formally called George "Stoner" in front of Francis, Irene, and others, the usual procedure with a servant. Irene knew what was going on but said nothing because "it wasn't my duty to say so. But Mrs. Rattenbury hurt my feelings."

In the early evenings, they all gathered in the drawing room. Francis shared his supply of cigars with George and invited the teenager to play cards with him. Meanwhile, Alma played the piano and chatted with Irene. It appeared to be a serene, uncomplicated household.

Early in their affair, George confided to Alma, "There's something queer about my brain that I'll outgrow if I keep taking medicine." He didn't specify what the problem was nor the type of medication.

"On thinking it over," Alma later said, "I became rather alarmed. I kept trying to make him tell me what he was taking, but he wouldn't say."

She expressed concern that he would become addicted, but he assured her, "I'm taking it less, only two or three times a year, and by the end of a few years won't have to take it at all."

"Otherwise, I couldn't have had him around the children," she said later.

According to her trial testimony, at Christmas, one month into her affair with George, Alma informed Francis, "Since you told me a few years ago that 'It's fine with me if you want to lead your own life,' I am." She didn't say she was doing so under his own roof with a servant whose wages were paid from his household allowance to her and with whom he spent the early evenings playing cards and smoking cigars.

After Christmas, Alma confided in Irene what Irene already knew — she was having an affair with George right in her own house with Francis nearby. At first, Irene didn't take it "very seriously," she later recalled. "I told her not to be so silly. I didn't take it seriously till afterward," by which she meant after Francis was murdered.

Francis's best friend, D.A. Wood, adamantly insisted that Francis never realized Alma and George were lovers. The January 27, 1935, letter that Francis wrote F.E. Winslow in Victoria, who was handling Francis's remaining business matters there, bears this out:

> I have enjoyed life over here and the wife has been a cheery courageous companion making life interesting. She is a truly grand character in spite of the fact that she has had a great deal of severe illness and many operations, cheerfully borne. Her many songs were all composed when ill and she is a devoted mother.

Perhaps his situation was karma, payback for his betrayal of Florrie.

Not long after Christmas, Alma began to worry about the big age difference between her and George. She told him she thought they should end their affair. "I'm older than you, married, and the mother of two children," she said, none of which she'd taken into consideration when she took up with him.

He had a temper tantrum whenever she raised the issue. She told Irene, "He's becoming absurdly jealous of Ratz" and had even "threatened" her "more than once." Alma became increasingly worried when George began carrying a knife with a four-inch blade and what seemed to be a real gun (it was a toy one), but she didn't tell him to get rid of them. "My nature is to avoid confrontations and hope that everything will be fine."

It wasn't. In early February, Irene was awakened late at night by a loud argument between George and Alma. She raced out of her room and down the short hall to George's bedroom. To her horror, she saw that George had his hands clenched tightly around Alma's neck. He was a powerful man, and Alma appeared in danger of choking to death. Irene reacted swiftly, yanking them apart. She told the trembling Alma to go to bed. What, if anything, she said to George is unknown. While all the commotion was going on, Francis was downstairs, totally unaware either due to his near total deafness or his usual alcohol stupor or both.

While "frightfully upset," Alma didn't tell George she wanted him out of her life immediately. She dithered, saying, "I was worried that he was becoming more agitated." Alma thought his erratic behaviour was due to his taking illegal drugs of some sort, especially when on February 12, shortly after he had been on the verge of strangling her, he said, "I have to go to London early this morning to get this drug." He didn't give it a name.

Alma was "so alarmed, so upset — it was dreadful" that she hurried to Dr. O'Donnell for help. "There's something I want to tell you. I'm afraid you'll be shocked and never want to speak to me again," she said.

"There are very few things I haven't been told in the course of my life and I'm not easily shocked," he replied.

She spilled out that she was sleeping with her chauffeur, that he'd recently tried to choke her and was now claiming that he was a drug addict.

"You're being very unwise," O'Donnell said.

She ignored his remark and went on. "I believe he must be taking drugs. He's gone to London this very day I believe to try to procure more drugs. Would you please see him and find out what drugs he's taking and warn him of the dangers?"

O'Donnell agreed to talk to George, although he pointed out, "I've read reports but have very little experience regarding the abuse of cocaine and other drugs."

The following day, O'Donnell saw George. He told him, "I've been informed that it's believed you're taking drugs."

"Yes," George replied.

"What drug?"

"Cocaine."

"Where did you learn this habit?"

"I found some at home. I tried it and it gave me pleasant sensations. I carried on with it whenever I could."

O'Donnell warned, "Cocaine is dangerous. I'll help if you want to give it up."

O'Donnell reported to Alma that George had said he was on cocaine. But because George seemed to her to be "better from then onward," she dropped the issue. "He said he couldn't get the drug, and I didn't want to agitate him in case he was longing for it," she said. "We went on just smoothly and I never brought the subject up again. He said he'd stopped it from then onward and, well, everything was all right. I thought he had."

Francis's friend, D.A. Wood, began to wonder why George "seemed to have free rein throughout Villa Madeira. The whole position of Stoner in the house was amazing. Although I visited them regularly, I didn't know that Stoner was only a chauffeur. Whenever I called, he was always smartly dressed in a blue suit. He was usually sitting about the house smoking cigars and reading a book. He was more like a guest than a servant."

Landlady Mrs. Price asked Alma, "Are you not getting too fond of that boy?"

"I consider that it's none of your business to interfere with my private domestic affairs," Alma snapped.

Mrs. Price later claimed that Alma also said, "I told you I'd make him love me and I have."

Alma adamantly denied this. "I absolutely did not. It's absolutely a falsehood."

The attitude toward adultery in England in the 1930s was hypocritical. The centuries-old double standard continued that said husbands could fool around but wives couldn't. The seventh of the Ten Commandments — "Thou shalt not commit adultery" — was applied to wives but not husbands. The exceptions in the era were the many married mistresses of the Prince of Wales, the future King Edward VIII, including most famously Wallis Simpson. The affairs were public knowledge. In the cockeyed way of looking at things, being the mistress of a monarch or a soon-to-be one was a source of pride. It had happened throughout history and not only in England. The husbands accepted being cuckolded because they received titles in exchange for their compliancy.

Women's magazines indulgently urged a wife to overlook her husband's infidelity.[3] Widely read Leonora Eyles (1889–1960), the advice columnist, "agony aunt," at *Woman's Own* magazine since its 1932 founding, wrote frequently on the subject in her column "Life and You." For example: "Most unfaithful men come back home after a time looking like little boys who have been at the jam cupboard and expect a spanking. Some men prefer the thrill of a glittering glass bobble to the steady glow of real gold; eventually they wake up and find that the glass bobble has splintered to nothing, and the gold is still left."[4] Eyles, by the way, was married.

There was no such forgiveness for women who committed adultery. Public opinion held that adulteresses should be treated harshly like Hester Prynne in Nathaniel Hawthorne's classic novel *The Scarlet Letter*, published in 1850: "Thus the young and pure would be taught to look at her, with the scarlet letter flaming on her breast, — at her, the child of honorable parents, — at her, the mother of a babe, that would hereafter be a woman, — at her, who had once been innocent, — as the figure, the body, the reality of sin."

Contemporary English writer F. (Fryniwyd, "Fryn," her version of her real name, Wynifried) Tennyson Jesse (1888–1958), a great-niece of renowned English poet Lord Alfred Tennyson, was a criminologist specializing in lurid crimes who was an exception to this way of thinking. Commissioned by W. Hodge, London, publisher of a series of books of trial transcripts, *Notable Trials*, to write a lengthy commentary introduction for its publication of the trial transcript, she said:[5]

> Mrs. Rattenbury was a highly sexed woman and six years of being deprived of sexual satisfaction had combined with the tuberculosis from which she suffered, to bring her to the verge of nymphomania. Now nymphomania is not admirable, but neither is it blameworthy. It is a disease. In spite of the urgency of her desires, which must have tormented her, Mrs. Rattenbury had not, as far as is known, had a lover since the birth of Little John. She certainly had had none the four years she had lived in Bournemouth, and she had no abnormal tendencies.... Most people in England, especially women, seem

easily able to feel superior to Mrs. Rattenbury. She had had "adulterous intercourse"; she had taken for her lover a boy, young enough to be her son; and the boy was a servant. That out of this unpromising material she had created something that to her was beautiful and made her happy, was unforgivable to the people of England.[6]

Jesse did, however, go on to call Alma "completely amoral."

Alma decided to take George on a several-days, luxury-lovers getaway in London. She didn't have any money to pay for the trip; in fact, she was substantially overdrawn by £67. 10s. and owed close to £50 for local purchases, half of it for dresses she had bought for herself on account, the rest for food, electrical repairs, and the dentist. No problem for her that she was broke. She had a handy source. Without compunction she asked the husband on whom she was cheating for £250 — five times her monthly allowance from him — lying that she needed it for an operation in London for her mastoiditis. In 1935, £250 equalled £18,180/CDN$32,000 today. Although she'd had such an operation just two months earlier, Francis believed her because it wasn't unusual for her to need them close to one another. "Stoner will drive me," she said. While it would halve his bank account, Francis wrote her a cheque for the full sum.

"My whole married life was spent twice a year, more or less, telling a lie like that," Alma said without remorse at her trial. "I had to pay for everything out of the £50 I received a month for housekeeping, and it never was enough. I asked for £250 because I thought then I wouldn't have to go through the beastly business of asking again in June, so I'd sort of kill two birds with one stone, as it were." She said she'd told Francis it was necessary to go to London "because I couldn't think of any other place to go." She airily added "I might have gone to Devon."

Alma deposited the cheque into her Barclays Bank account on Monday, March 18, then paid what she owed to the various Bournemouth shops. A lot of money remained, plenty for a spree by her and George.

George and Alma left the next day, Tuesday, March 19. She told Irene, who usually accompanied her on trips, that she didn't want her this time.

Alma seems to have been nonchalant that Francis was continuing to contemplate suicide. It should have been obvious to her because at his request she'd borrowed a novel on the subject, *Stay of Execution*, from the local Boots Booklovers Library. Boots, a national pharmacy chain, had in-store lending libraries.

Stay of Execution, published in 1933, was written by (Leonard) Eliot Crawshay-Williams (1879–1962), a former British Member of Parliament turned prolific author of novels, short stories, mysteries, farces, poetry, plays, and film scripts. Boots sometimes didn't carry a book until one year or more after its publication, which might explain why Francis was reading it in 1935.

Francis identified with the main character, Stephen Clarke, a depressed older man planning to commit suicide because he feels life has passed him by. He is sitting in his flat in the Chelsea neighbourhood of London, a revolver in his mouth, his hand on the trigger, when he is interrupted by the arrival of a friend who persuades him to give life another chance — "a stay of self-execution," to put off his suicide for a month and think things over. Stephen reluctantly agrees. During the month, he meets Cecily, an attractive woman much younger than he. She wants to marry him, but he is reluctant because of the big age difference. Francis was engrossed; it was as if Crawshay-Williams was writing specifically about him and Alma. Struck by the parallels, he resolved to discuss the book with Alma upon her return.

George and Alma had only driven 25 miles when their car, Francis's Fiat, broke down at Southampton, about one-third of the way to London. They decided to complete the journey by train. Upon their arrival in London, they checked in at the five-star Royal Palace Hotel near Harrods, the world-famous department store and shopping mecca for the royal family and the rich gentry. (The hotel was demolished in the 1960s.)

Alma signed the guest register as "Mrs. Rattenbury and brother." They were given rooms 530 and 532, almost opposite each other. Alma was accustomed to luxury, but for Stoner it was a whole new world. He had crossed the usually impenetrable social divide separating "downstairs" and "upstairs." He was addressed as "sir," which he had never experienced before. He might have pinched himself to make sure that it was real and not a figment of his imagination.

Taking George on a shopping expedition to Harrods, she bought him a complete expensive wardrobe. In the men's shoe department, she purchased two pairs of shoes and two pairs of shoe trees. In men's clothing, she got him three pairs of "crêpe de Chine" (silk) pyjamas at 60 shillings each. This might not sound like much, but it was equivalent to £215/CDN$370 today.

Alma also bought him three shirts, three ties, and silk and linen handkerchiefs. In men's underwear, she paid for three pairs of socks, two pairs of gloves, and two sets of underwear. In gentleman's ready-to-wear, Alma chose a light-grey suit with a broad stripe and a dark-blue suit for him. When George said he'd like to wear one of the suits that evening, the salesclerk arranged for necessary alterations and had it delivered to the Royal Palace in time. The expedition wound up with the purchase of a tan-coloured mackintosh, the British term for an all-weather coat. In all, Alma spent £40. 14s. 6d. on new clothes for George, almost as much money as he earned in an entire year, equivalent to £2,865/CDN$4,965 today.

For herself, she bought some belts and one dress for £2. 9s. 6d. from the "Inexpensive Dresses Department." It was arranged for the clothing purchases, except for what George intended to wear in London, to be sent to Villa Madeira. Monday arrival was promised.

Alma then gave George £20 in four £5 notes to buy her an engagement ring at Kirby and Bunn, a jewellery store at 44 Old Bond Street in the heart of an upscale shopping district quite close to Harrods. He purchased a single-stone diamond engagement ring with diamond shoulders costing £15. 10s., equivalent to £1,080/CDN$1,870 today. The judge at their trial called the whole expensive expedition "the orgy in London."

George requested that it be resized for Alma, whose fingers were a bit thicker than most women's, and delivered to "Mr. G. Rattenbury" that evening at the Royal Palace. The British measure ring size by alphabet letters. Alma was size "N," equivalent to size six and a half in Canada and the United States; size six is more usual.

That night, George put on the new suit Alma had bought him and they held a private commitment ceremony in which he put the ring on her ring finger. "The love between us was beautiful," Alma later wrote him from prison.

It is highly unlikely that Alma would have married George if she could have. As Tennyson Jesse put it,

> Mrs. Rattenbury was a woman of the world. The last thing she would have wanted was to have married a chauffeur, twenty years younger than herself; she was, to use a slang expression, "sitting pretty." She had a kind husband who allowed her to live her own life. She had a young and ardent lover who satisfied her emotionally and physically. She had two children to whom she was passionately devoted. She was being supported as extravagantly as she could have hoped for. She was, as she rather pathetically said in evidence, "happy then."
>
> For her husband she had a maternal affection — it must be remembered that in all her loves Mrs. Rattenbury was essentially maternal. She spoiled and protected Stoner; she adored her children; she comforted her husband; she tried to give Irene Riggs as good a life as possible; she was kind to every stranger who came within her gate.[7]

During the next few days, Alma and George dined, danced, and went to plays and movies. When they couldn't decide what to do, George tossed a coin and said, "Let Fate decide." They also had lots of sex, unhampered by the constrictions at home.

Throughout the trip, Alma kept in touch with Francis and Irene by telephone, maintaining the pretext that she was in London for health reasons. She wrote affectionate letters to her sons — "If the weather continues, we'll be swimming in the sea soon" — enclosing stories, drawings, and fragments of songs she created for them. By the end of the four-day trip, Friday, March 22, she had no money left.

The lovers arrived back at Villa Madeira Friday night around 10:30 p.m. Francis wasn't in the drawing room, so Alma went into his adjacent bedroom. He was semi-awake. According to her, he didn't ask about the trip. "He was jolly. He was always jolly late at night." In the United Kingdom, "jolly" is slang for "drunk." She said good night, then headed upstairs to her bedroom, while George went upstairs to his and Irene to hers. All seemed quiet and calm.

This was when Agatha Christie was beginning her mystery-writing career. Villa Madeira was like the setting in many of her books. A house that seems from the outside to be serene is about to become a murder scene in which the master is the victim.

POOR RATZ

At first, the afternoon of Sunday, March 24, was like every Sunday at Villa Madeira.[1] As usual on Sundays, Irene Riggs left at 4:00 p.m. to visit her parents. As usual, George brought afternoon tea with sandwiches and cakes upstairs to Francis and Alma who were sitting on the big balcony adjoining her bedroom because the weather was warm. Little John playfully ran in and out of the room for a while.

After George left the room, the basket holding the door ajar slipped out and the door swung shut. He believed that the door was shut purposely so that Alma could have sex with Francis in privacy.

What really was happening was that Francis was reading page 296 in the 318-page *Stay of Execution* to Alma, which he believed largely mirrored their situation. On page 296, Cecily, the young woman attracted to the much-older Stephen Clarke, told him she wanted to marry him. He said it wouldn't work. Francis read the following:

> "What sort of person do you think would stand you?" she asked.

"Oh — some elderly frump who couldn't get anything else. A staid motherly soul, who'd treat me like a child...."

"You don't think marriages between young girls and — and men a good deal older than themselves are possible?"

"They're possible all right. For some reason elderly men have a peculiar attraction for young girls. That may be due, nowadays, to the quality of young men of the day; but I don't think it is. It's always been so. And — the old men like to marry young girls; and after a bit it's hell for both."

"Why?"

"Because it's naturally annoying to a young girl to see her husband mouldering while she still feels frisky. To see the bare patch on the back of his head growing bigger and shinier. To have the shock, one day, of coming across most of his teeth grinning at her out of a glass of water. And there are other things besides."

"What things?"

"Well — if you will have me enter into physiological details — a woman, let's put it, always more than a man. And when a man's a good deal older, she wants a good deal more than him. A good deal more than he can give her. It takes all his time for a young man to keep pace with a young girl. And an old man hasn't a chance of doing it. And then — she usually goes somewhere else to make up the deficiency."

On finishing, Francis said, "I admire a person who commits suicide."

Alma "tried to think of ways to turn his attention away." She suggested, "Let's go to London."

"No."

"Let's go visit Jenks tomorrow. He might be able to help you with the flats you want to build." Shirley Hatton Jenks, a lawyer who had been advising Francis for a while, owned a country estate, Pilsdon Manor, near Bridport, a town 43 miles west of Bournemouth. Alma and Francis had visited before, always sleeping in separate bedrooms.

"All right," Francis said.

While she was in prison awaiting trial, Alma told a visitor, Daphne Kingham, that Francis said he wanted Alma to sleep with Jenks in order to persuade him to provide a large sum of money for the flats. She also mentioned that George Stoner was eavesdropping on the other side of the closed door.

In 1978, Daphne told Anthony Barrett this when he interviewed her for *Tragedy in Three Voices: The Rattenbury Murder*, published in 1980. Barrett left it out of the book because Alma's children, Christopher and John, were still living. Christopher died in 1995. Barrett told British writer Sean O'Connor in 2017, saying that "with only John still alive, it's appropriate to reveal the motive that provoked Stoner to attack his employer."[2]

Alma called Jenks between 6:30 and 7:00 p.m. from Francis's bedroom, the only room with a phone, leaving open the connecting door to the adjacent drawing room where Francis was waiting. George eavesdropped. Having thought Alma had had sex with Francis that afternoon, he suspected they would do so again at Bridport and/or Alma would sleep with Jenks. George was probably especially upset because just a few days before he and Alma had had a commitment ceremony with the engagement ring she had given him money to buy.

Stoner barged into the bedroom, brandishing a gun. Alma didn't realize that it was actually a toy pistol. "I'll kill you if you go to Bridport," he burst out.

Before he could continue, she led him to the dining room, away from Francis. Upon arrival, he accused, "You closed your bedroom door this afternoon to have relations with him."

"I assure you that I didn't," she coolly responded. "You must put that revolver away and not make an ass of yourself."

"Don't ever close it again, and if you go to Bridport, I won't drive. I don't want you to go with him. I don't want you to share the same bedroom."

"You're unnecessarily jealous. I assure you I'll have a separate bedroom."

Later, Alma said she felt she'd calmed George down. "He seemed to believe me and to be all right. It had been quite unpleasant, but it was now all right."

Alma left and returned to Francis, behaving as if everything was normal — she probably could have been an excellent professional actress. Making small talk to drive away "his blues," she said brightly, "How nice it is we're going to Bridport tomorrow."

Since it was her practice to lay out Francis's clothes for trips, she went to his bedroom, selected a suit from his closet, and hung it outside, as she usually did, for Irene or George to pack. She then went upstairs to her bedroom and began to select her own clothes. Then she put John, home from Cliff House for the weekend, in his bed in her room after his usual 7:15 bath. As usual, he fell deeply asleep. Next, she returned to the drawing room to play cards with Francis. He was "quite jolly [drunk]." Dinah the dog wandered around as she always did.

During this time, George drove Francis's car to Ensbury Park. At 8:00 p.m., Frederick Clements, a retired police sergeant taking a regular evening stroll, spotted Stoner parking outside his parents' house at 104 Redhill Drive. It would have taken Stoner very little time to drive there, since 104 Redhill and Villa Madeira were only three and a half miles apart.

Clements had known George since the latter was 14. "I saw him at least three or four times a week, almost daily. He was a decent and respectable boy of the highest character." The retired policeman saw nothing out of the ordinary in George's nocturnal visit and walked on.

However, George's destination wasn't his parents' home. He cut through the unlocked backyard gate to the house of his grandparents, Elizabeth and Samuel Stevens, at 109 Pine Vale Crescent.

Arriving shortly after 8:00 p.m., he asked, "Mother, will Dad lend me a mallet?" George called his grandparents with whom he'd lived during much of his childhood Mother and Dad. "I want it to drive in some pegs as I'm going to erect a tent," by which he meant Little John's sun shelter.

The weather was warm enough for John to have an afternoon nap outdoors, so the request didn't strike Elizabeth as odd. "Yes, Dad will," she said, then went outside to the cluttered, unlit backyard tool shed to grope around until she found one.

Immediately after she gave the mallet to him, George left. It was 8:35 p.m. Elizabeth was later able to recall exactly because "when he went out, the bus was coming down. He must have met the bus as he was going out of the gate and that's five minutes after every hour and every half hour. The bus must have passed him as he was going out."

The wooden mallet belonged to her son, Richard, George's uncle, who hadn't used it since Christmas. It was four inches in diameter, six and a half inches in length, and weighed two pounds, seven ounces.[3]

While George was on his mission, Alma and Francis completed their card playing. As usual, Alma opened the French windows for Dinah to go into the back garden to do her duty. As usual, she didn't lock the windows. "Good night, darling," Alma said to Francis, kissing him, then going upstairs to the bathroom. She didn't have a bath, so she wasn't, she said, "there very long." After that, Alma proceeded to her bedroom and took off her shoes and stockings. She shut the door as she "invariably" did, got into bed still in her lounging pyjamas, popped out to pack more clothes for Bridport, and leafed through a magazine while she waited for George to join her.

Stoner got back to Villa Madeira around 9:00 p.m. Knowing that this was around the time Alma usually departed the drawing room to go to bed, he went to the backyard, saw Dinah, and spied through the French windows to check if only Francis was there. He saw Alma kiss Francis, which probably fuelled his jealousy. As usual, Francis was in his favourite fireside armchair, his back to the windows. As usual, he had been drinking; there was a partly empty glass of whisky on one arm of the chair. *Stay of Execution* was on a nearby table.

George knew the windows were never locked. After he could tell that Francis had fallen asleep, he tiptoed into the room. He put on his leather chauffeur gloves so his fingerprints wouldn't be on the mallet, took it out from his suit jacket, and smashed it down on the back of Francis's head three times. *One! Two! Three!* No pause in between. The enormous impact blew out Francis's false teeth, which landed on the carpet. Blood gushed from his head, soaking his clothes, the chair, and carpet. George dropped the bloody mallet beside the settee in plain sight. Normally, Rule No. 1 for assailants is to take their weapons with them.

He climbed upstairs to his room and began to change into a pair of the crêpe de chine pyjamas Alma had bought him in London just days before. It was now between 9:30 and 10:00.

George was back in his room just before Irene returned from her time off. She'd been in bed only a few minutes when Alma entered around 10:15 to discuss the next day's excursion to Bridport. "I don't know whether Ratz or Stoner will be driving, but we're going to go," she told Irene. After about 10 minutes, Alma returned to her bedroom.

Shortly afterward, Irene left her room and headed downstairs to the kitchen for something to eat. As she walked along the hallway, she heard "unusual breathing." Thinking something might be wrong with Francis, she went to his bedroom, quietly opened the door, reached around to turn on the light while continuing to remain outside, and peered in to check that he was all right. It was the first time in her four years at Villa Madeira that she'd felt the need to do this. He wasn't in bed, which hadn't been slept in, so she concluded he must be in the adjoining drawing room. Irene listened but didn't go in because she thought the heavy breathing she heard meant he was sleeping and she didn't want to disturb him. Satisfied that all was well, she forgot about going into the kitchen and instead returned to her room upstairs.

A few minutes later, she went to the bathroom on the landing and saw George in his pyjamas "hanging over the bannisters at the top of the stairs, looking down."

"What's the matter?" she asked.

"Nothing," he answered. "I was looking to see if the lights were out."

Irene returned to her room.

Meanwhile, George entered Alma's room and got into bed with her. She thought he seemed agitated. "What's the matter, darling?" she asked.

"I'm in trouble. I can't tell you what it is."

"Oh, you *must* tell me."

They went back and forth like that for two or three minutes. Then George said, "No, you couldn't bear it."

She thought he was "in some trouble outside — his mother or something like that."

"I'm strong enough to bear anything," she assured him.

"You won't be going to Bridport tomorrow because I've hurt Mr. Rattenbury," he said. "I hit him over the head with a mallet."

"It didn't penetrate my head what he said to me at all until I heard Ratz groan loudly and then my brain became alive and I jumped out of bed," Alma later said. Her room was directly above the drawing room, and the sound had travelled upward.

Without stopping to fling a robe over her pyjamas and put on slippers, she ran downstairs into the drawing room and over to where Francis was slumped in his chair, blood gushing from his head. She tried to rub his hands; they were cold. She tried to take his pulse, shaking him to make him speak. Accidentally, she "trod on his false teeth," she recalled later, which made her hysterical. Gulping down a glassful of whisky, neat, she attempted to prevent herself from being sick. Then she spied the bloody mallet nearby on the floor.

Alma didn't take immediate action to get help for Francis. She didn't call for an ambulance, Dr. O'Donnell, the police, or even Irene. Her priority was to protect George. She turned away and headed upstairs to her bedroom to discuss the situation with him.

After Alma spoke to Stoner, he went to his room and hastily put on his trousers and shirt, but didn't bother to attach the shirt collar — men's shirt collars then were detachable — or put on his jacket. Then he waited, while Alma returned to the drawing room, poured herself more whisky, and began a performance to mislead concerning what had happened.

She called for Irene to come down, who rushed downstairs to the drawing room in her sleepwear. At first, Irene didn't realize there was something wrong. "Mr. Rattenbury was sitting in his armchair near the fireplace as if he was asleep," she later recalled. "He looked quite ordinary sitting in the chair."

"Whatever's the matter?" Irene asked Alma. Then she saw a lot of blood pooled on the floor at Francis's left and that his left eye was shut and badly bruised. She also noticed that Alma was in "a terrified state. She was a changed woman absolutely from when she'd spoken to me in my bedroom a few moments earlier. She was raving, 'Oh, poor Ratz. What's happened? What have they done to you?'"

It was now 11:30. "Call Dr. O'Donnell, hurry, hurry," Alma said to Irene.

O'Donnell likely wondered who was calling so late at night. When he answered, Irene said, "You're needed urgently at Five Manor Road. Please come at once."

He immediately telephoned for a taxi to take him to Villa Madeira. Cab driver Thomas Plumer was there in minutes.

While Plumer was speedily driving O'Donnell, Alma went into the next part of her performance. "Stoner, come down here." As soon as he did so, she distracted Irene for a moment to allow him to kick the bloody mallet behind the settee out of sight. That done, she told Irene, "Help us carry him to his bedroom."

Blood dripped onto the carpet as they did, forming a big stain. They placed the unconscious Francis on his side on his bed, removed his blood-soaked jacket and waistcoat, then wrapped a towel around his head and sheets around his body to absorb blood still pouring from his skull. Irene tossed the jacket and waistcoat into the main-floor bathroom's bathtub and filled it with hot water in an effort to remove the blood.

"Go get Dr. O'Donnell," Alma told George to give him an opportunity to remove the mallet from Villa Madeira. However, George didn't do this. Instead, he stuck the mallet behind some boxes at the trellis just outside the front door. By the time he got to O'Donnell's, the doctor had arrived by taxi at Villa Madeira. It was 11:45.

Irene had left the front door open for the doctor and was waiting for him in the vestibule. They hurried down the long hallway to Francis's room. O'Donnell was shocked when he entered: blood, blood, and more blood. Francis's head continued to bleed. The sheets around his body and the towel around his head were bloody, and so was the pillow under his skull. His left eye was badly bruised and so swollen that O'Donnell couldn't open it. Francis's breathing was laboured.

Alma, barefoot, ran about, gulping whisky from a glass clutched in her hand. "What happened?" O'Donnell asked her.

She didn't say. Instead, she cried out, "Look at him! Look at the blood! Someone has finished him!"

O'Donnell went to the telephone and called local surgeon Alfred Rooke to come at once. Alma knew Rooke because he had operated on her mastoiditis. In the drawing room, Irene removed the blood-drenched cretonne cover from Francis's chair, ran out the back door, tossed it in the dustbin, raced back to the drawing room, and tried to wipe away the blood coating the chair's back and arm.

Alma came in and gazed down at the pool of blood on the carpet. "Wash it out," she ordered Irene. "I don't want Little John to get a fright at the sight of blood."

Irene scrubbed and scrubbed, but the big stain remained.

O'Donnell walked in, and Alma went into the next stage of her performance, giving him a truncated account. "I went to bed early after spending a happy evening with Ratz, playing cards and talking about our planned trip to visit friends in Bridport tomorrow. I was awakened by a noise, a loud groan, from the drawing room beneath my room. I ran down to see what it was and found Ratz lying in his chair with his head leaning over to his left and a large pool of blood on the carpet. As I rushed into the room, I tripped over something. It was Ratz's false teeth, lying in a pool of blood. To block out the sight, I poured myself a stiff drink of whisky to try to calm myself. I tried to put the false teeth back in his mouth so he could speak."

Alma attempted to get O'Donnell to look at *Stay of Execution*, which she'd placed on the piano. "This afternoon Ratz read me a passage. He said he admired someone who had the courage to kill himself." Her purpose probably was to use what mysteries call "a red herring," a clue or information intended to be misleading. She wanted O'Donnell to think that Francis, influenced by the book, had killed himself. If she'd stopped to think, she would have realized that her story was utterly implausible. It would have been physically impossible for Francis to hit himself on the back of his head.

"I don't wish to see it," O'Donnell brusquely retorted. "I don't have the time to bother about it."

She put the book back on the piano, then "raved" — Irene's word — around the room, downing more whiskies.

O'Donnell's snap conclusion was that Francis had stumbled into the grand piano, severely banged his head, then collapsed into his chair. An accident, not an attack by someone with the intent to kill.

Rooke arrived a few minutes after midnight. He couldn't do more than a cursory examination of Francis because Alma kept getting in the way. "She made an examination impossible," Rooke later testified. "She was making utterly incoherent remarks but nevertheless was so solicitous that I said, 'If you want to kill him, you're going the right way to do it. Do let me get near him and attend to him.'"

"A perfect nuisance? *Embarras de richesses?*" Rooke was asked at Alma's trial.

"Exactly. I can't speak for the sincerity. There was the apparent wish to help. My entire preoccupation was with my patient."

Despite Alma's constant interruptions, Rooke was able to detect deep wounds in Francis's head beneath all the blood. He decided that "the only thing to do" was to summon an ambulance to take Francis to Bournemouth's Strathallen Nursing Home, where Rooke performed operations, for a closer look at his injuries. Located at 3 Owls Road, Strathallen was nearby, three-quarters of a mile, three minutes driving distance, from Villa Madeira. Rooke lived across from it. In the pervasive social divide in the United Kingdom between the upper and lower classes, nursing homes were privately run and catered to well-to-do patients like the Rattenburys for a substantial fee, while public hospitals were for the working class.

Glancing at his watch, Rooke saw that it was 12:30 a.m. He left O'Donnell to supervise when the ambulance arrived, raced home to pick up his medical bag, then scurried across the street to Strathallen. When the ambulance arrived 15 minutes later, Rooke rushed Francis into the operating "theatre." Since he was unconscious, Rooke didn't give him an anaesthetic. Monday, March 25, had begun. Rooke started examining Francis at 12:45 a.m., 75 minutes after Irene telephoned O'Donnell.

O'Donnell had requested Alma to let George drive him to Strathallen. He arrived in the operating theatre as Rooke prepared to examine the injuries closely by shaving off Francis's hair and cleaning up the blood so they would be visible. "I found three very bad, deep gashes," he testified later. "The worst was above the left ear. It had irregular jagged edges and was three and a half inches long. The bone was exposed in the deep parts of the wound and there was an obvious depressed fracture of the skull. I was able to feel where the bone had been driven into the brain. A formidable, very serious wound. The next wound was a deep laceration right down to the bone in the middle of the back of Mr. Rattenbury's head. The third one was similar to the second, a little to the right. His left eye was completely bunged up to such an extent that I couldn't pry apart the lids to look at the condition of the pupil. Some of the profuse bleeding in the skull had flowed into the eye."

When O'Donnell told him his theory that Francis had hurt himself, Rooke said he was wrong. "The wounds aren't the result of an accident but the result of a deliberately violent attack of three extremely powerful blows struck from behind with a heavy, blunt instrument, likely with the intent to kill." He instructed O'Donnell to call the police.

NOT OBLIGED

t was around 1:15 a.m. when the Bournemouth police got the call.[1] Veteran Constable Arthur Ernest Bagwell was dispatched immediately in response to O'Donnell's phone call. In those days, British police forces had few cars. Bagwell employed the main mode of transportation — a bicycle. He arrived at Strathallen about 1:30 a.m. and was taken right into the operating theatre to view Francis on the table so he could see that the man had indeed been savagely hit on the head. Rooke repeated, "The wounds are the result of a deliberately violent act with the intent to kill."

Having verified that the attack was a crime necessitating a police investigation, Bagwell bicycled to Villa Madeira, getting there at about 2:00 a.m. When the front door was opened, he saw two women, Alma and Irene, standing side by side. Alma was still in her silk lounging pyjamas but had put over them what Bagwell thought was "a light cape, something like a dressing gown or dressing jacket." She was no longer barefoot and now wore red slippers.

Alma took Bagwell into the drawing room. He noted that she "was under the influence of drink to a mild extent." Formally, he said, "I have just come from the Strathallen Nursing Home where your husband has been taken this evening where he is suffering from serious injuries. Can you furnish me with any particulars as regards to how he came by them?"

She gave him a very condensed response that was true as far as it went but far from the entire truth. "At about 9:00 p.m., I was playing cards with my husband in the drawing room and then I went to bed. About 10:30 I heard a yell. I came downstairs into the drawing room and saw my husband sitting in the chair. I then sent for Dr. O'Donnell. He was then taken away."

At this point, Inspector William James Mills of the Bournemouth police arrived. Upon entering the drawing room, he had this first impression of Alma: "She was very excited and appeared to have been drinking." He asked her, "What has happened?"

"I was in bed when I heard someone groaning. I came downstairs and found my husband in the easy chair. He was unconscious and blood was coming from his head."

Mills noticed that the left-hand French window was ajar. "Was this window open when you came down?"

"No, it was shut and locked."

In saying this, she threw away the opportunity to depict that the attack was done by an intruder, which meant someone in the house was responsible. Mills was quickly coming to regard Alma as the prime suspect.

He stared intently at the big bloodstain on the carpet by the left side of Francis's chair and the ones on its left arm and back. The chair's seat reeked of urine. He and Bagwell went to the bathroom down the hall and found Francis's washed and wrung-out jacket and waistcoat. Bloodstains were still visible. Then they went outside to search the grounds where they peered in the dustbin and found a man's blood-soaked shirt collar and the blood-smeared chair cover. Returning to the drawing room, Mills walked over to look at a book opened face-down on a small table near the chair. It was *Stay of Execution*, revealing page 296, which Alma had tried to show O'Donnell. She'd moved it from the piano to make it easier to see.

Indicating he would be back soon, Mills departed at 2:45 a.m., going to Strathallen for an in-person update on Francis's condition. He spotted George sitting outside in a car's left-hand front seat, apparently asleep.

George had been there for close to two hours, waiting for O'Donnell. In the anteroom to the operating theatre, Mills encountered O'Donnell. "I've been down to Manor Road. That woman is drunk."

During Mills's absence, a bizarre scene was occurring at Villa Madeira. Reeling drunkenly, Alma staggered to the record player and put on Frank Titterton's recording of "Dark-Haired Marie," her passionate love song.

As it played, she swayed over to Bagwell and attempted several times to kiss the tall, husky, moustached middle-aged policeman. He had never encountered such a situation before in his long career and was uncertain how to handle it. To get away from her "attentions," as he later put it, he told her he was going outside to find another police officer, saying, "I thought that saying that might calm her a bit."

Instead, the scene grew wilder. Alma attempted to chase him but was prevented by Irene, who locked all the doors, pocketed the keys, pushed her mistress into a chair in the dining room, and sat atop her to prevent her from breaking loose. It must have been quite a struggle between the two women, yet Bagwell insisted he "didn't hear any kind of disturbance."

After "about three minutes," Bagwell returned. He found Alma sitting alone in the drawing room. "I know who did it," she blurted. As he should have, he immediately cautioned her that she had the "right to silence." She paid no heed. "I did it with a mallet," she went on in what became a disjointed jumble. "Ratz has lived too long. It's hidden. No, my lover did it. It's urine on the chair. I would like to give you £10. No, I won't bribe you."

She had just finished when Inspector Mills returned. It was now 3:30 a.m., Monday, March 25. He found Alma in the hall "in a very agitated condition and under the influence of drink, slightly worse than she'd been at two o'clock."

"Your husband has been seriously wounded and is now in a critical condition," he told her.

"Will this be against me?"

"I caution you. You are not obliged to say anything unless you wish to do so, but whatever you do say will be taken down and may be given in evidence."

"I did it. He gave me the book. He has lived too long. He said, 'Dear, dear.' I will tell you in the morning where the mallet is. Have you told the coroner yet? I shall make a better job of it next time. Irene doesn't know. I made a proper muddle of it. I thought I was strong enough."

By now, Little John, upstairs in Alma's bedroom, was wide awake, confused, and frightened by all the activity. When interviewed in 2007 by York Membrey for the *Times* of London, he said, "I remember the night my father was murdered because the lights went on in the house and I woke up. Nobody would tell me what had happened, but I had this cold feeling that something terrible had occurred."

When Dr. O'Donnell and George returned a little later, the record player was no longer on, but the radio was. O'Donnell counted four policemen in the house, among whom Alma was "staggering about," he later said, "running from one room to another." As soon as Alma heard his voice, she rushed to him. He tried to explain Francis's condition, but she couldn't take it in. The doctor felt she was too intoxicated and exhausted to be interviewed by Mills. He helped her upstairs, put her to bed, and injected half a grain of morphia, a substantial dose, expecting it would knock her out for many hours.

Instead, after he left, she jumped out of bed and went down to the drawing room. O'Donnell intervened before Mills could resume his questioning. "Look at her condition. She's full of whisky, and I've given her a large dose of morphia. She isn't fit to make a statement to you or to anybody else. Morphia makes a person fuddled and muddled, not able to think properly. You can't place any reliance on a statement made by a person under the influence of morphia." He led Alma back upstairs and sat by her bedside until she fell asleep.

Police interrogations weren't regulated much in the United Kingdom until 1984 when the Police and Criminal Evidence Act laying out the rights of suspects came into effect, including the right to legal representation and limits on detention before charge. However, both in Alma's time and today, police are legally allowed to take statements from anyone, drunk or sober, regarding a crime. Thus, all O'Donnell could do was express his displeasure.

Downstairs in the kitchen, George whispered to Irene, "I suppose you know who did it?"

"Well?" she responded.

Nothing more was said by either.

At 4:30 a.m., Donnell left for home. Within minutes, Bagwell went into Alma's bedroom and searched under the bed in case the mallet was there. Moments after his fruitless search, plainclothes Bournemouth Detective Inspector William Goldsworthy Carter, appointed the senior officer on the case, arrived, by car, showing his importance. Carter had been on the police force for 23 years and an inspector for nearly five.

Alma woke up at 6:00 a.m., having had less than two hours of sleep. Carter was sitting by her bed, observing her. Neither spoke. After 10 minutes of this silence, she said, "I feel sick." She made sounds as if she were going to vomit.

Carter sent Police Constable Sydney George Bright, on guard in the room, to get a bowl. Irene was present, too. "Riggs, bring coffee," Carter ordered.

Alma sipped one cupful. Later, Irene said, "Her hand was shaking so much that the saucer shook."

Carter recalled it differently. "Mrs. Rattenbury's hand was steady, but she wasn't normal enough to make a statement right then. I decided to wait a couple of hours."

"I want a bath," Alma said.

"You'll have to be supervised. I'll call for a policewoman to come."

At 6:15 a.m., Bagwell found the mallet stuffed behind boxes near the trellis outside the front door.

Upon the arrival of the policewoman at 7:00, Bagwell and Mills left for the police station. Irene and the policewoman helped Alma, "staggering," according to Irene, to the bathtub.

While Alma was bathing, Carter went to the kitchen to interview George, recording it on pages 64, 65, and 66 in his notebook:

> I am a chauffeur handyman employed by Mr. Rattenbury of 5 Manor Road, Bournemouth. I retired to my bedroom about 8:05 p.m. on Sunday, 24 March 1935, leaving Mr. and Mrs. Rattenbury and the boy John in the drawing room. About 10:30 I was roused by Mrs. Rattenbury shouting to me to

come down. I came down into the drawing room and saw Mr. Rattenbury sitting in the armchair with blood running from his head. Mrs. Rattenbury was crying and screaming and said to me, "Help me get Ratz into bed, he has been hurt." I then took the car and went to Dr. O'Donnell's house. He had left before I got there. When I returned, I cleaned the blood from the floor on the instructions of Mrs. Rattenbury.

Mrs. Rattenbury was sober and, as far as I know, she had not been drinking. When I went to bed, she was in a normal condition. I have never seen a mallet on the premises. I heard no sounds of a quarrel or noises of any kind. Since September 1934, I have been employed by Mr. and Mrs. Rattenbury. They have been on the best of terms. I said to her, "How did this happen?" She said, "I don't know."

Carter handed the notebook to George to sign. Despite most of what he said being untrue, George signed.

After Alma's bath, Irene helped her back to her bedroom to put on a brown dress. Alma sat on the bed, and Carter returned at 8:15 a.m. "She appeared to me to be definitely normal," he testified later. He identified himself and cautioned her about the right to remain silent. "She appeared to understand," he said.

Irene contradicted him at the trial. "She was by no means normal."

"Mrs. Rattenbury," Carter said, "I charge that you did, by wounding, do grievous bodily harm to one Francis Mawson Rattenbury in an attempt to murder him on Sunday, 24 March 1935."

By law, Alma had the right not to give a statement in response — it can be used as evidence in a trial — but she chose to give one. A policeman is required to record a statement. Today, a video camera is used; in Alma's era, police wrote everything down in a notebook and asked the accused to sign it. "About 9:00 p.m. on Sunday, 24 March 1935, I was playing cards with my husband when he dared me to kill him as he wanted to die. I picked up the mallet. He then said, 'You have not got guts enough to do it.' I then hit him with the mallet. I hid the mallet outside the house. I would have shot him if I had a gun."

Her scenario was patched together from Francis's frequent assertions that he wanted to commit suicide, her having said, "You don't have the guts to do it," and *Stay of Execution*.

After Carter read back her statement, according to him she asked him to hand his notebook to her, read the statement silently, then aloud, and concluded by signing it. "She read it aloud clearly," he later testified. "I've had a good deal of experience in the hearing of statements by persons and the taking of statements, and as far as I could tell, she appeared to understand what she was saying and doing."

Declaring that he was going to take her to the Bournemouth police station to book her, Carter instructed Alma to put on the fur coat and a hat that Irene had gotten out for her. "To book" is to "record the name and other details of a suspected offender and the offence for later judicial action."

Alma wobbled when she stood and needed assistance descending the stairs. But Constable Bright, who was standing below in the hallway, testified later, "She showed no signs of having been both drunk and drugged a few hours previously. Assuming that she was not under arrest and knew how to drive a car, I would have let her."

"After being helped downstairs?" he was asked.

"Yes. She was in such a condition that she had to be helped slightly."

"Why should you say that was?"

"I couldn't say what her condition was caused by."

Irene and George were standing at the bottom of the stairs. "Don't make fools of yourselves," Alma whispered when she reached them.

George responded, "You've got yourself into this mess by talking too much."

Although speaking softly, they were overheard by Constable Bright, standing nearby.

Alma whispered to Irene, "Tell Stoner he must give me the mallet." She was unaware that it had been discovered by Constable Bagwell, who had given it to Carter.

As she was escorted by the police from the house to the police car, she glanced back and caught sight of young John at the front doorway ready for George to take him to school now that it was Monday. He looked confused about where his mother was going and when she'd be back. They would never see each other again.

George drove John to school as if nothing was out of the ordinary.

During the brief five-minute trip to the central police station on nearby Madeira Road, Alma was silent.[2] At the station in the presence of Superintendent Deacon as a witness, Carter cautioned and charged her once again. "That's right," she said. "I did it deliberately and would do it again."

There is a distinction between being charged and being arrested. Being arrested means the police believe the person likely committed a crime. They might or might not decide to bring criminal charges after an arrest. In addition, a person can face criminal charges without being arrested. The police can allow the person to go home until the court hearing on the charge, in which case bail is often required, or keep him or her in custody until the hearing. When people are charged with crimes and held in police custody, they must be brought to the first available court for a decision on whether they should continue to be held or remanded in custody. The U.K. Public Prosecution Service asks the court to remand the person if it believes there's a risk if released of the person "running away, interfering with or threatening a witness, perverting the course of justice, committing further offences, being a threat to public order." Regulations say that the time between the person being charged and the hearing can be up to 34 days, up to nine days for magistrates to announce their decision, and up to 119 days between the sending of the case to the Crown Court and the start of the trial.

GHASTLY NIGHTMARE

lma felt trapped in "a ghastly nightmare."[1] She was to appear for her hearing in Bournemouth Magistrates Court at 11:00 a.m., just three hours after she was booked. Court hearings on charges are supposed to occur quickly after the charge is laid. Alma was on a swiftly moving legal conveyor belt.

The United Kingdom's legal system says an accused "has the right to have a solicitor [attorney] and reasonable time to discuss the allegations against you with your solicitor. The police should not normally question you until you have taken advice. Your lawyer will also be present during the police interview, and you can suspend the interview at any time to consult with your solicitor without the police officers present. Even if you initially did not ask to see a solicitor, you can change your mind and ask to see one at any time."

With the clock ticking, Dr. O'Donnell, who thought of himself as Alma's friend as well as doctor, hurried to Robert Lewis-Manning, 39, a partner at a prominent Bournemouth law firm, Other, Manning & Boileau-Tredinnick.[2]

Manning agreed to represent Alma and was at the court when she was led in for the hearing, looking dazed. It had taken only a few minutes to transport her from the police station jail on Madeira Road to the courthouse at nearby 32 Stafford Road.

The hearing was over in a mere three minutes. Detective Inspector Carter was the only witness. "Mrs. Rattenbury confessed to attacking her husband, saying, 'I did it deliberately and would do it again,'" he told the court. Based on his one sentence, Alma was remanded in custody until April 2 and was taken back to prison.

O'Donnell was allowed to visit her two hours later at 1:00 p.m. It was obvious to him that the effects of his morphia injection remained. "She couldn't stand," he testified later. "She tottered when she tried to stand. She swayed about. She was supported by Inspector Carter and a policewoman. She tried to be sick — to vomit. Her pupils were contracted." Morphia can cause eye pupils to contract or dilate.

Alma was given 20 minutes to talk with O'Donnell. Her chief concern was her children. They shared the opinion that it would be best for both boys to stay at school for the time being and for John to board over the weekends at Cliff House in addition to weekdays, rather than come home. She wrote Irene and George each a £5 cheque and asked O'Donnell to deliver them.

Following O'Donnell's departure, Alma was transferred speedily to Holloway Prison in the north London district of Holloway, built in 1852 by the City of London for both men and women, converted to women only in 1902. Located on 10 acres adjacent to Camden Road, a major street in north London, it had capacity for over 950 inmates, making it Western Europe's largest women's prison. It was for remand, convicted, and those sentenced to death. In the early 1900s, it was notorious for its brutal force-feeding of incarcerated suffragettes. Past tense because Holloway was closed in 2016.

Constructed of stone, with its crenelated towers, battlemented walls, and turreted entrance gateway, Holloway from the outside resembled a Gothic-style, fairy-tale castle, earning it the sardonic nickname "Camden Castle." Inside was a different story. There were six wings, radiating from the central tower in a star shape, each with four storeys of long rows of single-person cells, very narrow with a high, barred window. The prisoners did manual labour and had their meals brought to their cells. Holloway was a "death house," a prison that carried out executions, which were by hanging. The trapdoor of the gallows opened into an empty cell that served as a pit for the body. Two people could be hanged side by side.

All prisoners wore a "Sister Dora cap," a type of nurse's hat that resembled a hairnet, a checked apron with a bib, black knitted stockings, calico knickers (underpants) that tied around the waist with tape, and prisoner-made shoes, flat with straps. There were different dresses for each type of inmate. Those awaiting trial, remand prisoners like Alma, were given grey dresses with a thin white stripe.

Prisoners had to get up at 6:00 a.m., and lights-out was at 9:00 p.m. The mattresses were lumpy, the pillows (one per prisoner) felt like rocks, the food was terrible, and the inmates had to do chores. Alma's was to wash floors, which she had only done before in her life while volunteering as an orderly in the First World War.

It was the complete antithesis of Alma's pampered lifestyle of high fashion and late-to-bed, late-to-rise hours, coffee served to her in bed when she woke up around noon. Cigarettes and makeup weren't permitted. However, she was allowed to go for solitary strolls in her fur coat in the exercise yard. In class-obsessed England, even in prison the upper strata got perks, but not the lower.

Nobody told her anything about Francis's condition. He was alive but only barely.

Meanwhile, in Bournemouth, Inspector Carter had compiled an itemized list of things he had taken from Villa Madeira for analysis: "One wooden mallet, one cretonne chair cover, one gents' jacket, one gents' waistcoat, one shirt collar, one pair braces, one pair trousers, two cushions, two swab cloths, one book (*Stay of Execution*), one lady's pyjama suit, one pair lady's red shoes, one kimono, one glass containing whisky, one armchair, one carpet, six cheque books."

With Francis in hospital near death, Alma arrested, and John and Christopher at boarding school, as of 9:00 a.m., Monday, March 25, Irene and George were the only people at Villa Madeira. At 11:45 a.m., Henry

William Hoare, the ambulance driver who had taken Francis to Strathallen, called to collect his fee of £1. 1s. George pulled out from his pocket the £5 note O'Donnell had delivered earlier from Alma and asked Hoare, "Can you change a fiver?" On schedule, the purchases Alma had made for him at Harrods arrived.

On Tuesday, March 26, Alma poured out her despair in a repetitive, stream-of-consciousness, 737-word letter to George. She was too upset to think about paragraphs or spelling:

> Oh Darling this is awful.
>
> I must see you I'm so ill. Tell me how Ratz is, also is Dr. D., Long [a London acquaintance] or someone arranging bail. Am writing small — cos not too much paper. But Bail must be arranged by April 2nd. I keep thinking this is some ghastly nightmare from which I must awake. Oh! Darling I'm going potty. In your foggiest dreams you couldn't imagine life here. All letters are censored. So can't write much even though long to. But Oh! Just to see you darling, why did this awful thing happen. I couldn't keep my handbag or anything, tell Irene. I must see my babies — simply must. My head is going round in circles, if they'd only let me sleep. But you know I'm not strong enough for this rough life and work. I'm so weak. Oh! Darling, why why did this ghastly thing happen. If only I could die. Please let me die. When I go home on Tues. can't you arrange to see me, Dr O.D. could find out details for you. Perhaps I could see you here. Why did they bring me here? Couldn't I have stayed in Bournemouth? Why bring me here? Do write to me darling. I love you so. Why why oh! Why did this have to happen. I am in a sick ward here — 10 beds — but not allowed to lie down and I'm so weak I can hardly stand. If only I could have a smoke. If if if. Oh! God why am I here, it all seems some ghastly joke. Find out about my bail. The lawyer Dr O.D sent should be able to tell you something. Keep your chin up darling — will meet again. My God its cold, oh

for a hot water bottle. Find out how Ratz is — everything (as far as my muddled brain will allow) depends on how Ratz is. Oh make him pull through. Please send me some papers. Tell Irene to write. Tell Dr O D also. Perhaps he could arrange I could have a smoke. The grey uniform and cape about kill my mind. I want to write so much — but knowing one's letters are read — crabs one's number. I do pray Ratz pulls through — all depends on that. I must get out of here — it's all so wrong. My babies — everything. Did you arrange for [Little John] to stay at school next Saturday. Two things in this ghastly nightmare stands out. LJ's face at the front door. And your kiss. Oh God will I never see either again. Will my brain stand the shock. Tell me everything that has happened. Send me the papers. Oh! God darling why did this happen, is it only last Tues. we were going to town laughing, without a care in the world? And now I'm a criminal. Awful clothes, dreadful food — a bath once a week. Not even a watch. No mirrors — no face powder — nothing allowed — and not seeing you or hearing your voice — yr dear voice — oh! Why did this happen. Why can't I even cry. And my children, will I be out by the 3rd? That bail must be arranged. Oh I wish to God I were dead. Nothing could be bigger hell for me, than to not see you or my children. They wouldn't let me see you before I left. Oh! Darling, darling, can't something be done — Please please help me. I'm so desperate. Perhaps you could get Dr O D to find out what train that woman policeman comes to town on, and which she returns to Bournemouth on with me. Oh! The clang of keys. You might get on the same carriage, Oh! Darling, I want to see you so. — I don't think you'd recognize me. I can hardly walk for weakness. God bless you Gold Bless you God Bless you — & my babies. My love is always with you, please write often. I do love you and want you so, just the comfort of your dear arms for five minutes. Angel, Angel, why am I here — and why did this have to happen to u? Let me

know how Rz is — so much depends on that. Au revoir — my
previous one. Give my love to Irene — only allowed to write
three letters a week. So explain to Irene — for I must write to
you my beloved.
Yr Lozanne

It comes through loud and clear that Alma only wanted Francis to sur-
vive so George wouldn't be charged with murder.

During the same day, as George and Irene returned from Wimborne, a
short distance north of Bournemouth, George detoured to Ensbury Park.
He showed her the home of Frederick Clements, the retired policeman who
had seen George on Sunday night while on a regular evening stroll, then
drove a few blocks farther to his grandparents' home. "I got the mallet from
my grandfather's workshop," he said.[3] Next, he drove around the corner and
showed her how close his parents' home was to his grandparents' place.

"Will your fingerprints be on the mallet?" Irene asked.

"No, I wore my chauffeur gloves."

"Why did you do it?"

"Because I saw Mr. Rattenbury living with Mrs. Rattenbury in the
afternoon."

"Living with" was a euphemism then for "having sex."

Irene mulled over what to do. If she went to the police, it was likely she
would have to disclose that Alma had been having an affair with George,
which wouldn't look good for Alma.

At the end of March 26, Ratz was still alive.

On the morning of March 27, Holloway's governor (warden), Dr. John
Hall Morton, who was also the prison's chief medical officer, had Alma
brought to his infirmary office. Morton's impression was that she was "very
depressed and somewhat confused." He checked her arms, looking for a
trail of needle marks that a drug addict would have, but found only a mark
from O'Donnell's morphia injection at 4:00 a.m. on Monday. As Alma had
alluded to in her letter, mail to and from inmates was scrutinized by prison
officials. Having read her letter to Stoner, Morton encouraged her to "tell
the whole truth."

"The truth is that it was my fault absolutely," Alma responded.[4]

"Your letter is a little too morbid to send," he told her. "Rewrite it when you're in a calmer frame of mind."

So Alma wrote a new letter, shorter, and with paragraphs:

> Darling,
>
> This is torn from part of a letter I wrote to Irene today. The letter I wrote you yesterday, the gov told me was a little too morbid! — So as I [Irene's] was of the same tone, it seemed the only thing to scrap that also. Sorry you couldn't have my 1st letter, though. I was desperately worried about you — but Irene cheered me up this morning.
>
> It was rather unfortunate she came at the same time with Katherine [Miller-Jones, Ratz's niece], it made it more difficult to talk. But oh! I must see you tomorrow with the lawyer. I think he could advise. Oh! Darling, I am so desperately miserable — Why should this have happened — oh! Why why. All letters are censored — both coming and out. Do you think the lawyer can arrange bail? Will you be in court on Tuesday? I must see you even if we can't talk. If you come to town with lawyer he might advise you and make it alright for us 3 to talk together. I hope this letter reaches you in time, for as you can see by the enclosed — he is coming tomorrow. Also, it is customary to ask permission of the governor before seeing a prisoner. If you hav'nt already done that, Manning could do it for you darling one. God bless you my sweet one, may God make the time speed away and get us all out of this awful nightmare. Two things stay in my mind — L.J.s dear little face, as he was leaving for school, and yr last kiss.
>
> My love be with you always.
>
> Lozanne

Morton permitted this letter to be sent.

By evening, Irene had decided she needed to confide in somebody and that it should be a Catholic priest because he would be bound to keep what she said in the confession booth secret. Also, he wouldn't recognize her because she actually was a member of an Anglican church. She left the house at 9:00 p.m., likely for Bournemouth's oldest Catholic church, Sacred Heart, located at 1 Albert Road, close to Villa Madeira.

In those days, there was same-day postal delivery in England with several deliveries daily, concluding at 9:30 p.m. It's likely that Alma's letter to Stoner was delivered while Irene was seeking advice from a priest. Its contents greatly upset him, so much so that for the first time in his life he took a drink — whisky neat from the Rattenburys' bar. Then he downed many more.

When Irene arrived home at about 10:30 p.m., she found George in his bedroom, plastered. "She's in jail, and I'm the one who put her there," he slurred. "Irene, you know I killed Mr. Rattenbury. I should never have let her say she had. You must get me up early in the morning as I want to go to London to see Mrs. Rattenbury and give myself up."

Irene telephoned the police at 11:20. "You must come. Stoner is drunk and saying mad things." Two constables were dispatched. "I don't want to stay here alone with Stoner," Irene told them after they arrived, then phoned her brother and asked him to come stay at the house.

The constables went upstairs to George. He had vomited and repeatedly asked how Francis was, saying nothing beyond that. Irene stayed at the foot of the stairs eavesdropping, apprehensive about what he might say.

All Irene said to George after the police left was, "I bought flowers and bobby pins for Mrs. Rattenbury and I'd like you to take them to her when you go to Holloway tomorrow." Moments later, Irene's brother arrived.

At the end of that day, Francis was still alive.

The next morning, at 6:30, Thursday, March 28, George drove Irene's brother to work. He arrived back at Villa Madeira at 7:00, collected the flowers and bobby pins, and got on the 7:25 a.m. train to London.

At the very same time, Alma was writing another brief letter to Stoner, this time without a salutation:

I am trying to have the lawyer's letter I received today sent to you darling, so that you can make arrangements to come up with him, or make arrangements with the governor. But I must see you darling. Please write to me. This is the 3rd letter I have written — I hope you receive this. I hardly know how to write now. Let me know how Ratz is getting along. No more now. God bless you — my love be with you always.

Lozanne

Have you talked with Dr O'D about how Ratz is? Goodness there is much I want to know. Please ask Irene to give you a few bobby pins for my hair. I think they should be allowed.

Francis had clung to life for three and a half days. He died at 8:15 a.m. on March 28. This escalated the attack on him from attempted murder to murder. Inspector Carter viewed the body, then contacted Robert Lewis-Manning, Alma's lawyer, telling him that Francis had died. He also informed Dr. O'Donnell and Francis's niece and nephew, sister and brother Katherine Miller-Jones and Keith Miller-Jones, the children of Francis's older sister Katherine, who shared a flat in London.

The train trip between Bournemouth and London's Waterloo Railway Station with stops along the way takes about two and a half hours. Thus, George would have arrived at Waterloo Station around 10:00 a.m. From there, he would have taken the Underground to Tufnell Park Station in northern London. There was no public transit from there to the prison, so George had to proceed on foot, a 15-minute walk.

George arrived at 11:30 a.m. but wasn't permitted to see Alma. He left the flowers and bobby pins for her and caught a midafternoon train back to Bournemouth.

Between 1:30 and 2:00, O'Donnell dropped in on Irene at Villa Madeira. "I believe you know far more than you have let on," he said. "Do you think that Mrs. Rattenbury attacked her husband?"

"I know she didn't!" Irene firmly replied.

"If you have any information, it's your duty to tell the police."

Irene hesitated.

Intuiting the reason, O'Donnell said, "Discretion is of little importance in comparison to Mrs. Rattenbury's life, which is at stake."

"Mrs. Rattenbury and Stoner were lovers," Irene finally replied. "Stoner told me that he had struck Mr. Rattenbury and where he got the mallet."

O'Donnell immediately called the police to come. It was 2:35 p.m. when Irene gave them a formal statement. "Mrs. Rattenbury and Stoner were on very friendly terms for the past two months, and I only saw them kissing each other once," she started off. "He told me he killed Mr. Rattenbury with a mallet."

Under British law, if the police "reasonably believe that the premises may contain evidence, they may search to the extent that is reasonably required to discover any such item of evidence." Based on Irene's statement, the police had the right to search George's room. They did so and found evidence: receipts for the stay at the Royal Palace Hotel and for the engagement ring, the latter made out to "Mr. G. Rattenbury."

To find out more about the mallet, the police brought Stoner's grandparents, Samuel and Elizabeth Stevens, and their son, Richard, George's uncle, to the police station for questioning. They first spoke to Elizabeth. "Did your grandson come to your home the night of the murder and ask to borrow a mallet?

"Yes," she replied.

The police then showed Richard the mallet that Constable Bagwell had found hidden behind the trellis at Villa Madeira's front door.

"Yes, that's mine," he told them. "The last time I used it was at Christmas."

The police turned to Elizabeth, "Is this the mallet your grandson borrowed?"

"Yes," she admitted.

If a death is thought to have occurred as a result of criminal activity, a post-mortem — an autopsy — is assigned to a "forensic" pathologist, a specialty that determines whether the cause of death was criminal in nature. It's an essential tool in murder cases. The term wasn't in use in the 1930s, but the methods were.

Bournemouth police surgeon Harold Simmons did the forensic post-mortem. When he began on Francis at five o'clock, it was nine hours since the man had died. Inspector Carter observed the autopsy, as did O'Donnell and Rooke.

For forensic pathologists to get a close-up view of injuries to a head, they remove the covering scalp by cutting an incision in one stroke all the way from behind one ear, across the forehead, to the other ear and around the back, enabling them to lift off the scalp.

"There were three definite wounds on the skull," Simmons later testified. "Those injuries meant three separate blows. They couldn't have been inflicted with less than three separate blows. They could have been inflicted with a blunt heavy instrument with a rounded edge. The injuries indicated that Mr. Rattenbury was sitting in the armchair with his head inclined to the right, probably dozing, and that the assailant was above him when the blows were inflicted. There was a considerable amount of blood. There was a nine-inch fracture. This wound must have been made with considerable force as it is contra coup [the brain had been bruised on the opposite side of the scalp from the impact]."

"What sort of a man was Mr. Rattenbury?" Simmons was asked at the trial.

"He was a well-preserved, strong man for his age, with no evidence in his physique of anything like his age. I knew he was 67 or so. He was five feet, 11 inches in height."

"And the body was healthy, was it?"

"The body was healthy."

Simmons went on. "There was no evidence of marks of any kind of injury on the body such as would indicate a struggle or resistance except three small bruises in the neighbourhood of the left knee, which might easily have been caused in moving his body from one room to another while he was still alive. The large quantity of urine passed is evidence of a loss of consciousness. Immediately following a concussion or compression of the brain, the sphincter muscle of the bladder is relaxed and the urine escapes."

"Is there any possibility of the wounds having been inflicted by himself?"

"None whatever."

In instances of indications of criminal involvement in a death, photographs of the wound(s) and tissue samples are taken for submission as evidence at a trial. Simmons took pictures and gave a piece of Francis's scalp on which there was some grey hair and the skull cap, the upper domelike portion of the skull, to Carter.

Carter had learned George was on the train that would arrive at Bournemouth's railway station at 6:35 p.m. He waited on the platform for it. As George stepped off, Carter went up to him and asked, "You know me to be a police officer?"

"Yes," George replied.

Carter "cautioned" him about his right to remain silent.

"I understand."

Then Carter drove him to the police station, charged him with murder, and searched him. He found two photographs of Alma, a letter she had written in prison for him, and a gold watch, Alma's father's watch that she had given George on permanent loan.

"Careful," said George. "It was given to me by Mrs. Rattenbury and is worth £20."

The next day, Friday, March 29, George was taken at 11:00 a.m. to Bournemouth Police Court for the charge to be formally read against him, the same time that Alma had been. He was dressed in the grey-striped suit, blue-striped shirt, and blue tie that Alma had bought him in London the previous week. George stepped lightly into the dock, the British term for the enclosed courtroom prisoner box, and smiled recognition to his parents in the public seats. The press reported that his face was pale, his blond hair brushed back smoothly, and that during the brief proceeding he stood with his arms resting on the side of the dock. When the charge was read by the clerk — "That you did by wounding murder one Francis Mawson Rattenbury on 24 March 1935" — someone at the back of the court yelled, "It's a lie!"

As had happened with Alma, Carter was the lone witness. He said that Rattenbury had died the previous day, March 28, and asked for George to be remanded.

George requested legal-aid representation under the Poor Prisoners' Defence Act, in existence since 1930. (E.W.) Marshall Harvey, senior partner in the Bournemouth law firm Marshall Harvey & Dalton, Solicitors, agreed to represent him.

When the hearing concluded at 11:10, George was put in the custody of Detective Constable George Henry Gates, who took him into the adjacent detention room. "You know Mrs. Rattenbury, don't you?" George asked.

"I do," Gates replied.

"Do you know that Mrs. Rattenbury had nothing to do with this?"

Gates immediately cautioned him of his legal right to remain silent, but George chose to speak. "I don't care, if you know what I mean, yet I do care. When I did the job, I believed he was asleep. I hit him and then came upstairs and told Mrs. Rattenbury. She rushed down then. You see, I watched through the French window and saw her kiss him good night, then leave the room. I waited and crept in through the French window, which was unlocked. I think he must have been asleep when I hit him. Still, it ain't much use saying anything. I don't suppose they will let her out yet. You know there should be a doctor with her when they tell her I'm arrested, because she'll go out of her mind."

The police now had an extraordinary situation on their hands: each person charged with Francis's murder was protecting the other rather than foisting the blame as usually happens. It was an indication of how much George and Alma genuinely loved each other.

George was transported to Dorchester Prison. Serving Dorset County, which included Bournemouth, the all-men's prison opened in 1795 and was 25 miles west of Bournemouth. It had capacity for 300 inmates and had conducted hangings until 1858. It was closed in 2014.

Carter's day wasn't over. He called Alma's lawyer, Robert Lewis-Manning. "I'm going to Holloway Prison this afternoon to charge Mrs. Rattenbury with murder. She has the right to have her lawyer present. Meet me at Holloway a little after five o'clock."

When Alma was brought into the interview room at 5:40, Carter told her, "Mr. Rattenbury died this morning. I charge you with murder." She had the legal right to remain silent, so she did.

When it published its evening edition, the *Bournemouth Daily Echo* only knew the story through George being sent to Dorchester Prison, but that was ample material for it to run a multi-tiered headline in big block letters at the top of the front page:

SENSATIONAL EAST CLIFF TRAGEDY
DEVELOPMENT
RATTENBURY'S DEATH
HIT ON HEAD WITH MALLET
MAN REMANDED AT BOURNEMOUTH

In British Columbia, the *Vancouver Sun* also had a multi-tiered headline:

RATTENBURY MURDERED IN ENGLAND
NOTED ARCHITECT BELIEVED SLAIN BY HIS
CHAUFFEUR
WIFE CHARGED WITH WOUNDING
VICTIM WON PROMINENCE AS DESIGNER OF
PARLIAMENT BUILDINGS

Odds are that Daisy Maclure thought, *I knew it would end badly.*

WHO COMES FIRST?

On Monday, April 1, Bournemouth's coroner, F.G. Lefroy, opened an inquest, with a jury he convened, into Francis's death. The use of juries to assist coroners in determining the cause of a person's death dates back to medieval times in England, but since the late 1920s they had rarely been employed. Given the magnitude of this case, Lefroy decided to have one.

"Since the circumstances of Mr. Rattenbury's death are now a matter of criminal proceedings," he said, "this inquiry will be confined to one of identity, evidence of death, and medical cause of the evidence of death." He then scheduled the hearing for Wednesday, April 10.

On April 2, the police returned to Villa Madeira to check if Alma's medicine chest, which she kept in her bedroom, contained evidence of cocaine and/or heroin use by her. At the back, they discovered a hypodermic needle. Irene testified at the trial, "Christopher's doctor told Mrs. Rattenbury to get a needle to give Christopher regular injections for a glandular problem in his left leg."

On April 4, a man named Frank Hobbs came to the police with a sensational story about Alma that depicted her as what today we would call "a cougar," defined as "a woman of middle age who actively seeks the casual, often sexual, companionship of younger men, typically less than 35 years old; by implication a female 'sexual predator.'"

In October 1932, I saw an advertisement in the *Bournemouth Echo* for a cook general wanted for Five Manor Road. I was 34 then. I telephoned for an appointment and later arrived at the house to meet Mrs. Rattenbury. The next day I received a letter offering me the job. The following day I started work at the Villa Madeira and was given the spare room next to hers.

Practically from the first day I entered service, Mrs. Rattenbury would spend a great deal of her time talking to me in the kitchen and taking me into her confidence. She wrote songs and asked for my opinions about the lyrics. She confided in me that she had been married before and that her mother had arranged the marriage between her and her husband.

After two or three weeks, I went out for my half-day off one Wednesday afternoon. On my return I found Mrs. Rattenbury in the kitchen where she was clearly anxious to see me. She said, "I have been waiting for you to come in." Thinking that she had some orders for me, I said, "Yes, madam." But she replied, "Don't call me madam. You are the same equal as myself. Don't you realize that you were one of the many applicants for the situation? The other applicants' references were far superior to yours but I chose you because you have sex appeal." I said, "You are not yourself and don't know what you are saying." She said, "I know what I am saying quite well. I want you and I mean to have you."

I asked her if she was aware that her husband and children were in the house. I insisted that I wasn't that sort of man and wouldn't even think of sleeping with her. I left the kitchen and went up to my bedroom. Only a couple of minutes later, she came into the room. I tactfully pushed her out and locked the door. Throughout the night she continued to tap on my door, but eventually she gave up and went to bed.

The next morning I carried on my work as if nothing had happened. She never got up before noon, but after this incident she stayed in bed for three or four days. When she finally appeared, she came to me in the dining room where I was preparing breakfast and apologized. She said she had lost control of herself and I was "a perfect brick" for not doing what she wanted me to do. I assured her that the matter was closed as far as I was concerned and carried on with my work.

Two weeks later I was approached by Mr. Rattenbury who said that, owing to the economic depression, they could not afford to keep me. He said Mrs. Rattenbury would do the cooking and she would get a woman in to do the housework. He then gave me two weeks' wages in lieu of notice.

I was convinced that he knew nothing of the incident that occurred between her and me. He had always been pleased with my work. I was convinced that Mrs. Rattenbury must have persuaded him to dismiss me. That afternoon I packed my things and left.

I am making this statement in fairness to the chauffeur who is charged with Mrs. Rattenbury. Had I fallen in with her suggestions, I might have become infatuated and easily agreed to do anything which she might have suggested.

Was this story true or was it fabricated? Make of it what you want — Hobbs wasn't called as a witness at the trial. Perhaps it was thought he was irrelevant or maybe he wasn't believed or both.

During the first week of April, George was examined at Dorchester Prison for signs of cocaine addiction by Dr. Lionel Weatherly, a retired physician who had been president of the Society of Mental and Nervous Diseases and of the psychology and neurology section at the 1934 annual meeting of the British Medical Association. He had owned a private mental hospital. But although he had "62 years of experience as a medical man" and had "lived among mental cases practically all my medical life," he had done no general practice since 1886 and had only had "three cases of cocainism under care" in his entire career. The medical study of cocaine addiction was in its early days in the 1930s. Some scientific papers had been published, but few doctors had personally handled cocaine cases. He wrote down that George's pupils were "dilated," which can be an indicator of cocaine use. "His paranoid behaviour and feelings of morbid jealousy on the afternoon before the murder were completely consistent with his having taken cocaine," Weatherly added.

On Sunday, April 7, Frank Titterton, the tenor singer who had recorded a number of Alma's songs, chose to sing one, "Avelette," with lyrics by Edward Lockton, during his performance with the BBC Orchestra broadcast by BBC Radio.

> Avelette, the night is slowly falling,
> On your garden sinks the twilight dew.
> Now the last sweet bird of day is calling
> Singing through this happy hour to you!
> Far o'er the mountain the morn appears
> And lays down her mantle of white
> The world seems a garden of heaven
> I whisper again my good night.
>
> Avelette, rest on till dawn,
> Through the hours of sleep.
> May the breezes sing to you all night long
> For the sweetness of the flow'rs
> They will waft unto you
> And murmur from the trees in a song.
> Your dreams shall be dreams of love's delight;
> My heart all the while will linger near,
> For angels from above
> Will guard you with their love
> Avelette, sleep on till dawn is here.[1]

Between the concert and Alma's upcoming court appearance, Titterton and Beatrice Esmond, telling prison officials they wanted to discuss the publication of some of Alma's songs, were allowed a short visit with her. Beatrice brought flowers, which were confiscated. When Alma walked into the interview room, she extended her arms wide in greeting but wasn't permitted to touch them. "How dreadful it is to meet like this," she said.

Titterton later recalled, "She looked wan and was worried about the children. She spoke little about the charge against her. She discussed plans for the publishing of her songs, and again and again she spoke of what she would do 'when it is all over and I am free again.'"[2]

Alma told them she particularly missed cigarettes and music. "The only way of passing the time is to recite my songs over and over again to myself."

Titterton bent over and softly hummed a verse from one of her songs. "Lozanne went into ecstasies," he said. "It was pathetic to see."

"I am sleeping badly, and it would help if I was allowed to compose songs," Alma said. "I am so hungry for music."

"Is there anything I can send you?" Beatrice asked.

"Strongly perfumed soap. I hate the overpowering smell of disinfectant." The guards ended the visit after 20 minutes.

Afterward, Titterton sent her a package of lyrics "to occupy yourself setting them to music." They got no farther than prison officials, who returned them.

Alma wrote sweet, loving letters to her children; for example:

> Darling Little John,
> This picture reminded me of Dinah's little puppies, so I cut it out for you. I suppose you are using your garden tools now, unless the weather is cold at Bournemouth — like it is here.
> Bye for now, Chipmonk — soon we'll be together again.
> A big kiss and hug from your old mummie who loves you.
> Lozanne
> God keep you night and morning
> God keep you everywhere.

Bournemouth Coroner F.G. Lefroy formally opened the inquest into Francis's death on April 10. It lasted only minutes. Francis's nephew, Keith Miller-Jones, identified Francis's body, Lefroy invited the jury he had convened to view it, and adjourned the inquest.

Bournemouth wasn't a crime centre, but sensational murders had occurred there before. For example, the 1921 "Telegram Murder Case," in which the victim, who had advertised for a position as a school cook, was lured to Bournemouth by a telegram inviting her to come for a job interview. The sender murdered her.

There have also been sensational murders since. The most notorious were the 1946 "Lady-Killer Murders," in which one of the two mutilated, then suffocated female victims was a Bournemouth woman. Because the murderer was handsome, a "lady-killer" in slang, the press was making a grisly play on words.

When they occurred, the "Telegram" and "Lady-Killer" murders dominated the headlines and were the talk of the country. But they're unremembered today, whereas the Rattenbury case remains a *cause célèbre*. In August 2006, *Dorset Life*, a regional magazine for the area where Bournemouth is located, called Francis Rattenbury's killing "Bournemouth's most sensational and famous murder in its history." It still is and it is in Wikipedia's list of notable murders in the United Kingdom since 1800, one of five singled out for the period 1931–1940.

The salaciousness of the case drew the attention of Britain's national tabloids, always on the hunt for the racy, gruesome, and sensational, the reason they sold so well. The main national tabloids at the time — all still around today — were the *Daily Mirror, Daily Mail*, and the *Daily Express* and *Evening Standard*, the last two then owned by Canadian expatriate Max Aitken, Lord Beaverbrook. The papers were in a tough battle for readers during the ongoing Depression. Murder at the Villa Madeira was welcome fodder.

Interest was also stoked by striking similarities to two recent bestsellers. *Lady Chatterley's Lover* by English writer D.H. Lawrence, published seven years before in 1928, recounted the steamy affair between a sex-starved, rich married woman and her lower-status gardener, just like the upstairs/downstairs coupling of Alma and George. *The Postman Always Rings Twice* by American James M. Cain, published in 1934, the year before Rattenbury was slain, told the story of a beautiful, young wife using her sex appeal to get a drifter to help her kill her elderly husband. Life seemed to be imitating fiction in Rattenbury's murder.

The media circus began on April 11, the day after the inquest, with a preliminary hearing before local "magistrates," so-called although they had no legal training. Magistrates were respected community members. A preliminary hearing is the first step in the legal process in a criminal case to determine whether it should be "committed" to a full trial. The use of the word *commit* is derived from Middle Ages English Latin, *committere*, "to entrust, to put into custody," from *com* ("with") and *mittere* ("send").

As early as 9:30 a.m., an hour and a half before the court was due to open, a small group of women had already gathered outside the site, Bournemouth's magistrates' court at 32 Stafford Road, in their eagerness to obtain seats.[3] An hour later, the queue had grown to about 150 people. Some had brought food, five policemen were present to control entry, and only a few people were admitted. The tabloids had dispatched a total of 25 journalists.

George arrived in a police van, locked inside a steel cage at the back. Underscoring the class division between him and Alma, she was driven in a large saloon car, the British term for a large vehicle with seats for four or more people. A wardress sat on each side of her. Seeing the crowd, she shrank back as far as she could in her seat; one of the wardresses hurriedly drew across the car's side window curtain to conceal her from view.

On a long table between the magistrates' bench and the spectators' seats, there were exhibited a pair of folded, faded brown trousers; two suitcases; green and brown crêpe de chine pyjamas; men's shirts; red and blue ties; a stained pack of playing cards; *Stay of Execution*; and a heavy wooden mallet. Beside the table was Francis's blood- and urine-stained armchair with its cushion.

Alma was brought into the dock first. She was dressed stylishly in a beige dress with a large pink carnation attached. Pink was her favourite colour. "When Stoner came in, their eyes met, but there was no sign of recognition between them," the press reported.

The British government's Department of Public Prosecutions (DPP) was represented by G.R. Paling. Under the law, there are "summary offences," less serious, such as "solicitation of prostitution, being found in a common bawdy house," and "indictable offences," the most serious of criminal offences, such as murder, robbery, treason, and drug trafficking. Paling wanted Alma and George to be "indicted" jointly. Manning and Harvey each wanted the other's client to be listed first on the indictment on the premise that a jury likely would construe that person was worse than the one listed last. "Stoner should be listed first because he was the first to be charged with murder," Manning maintained.

"Mrs. Rattenbury should be named first because she was charged with attempted murder before Stoner was arrested," Harvey countered. The magistrates sided with him; Alma was listed first.

While there's a drawback to being listed first, there's an offsetting advantage. At the trial, the lawyer for the person listed first is scheduled last in the presentation of closing arguments. Chances are that his or her words are fresher in the jurors' minds when they deliberate a verdict. Based on this theory, Alma could be in a stronger position than George.

Both Alma and George pleaded not guilty. The press wrote, "Stoner stood relaxed and apparently unconcerned. Mrs. Rattenbury fidgeted with the collar of her fur coat."

Paling handed the magistrates a diagram of Villa Madeira. He dwelled on Alma and George's affair, read aloud police reports and Alma's statements, identified each exhibit, and theatrically held high the mallet, saying, "To say the least of it, this seems to be a formidable weapon." He then read George's statement. "His saying that he went to bed at 8:05 p.m. on the 24th cannot be true because it has been shown that at 8:30 p.m. he collected the mallet at his grandparents' house."

Paling dramatically concluded, "The relationship between the accused was not confined to that adopted or expected between a servant and the wife of his master. When you come to view the evidence as a whole, I shall ask you to bear in mind the motives that ordinarily actuate human beings in the conduct of their affairs and to come to the conclusion that there is evidence which ought to go before a jury to show that Mrs. Rattenbury as well as Stoner is a principal in the commission of the offence with which they are both charged."

His speech lasted until the end of the day. Another two days were dedicated to testimony by the Harrods sales clerks, the reception desk clerk at the Royal Palace Hotel, the salesman at Kirby and Bunn where Stoner bought the engagement ring, police, and Alfred Rooke who had done the initial examination of Francis. Rooke indicated on his own head where Francis had been struck.

In a preliminary hearing, the defence lawyer is entitled to cross-examine the Crown's witnesses, but Manning and Harvey didn't. At the end of a preliminary hearing, in the British legal system, the magistrate(s) decide whether to send — "commit" — the person for trial in a higher court. The magistrates said they would announce their decision about Alma and George on April 24.

The newspaper headlines at the time were:

SEASIDE DRAMA
A BOURNEMOUTH SENSATION
SENSATIONAL ALLEGATIONS BY PROSECUTOR
MR. RATTENBURY'S HEAD WOUNDS
MRS. RATTENBURY'S PINK CARNATION
ALLEGED PURCHASES BY ACCUSED COUPLE AT
    LONDON STORE
A GOOD-NIGHT KISS
THREE SEPARATE BLOWS
PYJAMAS AT 60/ — A PAIR[4]

Easter school holidays were about to start. Manning arranged for John to stay with Keith Miller-Jones, his godfather, and Keith's sister, Katherine, at their flat in Belgravia, a very affluent London neighbourhood. Keith and Katherine were in their thirties, and Keith was a solicitor. Manning asked Mrs. Daphne Kingham, "Pinkie," the sister of Christopher's father, Alma's second husband, Thomas Compton Pakenham, to take care of Christopher. She, too, was in her thirties and well-to-do. Pinkie, her husband, and seven-year-old son, Michael, lived in Berkshire County, 40 minutes by train to

London. Windsor Castle is in the county. Pinkie had never met Alma or Christopher; nevertheless, she agreed to accept Christopher.

"Can I do anything to help Alma?" Pinkie asked Manning.

"Go and visit and talk with her," he suggested.

The two women hit it off right away, since they had love for their respective children in common. "She clearly adored her children, and they in return were always asking about her and champing to be with her," Pinkie later recalled.[5]

The prison interview room was bare except for a long wooden counter that stretched from wall to wall and a chair on each side. A wardress, Mrs. Grieg, supervised. Pinkie had brought makeup in her purse for Alma to put on. She placed the purse on the counter and invited Alma to use the lipstick and other cosmetics. Holloway's regulations prohibited inmates from wearing makeup, but Mrs. Grieg didn't intervene. The guards at Holloway appreciated that Alma wasn't a difficult prisoner.

After Pinkie told Alma all about Christopher, she asked, "How have they been treating you?"

"I've been scrubbing floors. I don't know whether I should have been made to do this as I am officially innocent unless and until found guilty, but it was easier to acquiesce than to have a row about it." She added that she was convinced George wouldn't be convicted. "The worse that could happen would be a verdict of manslaughter."

Later, Pinkie said, "I was impressed by her personality and good nature but didn't find her particularly beautiful," not surprising considering recent events, and Alma's songs, she said, weren't much to her liking.

As she left the prison, Pinkie was accosted by a reporter. "Alma Rattenbury is the most talked-about woman in the country in the most sensational story of the day," he said. "We'll pay you £500 for your own story and hers." The tabloids regularly made such deals, then and now. It was a huge offer, equivalent to £36,364/CDN$63,692 today, indicative of how eager the tabloids were for any information and how certain they were that Alma's tale would sell like hotcakes. Pinkie ignored the reporter.

Holloway's governor, John Hall Morton, had overseen the controversial 1923 execution at the prison of Edith Thompson, convicted, along with her lover, Frederick Bywaters, younger than she, of murdering her husband, who was a number of years older than she. Many of the British public believed she was innocent; a million people had signed petitions for clemency. Bywaters had said she had nothing to do with the murder, and she had collapsed in her cell when the guards came to take her to the gallows. Morton had ordered her to be sedated, carried to the gallows, and tied to a chair. The newspapers reported that afterward her underpants were filled with blood, which they said indicated she must have had a miscarriage. There was a huge outcry about the execution.

Alma and George's case had obvious parallels to Thompson-Bywaters. But unlike with Thompson, Morton thought Alma was innocent. He was concerned that her non-cooperative attitude would result in her being convicted and sentenced to death.

Thus, he instructed the guards at Holloway's main gate to bring Pinkie to his residence inside the gateway when she next visited.[6] The home resembled a Tudor-style lodge. "I feel sorry for Mrs. Rattenbury," Morton told Pinkie. "I feel very strongly that she should not have been pressed by the police to make statements while she was under the influence of alcohol and morphia. She is sticking to her story that she murdered her husband despite Manning and his associates telling her repeatedly that by shielding Stoner she will only get herself hanged without being able to save him. Would you please convince her to talk?"

"I'll do my best," Pinkie said. She, too, believed Alma was innocent.

Pinkie decided the best approach was to appeal to Alma's love for her children. "It's not fair to the children," she said forcefully. "They have all their lives before them — are they to be known as the sons of a woman who was hanged for murder? You have no right to blast their lives to shield Stoner. You owe it to them to tell the whole truth, hiding nothing — and if you won't do anything for your own children, why should anybody else? You needn't expect me to keep on looking after Christopher for you!"

Afterward, Pinkie said, "I had to speak to her like that. It was the only weapon I had."[7]

Pinkie went on to question Alma about the crime. "It seems to me to have been totally unnecessary. Stoner had no reason to be jealous of your husband who had made no physical demands on you for several years."

This remark led Alma to say that George had overheard Francis asking her to sleep with Shirley Hatton Jenks to get money from Jenks for his flats project.

"You have to decide who comes first — your sons or your lover?" Pinkie repeated.

While she wrestled with her dilemma, Alma continued to write letters to John and Christopher, enclosing drawings and lines of music she'd composed and assuring them, "I will see you when I return from my holiday."

> Darling Little John,
> I missed not hearing from my baby this week, however, it will not be long before mummie is reading you stories again. "Peter Pan and all the Fairies" — and oh! So many hugs and kisses first, my chipmonk. God bless you. Be a good little boy and do what you are told.
> A big kiss from your old mummie who loves you.
> Lozanne

> Darling Little John,
> I was very pleased to receive two letters from you this morning — and the little pictures that you had coloured.
> Yes, it will be wonderful to see my baby again, and you will have grown inches and inches by then, for it seems a very long time since I saw you, chipmonk. However, in a short while, mummie will be with you again, and you'll have so much to tell me, and how your new teeth will have grown!
> Much love baby mine and God bless you.
> Your old mummie who loves you always and always.
> Lozanne

Pinkie's words had hit home. Alma wrote a last paragraph in a letter she wrote April 18 to Irene that would be a turning point. Since Manning had instructed her to stick to subjects in her letters that had nothing to do with the case to prevent anything being interpreted as incriminating, she began with a request for Irene to bring her tweezers, rouge, nail polish ("light colour"), small bottles of perfume ("should last longer"), slippers ("grey or fawn"), and "the brown shoes with laces." Then she abruptly changed direction in her concluding sentences: "Should think S's remorse at what he's brought down on my head, the children's etc. — smashed lives — would drive him a raving lunatic — a frightful responsibility to hold in one person's hands. God deliver me from such a hellish responsibility. I couldn't have courage to bear that pain; my own is more than enough in a hundred lifetimes as it is."

Irene gave the letter to the police.

On April 24, gawkers started turning up outside the magistrates' court three hours before the session was to begin at 11:00 a.m. Soon there was a large crowd as well as a throng of reporters. Despite summer-like heat, Alma wore her fur coat. "In the dock with flashing dark eyes and intensely red lips, she wore another pink carnation," the *Daily Express* reported.

On behalf of the director of public prosecutions, G.R. Paling asked the magistrates to commit Alma and Stoner for joint trial. As everyone had anticipated, they did.

On May 1, Alma and George were formally committed to trial to start May 27 at the Central Criminal Court in London, popularly known as the Old Bailey. Alma was also to be tried as "an accessory" for having "comforted, harboured, and assisted" George on the day of the murder.

Murder at Villa Madeira was more than a lurid crime. Theoretically, murder trials are supposed to be about the crime, not morals, but it was thought that a woman guilty of having sex with her lover while her young son was in a nearby bed was also capable of murder. There was no getting away from the fact that Alma had an amoral attitude to sex, but there were men who also did. A double standard was at play, which sparked an international debate on sexual mores, spotlighting the hypocrisy and misogyny toward women, still thorny issues today.

ADULTEROUS INTERCOURSE

On May 14, George was transferred from Dorchester Prison to century-old, all-male-inmates Brixton Prison in south London, opened in 1820. Holloway Prison, where Alma was, was in the north end of the city.

Dr. Hugh Arrowsmith Grierson, the prison's senior medical officer, examined George: "Normal and rational in behaviour, takes his food, has put on eight pounds, sleeps well."[1]

In the United Kingdom and Canada, there are two categories of lawyers. Those who perform most of their legal work in a law firm or own an office are called solicitors; those who represent clients in court as their counsels are barristers. Some lawyers do both. Robert Lewis-Manning, Alma's lawyer, and Marshall Harvey, George's, were solicitors only.

Manning obtained Sir Terence James O'Connor, 44, called T.J., a much-respected lawyer who concurrently was also a Conservative Member of Parliament, as Alma's lead defence lawyer. The perpetually broke Alma had almost no money and, of course, wasn't allowed under the circumstances to fund her defence with money from Francis's estate, of which she was the sole designated heir. Manning contacted her mother and family in British Columbia who agreed to pay her bills.

George was represented under legal aid, which he had requested, by Joshua Casswell, 49. Casswell had represented some of the families of victims in the *Titanic* disaster who sued the owner of White Star Line for damages. He then went on to primarily practise criminal law.

Opposing lawyers in one case sometimes worked together on another. O'Connor and Casswell had teamed up successfully earlier in 1935 to get the murder conviction of 21-year-old Reginald Woolmington overturned on a rare legal argument of the time — "presumption of innocence."

Many of the cases Casswell took on were, like George's, legal aid. "I always made a point of accepting these briefs whenever I was available, not only because they provided me with a challenge of a stimulating kind but because I considered them an essential part of my professional duties," he wrote in *A Lance for Liberty*, his 1961 memoir.

In his 1988 book *Murder at the Villa Madeira*, Sir David Napley, a lawyer who promulgated that George was innocent and Alma guilty, criticized Alma for not providing money for George to have a non-legal-aid lawyer. People paid attention because Napley had been president of the Law Society of England and Wales in 1976–77. A February 2020 article in the *Law Society Gazette* described him as a "celebrated legal figure, a star."[2] He had a particular interest in getting what he saw as miscarriages of justice recognized and believed George belonged to this category.

"If Alma was so deeply in love with Stoner, as some would have had others believe, would she not in securing the best-paid legal representation for herself have insisted that the same level of legal ability be made to available to her lover?" wrote Napley in *Murder at the Villa Madeira*. "Indeed, some might consider that the object of such great devotion would have been her first care, even before herself."[3]

Napley chose to overlook that Alma was having trouble enough raising money for her own defence. Co-defendants such as Alma and Stoner aren't allowed to have the same lawyer in case one is asked to testify against the other at their joint trial. Their trial is "joint" because they're "answering" the same charge based on the same facts. However, the defendants' lawyers aren't working as a team; each represents his or her client only, and to save the client may well attack the other defendant.

O'Connor shared Manning's opinion that Alma was innocent. "Nothing you say will affect Stoner's position," they said over and over to her. Every time, Alma said nothing. "She would have done anything or everything — even risking the death sentence — to save Stoner," Manning later recalled.

Manning and O'Connor concluded they would have to resort to what Manning later described as "callous directness," shock tactics. As Holloway's governor John Hall Morton had, they turned to Pinkie Kingham for assistance. "Tell Christopher as gently and tenderly as possible that his mother is in great danger and her lawyers need him to persuade her to tell the truth," Manning said. He hoped that "mother love would be stronger than any other feeling."

On May 16, with only 11 days to go before the trial started, Pinkie brought Christopher to Holloway to see his mother. They met in the bare interview room. She had one eye bandaged due to an infection and tried to appear cheerful. He implored her to tell all that she knew. As Manning and O'Connor had hoped, Christopher's visit broke down Alma's resistance. "I wish I had brought Christopher to her sooner," Pinkie said afterward.

When Manning next came, Alma told him, "For the sake of the children, I will tell the whole truth." She no longer denied that Stoner had committed the murder.

"He was silent, completely uncooperative," Casswell later wrote about George. He decided the best strategy would be to not have Stoner testify.

London's Central Criminal Court is popularly called the Old Bailey because it's old, much of it erected in 1673, and on Bailey Street, so named because it's on the site of a bailey, a rampart, constructed just outside the wall of the City of London in Norman times. Its appearance is both magnificent and intimidating.

The exterior is faced in Portland stone, a greyish limestone used extensively in the United Kingdom, including for St. Paul's Cathedral and Buckingham Palace. On top of its 67-foot-high copper dome, there's a 12-foot-tall gold-painted statue of Lady Justice holding a sword in one hand and the scales of justice in the other. She isn't blindfolded as she usually is depicted because the court wants to convey that it's "clear-sighted."

Carvings over the main entrance represent fortitude, the recording angel, and truth, while an inscription says "Defend the children of the poor and punish the wrongdoer" from Psalm 72:4. The entrance today is only open for ceremonial occasions but was regularly used at the time of Alma and George's trial.

The lobby is equally magnificent: marble floor, mosaic arches, and paintings signifying labour, art, wisdom, and truth. At the time of the trial, the Old Bailey had four courtrooms, all oak-panelled. Each had a large dock enclosed by low partitions for the defendants, with a connecting staircase to prisoners' holding cells below. There were separate waiting rooms for male and female witnesses and another for witnesses of "the better class." Lawyers had their own room, as did their clerks. There was an opulently appointed dining room for the judges. An extension was added in 1972.

Alma and George were tried in Court Number One, reserved for the most serious and high-profile trials, chiefly murder cases. It's small, so judge, jury, and defendants are quite close together.

The public's attention was captured by Alma and George's case, so getting a spectator seat was an obsession. As with much in the United Kingdom, the social barrier between the upper and lower classes placed the upper ahead of the lower. On Saturday, May 25, two days before the trial's opening day, there was a rush for seats from members of the top strata, keen to obtain "privilege seats" behind the lawyers. "It was as if they were trying to book the best seats in the stalls at a matinee," the *Bournemouth Daily Echo* wrote. "There is amazing interest." In Britain, "stalls" were a theatre's best seats on the main floor in front of the stage.

The lower strata had to be resourceful. Some stood all night at the entrance to the public gallery, intending to sell their places in the morning to later arrivals willing to pay scalper's rates. Others slept in the street. A street vendor sold coffee and rolls. Police maintained order.

F. Tennyson Jesse wrote in her commentary preceding the transcript *Trial of Alma Victoria Rattenbury and George Percy Stoner*: "There was probably no one in England and no one in court when the trial opened save Mrs. Rattenbury, her solicitor and counsel, and Miss Riggs who did not think Mrs. Rattenbury was guilty of the crime of murder."[4]

Monday, May 27, was warm and sunny. Pinkie Kingham joined the general lineup around 8:00 a.m. because her promised reserved ticket couldn't be found. Around the same time, Alma arrived from Holloway Prison and George from Brixton Prison. The difference in their modes of transportation underscored the class distinction between them. Alma was driven in a large saloon car, George in the steel locked cage of a police van. British police vehicles were nicknamed "Black Marias." There are many folklore explanations as to why, including a popular racehorse name; Maria Lee, the Black owner of a sailors' boarding house; a Black woman arrested Saturday nights for drunkenness; and the English version of a term used in an 1868 French detective novel.

There were separate holding cell sections for men and women. A cell had a minuscule wooden table and bench, both screwed to the floor, and a tiny, barred window.

The lead Crown counsel was Sir Reginald Croom-Johnson, 55, a barrister, Member of Parliament, and a noted philatelist with a specialist collection of British Solomon Islands stamps. He had written a guide, *Postage-Stamp Collecting Illustrated*, published in 1923.

The judge, Sir Richard Somers Travers Christmas Humphreys, who went by "Travers," 68, had in his lawyer days defended playwright/author Oscar Wilde (*The Importance of Being Earnest*, *The Picture of Dorian Gray*) against sodomy charges and prosecuted Edith Thompson. He was appointed a High Court judge in 1928 and received the customary accompanying knighthood.

The trial began at 10:30 a.m. As usual in Court Number One, the proceedings were opened with pomp and circumstance by an usher of the court:

> If anyone can inform My Lords, the King's Justices, or the King's Attorney-General, ere this inquest be taken between our Sovereign Lord, the King, and prisoners at the bar, of any treasons, murders, felonies, or misdemeanours, done, or committed by the prisoners at the bar, let them come forth and they shall be heard; for the prisoners now stand at the bar on their deliverance. And all persons who are bound by recognizance

to prosecute or give evidence against the prisoners at the bar, let them come forth, prosecute, and give evidence or they shall forfeit their recognizances. God save the King.

Everyone stood in respect as Humphreys, described by the press as "a small, alert figure," entered wearing the customary High Court justice outfit of a red velvet robe trimmed with white ermine fur; a "full-bottom" wig, a long handmade white one that hung over the ears to below the shoulders; and breeches, stockings, buckled shoes, and white gloves. He carried a triangular piece of black material known as the Black Cap, donned by judges when they impose a death sentence, and a small nosegay, a tradition going back centuries to when cases were held in the adjacent Newgate Prison and judges had a posy of sweet herbs to ward off the typhus rampant in the prison due to the large quantity of lice, bedbugs, fleas, mites, and rats biting and infecting inmates. A High Court judge is addressed as "My Lord" during a trial.

The lawyers wore black silk robes and "barrister wigs" made of white horsehair with frizzled crowns, rows of coiled curls at the back, and two queues (pigtails) at the bottom, perched atop their heads.

After Humphreys took his place, Alma was led up the stone stairway from the holding cells to the courtroom and was seated at the right side of the prisoners' dock. She had always made a point of being stylish, and this was no exception. A study in blue except for the fox fur stole around her shoulders, she wore a matching outfit of dark-blue coat, dark-blue silk dress with a dark-blue and white dotted scarf, wide-brimmed dark-blue straw hat, and dark-blue elbow-length suede gloves. During her two months in jail, her hair had grown from its original bob to long enough to braid around her ears. Her face was lightly powdered, she wore red lipstick, and had dabbed on perfume. Alma's fashionable appearance was suitable for a *British Vogue* cover. She glanced briefly around the court, then half hid her face with her fur stole.

George was brought up and placed at the left end. He and Alma were separated by a warden and wardress sitting between them. George wore the light-grey suit she had bought him at Harrods. She gave him a fleeting glance, but he didn't return it.

Daily Mirror reporter Barbara Back wrote,

> After the first glance she gave round the court, Mrs.
> Rattenbury remained half-hidden by her fur, and apparently
> quite unmoved. She is more than a pretty woman: her face
> is attractive with its large perfect eyes, short nose and thick-
> lipped mouth. She was said to be thirty-eight. She looked
> much younger. She wears her dark blue coat and hat with
> gloves to match with a certain chic.
>
> Stoner looks even less than his eighteen years. He has a
> pale gentle face.

The Clerk of the Court rose and said, "Alma Victoria Rattenbury and
George Percy Stoner, you are charged with the murder of Francis Mawson
Rattenbury on the twenty-eighth of March last. Alma Victoria Rattenbury,
are you guilty or not guilty?"

"I plead not guilty."

The press wrote that she had "a faint smile" as she said the words.

"George Percy Stoner, are you guilty or not guilty?" the Clerk of the
Court asked next.

"I plead not guilty."

The press said George spoke "in a clear voice."

Alma's counsel, T.J. O'Connor, and George's, Joshua Casswell, were sitting near each other at the counsels' table. O'Connor leaned over to Casswell
and said, "Mrs. Rattenbury is going to give evidence against your boy."

Casswell had never considered that this might happen. "This was the
first I knew," he later wrote in his memoir, "that Mrs. Alma Rattenbury
was going so far in her efforts to save her own neck as actually to give sworn
testimony against her ex-lover."

Hurriedly, Casswell rose to his feet and asked for separate trials. "Mrs.
Rattenbury's April 18 letter to Irene Riggs if read out might have a very bad
influence upon the minds of the jury as regards Stoner. It would be difficult
for the jury to disabuse their minds of it. Whereas if Stoner were tried alone,
the letter could not be used as evidence and the jury would not hear it."

Humphreys asked O'Connor, "Do you support this application?"

"I do not oppose it," O'Connor replied.

Humphreys then asked the prosecutor, Croom-Johnson, "Do you intend to use this piece of evidence?"

"The letter is no different from the other evidence in the case," Croom-Johnson replied. "I had intended saying something about it to the jury, but that is entirely at Your Lordship's discretion."

Humphreys said, "No, Mr. Croom-Johnson, it is for you to decide whether any particular matter brought to my attention is admissible in evidence or not. It is not for a judge to advise either side how they should conduct their case. I much rather prefer to leave them to conduct the case themselves and I am in a position, so to speak, of an umpire. Very well, I am much obliged. When that letter is tendered in evidence, I will rule whether it is evidence or not." He denied Casswell's application. "I see no ground for directing that there should be separate trials in this case."

Casswell later wrote in his memoir that he thought the one-sentence ruling was "rather terse."

The twelve-person jury included two women; the rest were men. The inclusion of women was a step forward for women's rights. Although women had been eligible for jury duty since 1919, there were efforts to keep them off based on the continuing chauvinistic view that "women are intellectually inferior to men and too emotional." The Clerk of the Court addressed them: "Members of the jury, the prisoners at the bar, Alma Victoria Rattenbury and George Percy Stoner, are charged with the murder of Francis Mawson Rattenbury on 28 March last. To this indictment they have separately pleaded not guilty, and it is in your charge to say, having heard the evidence, whether they, or either of them, be guilty or not."

Throughout the trial, Alma was called "Mrs. Rattenbury," while George was referred to as "Stoner," not "Mr. Stoner."

The prosecution goes first in a trial. Croom-Johnson rose to his feet to present the case for the Crown, going over Alma and Stoner's London excursion, then proceeding to Francis's murder. "It is the submission of the prosecution in this case that the relationship between Mrs. Rattenbury and Stoner had ceased to be that of the wife of the employer and the man employed but had become an adulterous intercourse. The prosecution submits that Mr. Rattenbury stood in the way of their indulgence in this guilty passion.

"Ladies and gentlemen, it looks as though Stoner, having borrowed the mallet, which undoubtedly was the instrument used to inflict the head injuries, brought it back, naming some purpose or other, to the house, and it is the contention of the prosecution that one or other of the accused delivered a blow or blows at the head of Mr. Rattenbury, and, if that is right, the prosecution suggests for your consideration that these two people, Mrs. Rattenbury and Stoner, with one common object and one common design, set out to get rid of Mr. Rattenbury, who, as I suggested earlier, stood in their way. That, members of the jury, is the contention of the prosecution in this case."

"Adulterous intercourse," "guilty passion" — these phrases were intended to reverberate in the jurors' minds throughout the trial.

Daily Mirror reporter Barbara Back wrote,

> After sitting in the court for several hours, you become unconsciously part of the machine. Your heart stops aching for the prisoners. You can look at them without feeling cruel or inquisitive. At first, I watched the judge, wondering if he would show, by the flicker of an eyelid, what he was feeling. Now I don't bother. I was lulled into a sort of coma by Croom-Johnson's droning voice. He was a very dull speaker, but he was seeking to establish a theory, not to make an effect.

The Crown's first witness was Harold Robert Homewood, assistant to the borough engineer of Bournemouth. "On 26 March, I went to Five Manor Road, Bournemouth, the house where Mr. and Mrs. Rattenbury had been living and I made a survey of the premises. I produce a plan which I made from that survey, Exhibit 1."

He was followed by Police Constable Arthur Edward Punter. "On 28 March, I went to Five Manor Road, Bournemouth, and took some photographs of the outside and inside of the house. I produce the positives which were taken from the negatives that I took. They are Exhibit 2."

Frederick Clements, the retired police sergeant who had seen Stoner on the evening of March 24 outside his parents' Ensbury Park house, was next, followed by Stoner's grandmother, Elizabeth Stevens, and uncle, Richard, who identified the mallet as theirs.

Then came Irene Riggs, the day's most awaited witness. "She entered the witness box, looking very smart in a bright-green dress and a white hat," Barbara Back wrote. Croom-Johnson began by asking how long she had worked at Villa Madeira, her duties, George's, and the layout of the house. He wanted to know the type of clothing Alma wore.

"Mr. Croom-Johnson appeared to be rather at sea with Miss Riggs's description of a jumper [British English for "sweater"]," Back wrote, "and nothing could make the learned counsel understand what a three-piece suit was until it was produced as an exhibit and held up piece-by-piece in front of the witness box."

Maybe Croom-Johnson was genuinely puzzled, but it's possible he was pretending in order to linger on this visible evidence of Alma's unconventionality.

Back continued: "Mrs. Rattenbury listened attentively to Miss Riggs's evidence and watched her all the time she gave it. But not once during the day did I see the boy, or she, glance at each other."

"Look at Exhibit 3," Croom-Johnson told Irene. "Do you recognize that watch?"

"Yes."

"Do you know whose it is?"

"Mrs. Rattenbury's."

A judge can take over questioning of witnesses at a trial if he or she feels elaboration is necessary. How long can this continue? Until the judge is satisfied. What if the lawyer doesn't want the witness to discuss what the judge is asking? He or she can stand up and object. Since the judge has decided he needed to intervene and ask clarifying questions, he will usually say "objection overruled," which means the judge will continue questioning the witness himself.

Using this prerogative, Humphreys interjected and asked Irene, "It is a man's watch, is it not? How do you know it is hers? Have you seen her wearing it?"

"I think it belonged to her father or grandfather or somebody."

"Where have you seen it?"

"On her dressing table."

"It is not a watch, obviously, a woman would wear. It is a very big, heavy man's watch."

"A heavy hunter," Croom-Johnson added. With that settled, Croom-Johnson moved on. "Look at Exhibit 4, which is an envelope. Do you know Mrs. Rattenbury's handwriting?"

"Yes."

"Is that envelope addressed 'Mr. George Stoner, Villa Madeira, 5 Manor Road, Bournemouth?'"

"Yes."

"Look at Exhibit 5. In whose handwriting is that?"

"I say the same as the envelope."

"Does that document bear this upon it — 'No. 880: Name, A.V. Rattenbury, Holloway Prison, 27.3.1935. I am trying to have the lawyer's letter received today sent to you, darling, so that you can make arrangements to come up with him, or make arrangements with the governor. But I must see you darling. This is the third letter I have written. Hope you receive this. I hardly know how to write now. God bless you. My love be with you always. Lozanne.'"

"Yes."

Croom-Johnson continued reading the letter. "'Have you talked with Dr. O'Donnell about how Ratz is? Goodness, there is so much I want to know. Please ask Irene to give you a few bobby pins for my hair. I think they would be allowed.' Do you know who Ratz is?" the prosecutor asked Irene.

"Mr. Rattenbury."

"How do you know that?"

"It was Mrs. Rattenbury's name for him."

"While you've been employed by Mr. and Mrs. Rattenbury, has there ever been a tent in the garden?"

"A sun shelter."

"Is a sun shelter put up with pegs?"

"Yes."

"What sort of pegs?"

"Just little ones."

"Ones, as far as you could see, that would be easily driven in?"

"Yes."

"Did you receive yourself a letter from Mrs. Rattenbury after she was arrested?"

"Yes."

"In whose handwriting is that letter?"

"The same as the others."

The moment Casswell had been fearing had arrived; he knew this letter would implicate his client, George. He interrupted to protest. "My Lord, if it is proposed to put this letter in, in my submission it is not evidence. We have now come to that piece of additional evidence which I have already drawn to Your Lordship's attention before. In my submission, that is not evidence. It cannot be evidence either against Mrs. Rattenbury or against my client Stoner."

"Of course," Humphreys said, "it will not prejudice your client. It is not evidence against him. The letter is prima facie admissible in evidence against Mrs. Rattenbury if it is a letter in her handwriting. It may help her or be against her — one does not know anything about it at present. Obviously, it is not. No objection is taken." (Prima facie denotes evidence that, unless rebutted, would be sufficient to prove a particular proposition or fact.)

"My learned friends have got a copy of this," Croom-Johnson said. "There is a great deal in it dealing with all sorts of personal details about wearing apparel and the like. If either of my learned friends want me to read the whole letter, I will do so."

"Mr. O'Connor, this is a matter for you," Humphreys said. "Your client is concerned with it. Would you like it all read?"

"I should like it read from the words 'Oh Lord, and tomorrow Good Friday.'"

"That is about two-thirds of the way down the first page?" Croom-Johnson asked.

"Members of the jury," Humphreys said, "you understand that the letter is now in evidence, therefore it will be available for you when the time comes for you to read it. You will be entitled to look at all of it. There is nothing in it that anybody wants to keep away from you. The reason it is not being read in entirety is that both counsel agree that it is immaterial. It is about clothes, or something of that sort. It has nothing to do with this case, and that is all. It is not being kept away from you at all, and when the time comes, if you like, you can read it all if it interests you."

Croom-Johnson proceeded to read the final paragraph. "'S.'s feelings must take some weighing up, but he'll be the same and not allow himself to think. Should think his remorse at what he's brought down on my head, the children's, etc. — smashed lives — would drive him a raving lunatic — a frightful responsibility to hold in one person's hands. God deliver me from such a hellish responsibility.'"

"Now that letter must be made an exhibit," Humphreys said.

It was marked Exhibit 43.

Irene had achieved what she'd intended when she'd given the letter to the police — place the blame on George.

Now it was O'Connor's turn to question Irene. "During the whole of these four years that you have belonged to that household, have Mrs. Rattenbury's relations with her husband been perfectly friendly?"

"Yes."

"With the exception of one trivial quarrel, have you ever known them to have a quarrel?"

"Just little funny affairs, but nothing."

"Just little two penny, ha'penny affairs?"

"Yes."

"You have known for some time, have not you, that the relations between Mrs. Rattenbury and Stoner were those of a woman and her lover?"

"Yes."

"And did Mrs. Rattenbury tell you that her life had been threatened more than once by him?"

"Yes."

"Was there an occasion —"

Realizing that the position of the man he was defending was getting worse by the minute, Casswell interrupted. "My Lord, I object. This apparently is evidence of something which was said to this lady by one of the accused."

"Well?" Humphreys said.

Casswell elaborated. "It does not appear to have been said in his presence and in my submission it cannot be evidence against him, and there is no purpose in bringing it out at all unless it is evidence against him."

"I am not concerned with the object of learned counsel in bringing out something which in my view is clearly admissible in evidence for or against his client," Humphreys said.

Casswell retreated, and O'Connor continued with Irene. "Did you say that on two or three occasions she told you that he had threatened her life?"

"Yes."

"Not two or three," Humphreys interjected. "I do not think she said that."

"About how many times, Miss Riggs?" O'Connor amended.

"I cannot say."

O'Connor asked her to recall the heated quarrel between George and Alma in February when George came close to strangling her.

"Stoner had a firm hold of Mrs. Rattenbury," she told him.

"Who separated them?"

"I separated them."

"Did Stoner used to carry a dagger about with him?"

"Yes."

"What kind of length was it?"

"A blade about four inches."

At O'Connor's request, Irene detailed the events on the night of March 24 as she saw them: Alma's chat with her, seeing George leaning over the upper stairwell, Alma calling her to come downstairs to the drawing room, Rattenbury slumped in his chair, blood everywhere, her calling Dr. O'Donnell to come help, Ratz being taken away in an ambulance, Alma's consumption of many drinks, her drunken attempt to kiss Constable Bagwell, Alma's fuzzy condition from the combination of drinks and O'Donnell's morphia injection at the time the police arrested her and took her to Bournemouth Prison.

O'Connor then asked about George's confession to her.

"On the Tuesday, I asked Stoner why he had done it," Irene said.

"What did he say?"

"He said because he'd seen Mr. Rattenbury living with Mrs. Rattenbury in the afternoon."

"Let me have this. On the Tuesday, was it?"

"Yes."

"Was he sober when he said that?" Humphreys asked.

"Yes."

It was now Casswell's turn. "You have said that Mrs. Rattenbury and her husband got on well together except on one occasion. On that occasion did Mrs. Rattenbury have a black eye?"

"She had an injured eye, yes."

"Had Dr. O'Donnell to be sent for?"

"Yes."

"Had she bitten her husband's arm very badly?"

"Yes. I don't know whether she bit him, but she did something to his arm."

"Because he was a quiet old gentleman, was he not?"

"He seemed to be, yes. He showed me his arm."

"It was bitten, was it not?"

"I don't know."

Casswell sought to portray Alma as a drug addict. He showed Irene the hypodermic syringe found in Alma's medicine chest. "We have been told that that was found in something in the nature of a medicine chest in Mrs. Rattenbury's room. Have you seen that before?"

"Yes."

"Where did you see it?"

"It's always been at the very back of the cupboard and to my knowledge was only used by her to give Christopher injections for a glandular problem in his left leg on his doctor's advice."

Casswell presented her with a picture Christopher had drawn of a man with an exaggeratedly long hypodermic needle bending over a boy sitting up in bed.

"It's the only one he did," Irene said. "He draws weird pictures. They're all over the house."

"You mean to say that no attempt was made to hide that case?" Casswell asked.

"No, no attempt at all."

"Was the case shut?"

"Yes, the lid was on."

"Did you know what was inside it?"

"I always have known."

When Casswell finished, Humphreys asked a series of questions about Alma's habits. "You have told the jury that Mrs. Rattenbury was sometimes excitable and sometimes drank too much alcohol?"

"Yes."

"And that she had drinking bouts. How long had that lasted — all the time you were there?"

"Yes."

"And how often did she have drinking bouts?"

"Sometimes she'd go a month or so without having one."

"And sometimes it was more often than once a month?"

"Yes."

"You also told the jury that at times she had what you call sudden attacks, when she got excitable and ran about, and afterward used to go to bed and sleep. Were those occasions when she had been drinking?"

"Yes, more or less."

"Did it seem to you that her condition at those times was due to drink?"

"Yes, I always thought so."

"That is what it seemed like. Did you ever know her to take drugs? Things like cocaine, morphia, and heroin?"

"No, not to my knowledge."

Humphreys adjourned the trial for the day. It was 4:40 p.m. Irene had been in the witness box three and a half hours, never once hesitating. Casswell later wrote in his memoir, "This domestic servant was one of the strongest witnesses I ever cross-examined."

Newspaper headlines reported:

LOZANNE FACES HER JUDGE

TRIED TO KISS POLICE, SAYS WOMAN WITNESS

A QUARREL AT MIDNIGHT

BOY CHAUFFEUR'S ORDEAL

"HUSBAND IN THE WAY," COUNSEL SUBMITS

NIGHT WALKS CLAD ONLY IN PYJAMAS

"THIS GUILTY PASSION": PROSECUTING
  COUNSEL

MRS. RATTENBURY "IN A TERRIFIED STATE"

LOZANNE WRITES FROM GAOL OF "SMASHED
  LIVES"

SEPARATE TRIALS REFUSED

On Tuesday, the lineup to get into the public gallery had swelled exponentially. "Many well-dressed women who arrived in cars were disappointed in their efforts to secure seats," the *Daily Express* reported. "Some women with picnic baskets containing vacuum flasks [thermoses] and sandwiches picnicked in court. Others crowded into their seats at the last minute before the judge entered."

The day's principal witness was Dr. O'Donnell. Croom-Johnson's junior counsel, Edward Anthony ("Tony") Hawke, did the questioning for the prosecution. He asked him to describe Francis's condition when he arrived in response to Irene's urgent phone call late March 24.

"There was a bloodstained towel wrapped around Mr. Rattenbury's head. His head was bathed in blood, which was clotted and clinging to his hair. He was unconscious — laboured breathing. His left eye was very contused, purple, and swollen. His pulse was slow and very irregular."

"You told us Mrs. Rattenbury was there?"

"Yes."

"What condition was she in?"

"Very exited and inclined to be intoxicated."

"Had she got any materials for becoming inclined to be intoxicated with her?"

"Yes."

"What had she got?"

"She had a whisky and soda in a glass in her hand."

"How was she dressed?"

"In her pyjamas without any shoes."

"Had she anything over her pyjamas?"

"No."

"Did you speak to her when you saw her?"

"I did."

"What did you say?"

"I asked her what had happened."

"What did she say?"

"She said, 'Look at him. Look at the blood. Somebody has finished him.'"

O'Connor's cross-examination covered a wide range. "You have examined her body on several occasions?"

"Many occasions."

"Have you ever seen any sign or suggestion of any sort that were marks of a hypodermic needle?"

"Never."

"Speaking generally, how would you describe her temperament?"

"Uneven."

"Excitable?"

"Yes, very."

"As her medical attendant, and one who has had every opportunity of seeing her temperament at close quarters, do you think it would be possible for Mrs. Rattenbury to take part in a crime of this description and then act perfectly peacefully and normally with her maid?"

"I do not consider it possible."

"Have you ever seen her in a condition as excited as she was on that night?"

"No."

"What were her habits as regards drink?"

"Occasionally she had too much."

"She was not a chronic drunkard but had bouts?"

"No — occasionally."

"Did she tell you that Stoner was her lover?"

"She did."

"What date was that?"

"February 12, 1935."

"Did she tell you of anything that Stoner had tried to do to her?"

"Yes."

"What did she say?"

"She told me that he had tried to strangle her."

"Tell My Lord and the jury in what condition you spoke to her at one o'clock on the following afternoon at the police station."

"She could not walk, she had to be supported into the room where I was, a police matron supporting her on the one side and Inspector Carter on the other."

"At that time, one o'clock, was she dazed?"

"Yes."

"Was she in a fit condition to make a statement?"

"I do not consider so."

"What do you say as to her fitness to make a statement at six, seven, or eight o'clock that morning?"

"I should not place any credence on a statement given under such circumstances."

"By any stretch of imagination, from what you saw of her at one o'clock, would it be true to say that at six o'clock that morning she could have been normal?"

"I should say no."

"Or at eight o'clock?"

"No."

That concluded O'Connor's questioning. It was now Casswell's turn to cross-examine the doctor. He began by asking, "With regard to Stoner, a boy of seventeen and a half, was that the sort of atmosphere that you would put a boy in?"

"Well, it is very easy to be wise after the event. I should say no to that question."

"If you had regulation of that household, you would not have had him sleep there in that household, would you?"

"I could not say no to that."

"No, you could not say no, I agree."

Casswell turned to the topic of George and cocaine. "Then the time comes in February when you are asked to speak to him because you are told that he takes cocaine."

"She did not tell me he took cocaine."

"She told you she thought he was a drug addict?"

"Yes."

"That is rather a terrible thing to be told about a lad just over eighteen, is it not?"

"Yes."

"Because one does not know where it will lead, does one?"

"Decidedly."

"Have you had much experience of cocaine poisoning?"

"No, I am thankful to say I have not."

"What symptoms did you look for?"

"I did not look for any."

"But you asked him, and he said he had been taking cocaine?"

"Yes."

"Did you believe him?"

"Well, I suppose I did."

"Did you ask him whether he had been up to London to try to get it?"

"He told me he had been up to London the day before to get it."

"Did he say whether he had managed to get it or not?"

"He said he had failed."

"Did he tell you where the money had come from to get it?"

"He did not."

"Did you ask him?"

"No."

"So the steps you took on his behalf were to warn him of the dangers of cocaine?"

"That is so."

"Do you think it is much good to warn a cocaine taker of the dangers of cocaine?"

"No, I do not think it is."

"What report did you make to Mrs. Rattenbury about this?"

"I reported to Mrs. Rattenbury that he had told me that he was taking cocaine."

"Is that all?"

"I told her where he had suggested he had got it from to commence with. I told her I had warned him of the evil effects and implored him to give it up."

"He suggested to you that he had first found it at his home?"

"Yes."

"A working man's home is not the sort of place where you would expect to find cocaine, is it?"

"No."

"Did you ask him how much he took in a dose?"

"No."

Crown Counsel Croom-Johnson sought to diminish the impact of O'Donnell saying Alma had been in no condition to be questioned by the police nor give a statement. "Is coffee a thing which might assist in getting rid, temporarily at all events, the effect of a drug?"

"Coffee, walking about, and a bath."

"A hot bath?"

"Yes."

Inspector Carter had had Alma do all of these.

"What effect does morphia have on the patient besides making the patient sleepy?" Croom-Johnson asked.

"It makes them fuddled and muddled and not able to think properly."

"Unable to tell a coherent story?"

"The brain will not function properly."

"Would you like to place any reliance at all on any statement made by a person under the influence of morphia?" Humphreys asked.

"No, My Lord."

"Did you make any inquiry as to how often he had taken cocaine since he had discovered it gave him a pleasant sensation?"

"No, My Lord."

"Does that mean you did not gather from him whether it was a matter of a week or of five years?"

"That is so. I did not ask him."

Humphreys said no more, and Croom-Johnson resumed his interrogation of O'Donnell. "You did not ask him?"

"I was only asked to find out what drug he was taking and to warn him about it."

"I gather you have no experience of people who are taking cocaine?"

"No."

Humphreys used his judge's prerogative to ask O'Donnell some more questions. "Surely your experience is enough, is it not, to know that it is important to find out whether a person has been taking it for a week or for five years?"

"He seemed perfectly normal to me that day. I had no reason to believe he was taking large doses of cocaine."

"Or that he had been taking it for some time?"

"I could not say that he had taken any from what I saw that day."

"He said he had?"

"Yes, he told me he had."

"He said he had been up to London to get it the day before?"

"Yes."

"Did you understand from him whether that was the first time that he had been up to London to get it, or not?"

"No, I did not ask him."

Humphreys said no more, and Croom-Johnson was able to resume. He queried O'Donnell about his injecting Alma with morphia. "When she came down, between the first time that she had been taken up to bed and the second time, did she seem less mistress of herself than when she went up?"

"Getting less."

"Was the drug taking effect?"

"Yes."

O'Donnell's testimony ended there. He was followed by the police officers in the case, starting with Constable Bagwell.

Croom-Johnson asked the constable to describe what he had seen the night of March 24.

"She said, 'I know who done it.' I immediately cautioned her. She said, 'I did it with a mallet. Ratz has lived too long. It is hidden. No, my lover did it. It is urine on the chair. I would like to give you £10. No, I won't bribe you.'"

Croom-Johnson picked up a book of photographs from the exhibits table. He opened it to Photograph No. 2, a picture of the mallet.

"I searched for the mallet and found it outside the front door on the left side hidden behind a box back of the trellis work," Bagwell said. "It was about 6:15 a.m. when I found it. There was a piece of flesh and hair on it."

On cross-examination, Alma's lawyer, T.J. O'Connor, asked, "In order to get to where the mallet was found, you have to bend down and get under an overhanging tree?"

"Yes."

"Do you have to squeeze through a narrow passage?"

"Well, it is a bit narrow there, yes."

"The gap between the trellis work and the wall is pretty narrow?"

"Yes."

"It is not the sort of expedition that anybody would be likely to undertake in their bare feet in their pyjamas?"

"The ground is quite even."

"Whoever went would have to crush in between the trellis work and the wall?"

"They would just have to bend down."

O'Connor moved on to when Bagwell went outside.

"I went outside for natural purposes."

"Why go out for natural purposes? Are there not two lavatories in the house?"

"It was impossible for me to go to the lavatory. This lady was pestering me the whole of the time."

When Detective Inspector Carter was in the witness box, considerable time was spent on whether Alma had or hadn't been capable of understanding when he questioned, then charged her, while she still had the large amount of morphia in her system from O'Donnell's injection a few hours earlier.

"What was her condition at 8:15 a.m. on the 25th when you charged her?" Croom-Johnson asked.

"She appeared to me to be definitely normal. She appeared to understand."

"Before we read the statement she made, did she speak coherently?"

"Yes, she spoke with deliberation."

"Had you any difficulty in understanding what she was saying?"

"None whatever."

"When you were in the hall on the way out to the police station, did you see anybody?"

"Yes, the accused Stoner and the maid Riggs at the bottom of the stairs."

"Did Mrs. Rattenbury say anything to them?"

"She did."

"What did she say?"

"'Do not make fools of yourselves.' Stoner replied, 'You have got yourself into this mess by talking too much.'"

O'Connor fiercely cross-examined Carter. "Have you ever seen this woman in your life before?"

"Never."

"The first time in your life you ever saw her was when she was asleep when you arrived?"

"That is so."

"You took a statement from her at 8:15 a.m.?"

"Yes."

"And you have told us that she was then normal?"

"I did."

"How can you judge whether a person you have never seen in your life before was normal?"

"I saw Mrs. Rattenbury when she woke up at 6:00 a.m. and she was then not in a normal condition, but it was at 8:15 a.m. that I decided she was in a normal condition, before I attempted to take a statement from her."

"Do you agree with Dr. O'Donnell that no reliance could be placed on any statement taken from her at that time, 8:15?"

"No, I do not."

"Did you know she had had half a grain of morphia?"

"I was told she had an injection of morphia. I did not inquire how much it was."

"Why not?"

"It did not concern me."

"Did it not concern you, if you were going to take a statement, to know how much it was?"

"No, because if I had not been satisfied that she was normal I should not have taken a statement from her."

On his cross-examination of Carter, Casswell raised questions pertinent to George. "Above the very chair where this man was killed, or badly hurt, over the mantelpiece were there two swords hanging up?"

"Yes."

"And also a pistol with a heavy butt?"

"Yes, there was."

"And the pistol with the heavy butt could easily have been used to give the man a very bad hit on the head?"

"Yes."

"And yet for some reason or other apparently this mallet was used?"

"Yes, that is so."

"I suppose there were other things about the premises which could have been used?"

"I suppose there were several."

"And when you came to look to see that man's head, as you did see it, I think, at the nursing home, there could be no doubt whatever that he had had violence done to him by someone?"

"I am not in a position to say anything about the head because it was swathed in bandages when I saw him at the nursing home."

Court was then adjourned. The newspaper headlines were:

"UNFIT TO MAKE STATEMENT"

ALLEGED CONFESSION "WORTHLESS"
"SHE TRIED TO KISS ME"
"INTOXICATED," DOCTOR SAYS
WHEN MRS. RATTENBURY WAS DRUGGED
STORY THAT STONER TOOK COCAINE

CAN'T RECALL

Wednesday, March 29, began with a question from the jury foreman.[1] "We notice the head of the mallet is split in two from side to side. The bottom half seems to slide easily along the handle. Could we know if it was in that condition when found by the police?"

Bagwell was recalled. "I did not notice that," he said. "I handled it very carefully, but I did not examine it to that extent."

"I think we will be able to clear this up from Dr. Lynch's evidence," Croom-Johnson said.

Roche Lynch, senior analyst at the Home Office, a British government ministry with jurisdiction over criminal investigations, had been requested by Detective Inspector Carter to examine the mallet. "I noticed the split, but there was no evidence the mallet was coming apart. It is an old crack. It weighs two pounds, seven ounces. On it I found a number of short white, grey, and darkish hairs, and a thick whitish substance which resembled a portion of skin. The hairs had been cut at one end which indicated they were from the head of a man who had periodically visited the barber. I compared hairs removed from Mr. Rattenbury's skull with the hairs on the mallet and found that they matched."

When it was his turn to question Lynch, Casswell asked if he was knowledgeable about cocainism, since George, whom Casswell was representing, claimed he was a cocaine addict.

"I am prepared to give assistance on the subject of cocaine addiction, although I have never personally examined addicts. My knowledge is based upon what I might call the toxicology of cocaine."

"Would you agree that a typical symptom of cocainism, somebody having taken cocaine continuously, is hallucinations of touch?" Casswell asked.

"It is part of what I call disordered sensation."

"Have you heard that called the *cocaine bug*?"

"The term *cocaine bug*, as I understand it, is in reference to alleged insects crawling under the skin."

"Quite so, only Dr. O'Donnell has never heard of it, or said he had never seen it in any textbook, but it is quite a well-known expression, is it not?"

"I think it is an expression which has come into use recently."

"Would you agree that one of the principal symptoms is insane jealousy at times?"

"Yes, and a suspicion associated with it."

"An unreasonable jealousy?"

"Yes."

"And delusions of persecution?"

"It has been recorded."

"And, in consequence, the carrying of weapons?"

"Quite possibly."

"Assume that a person has been deprived altogether of cocaine for a period of about two months, would you observe any symptoms?"

"Oh, he would become by then, in all probability, seriously ill. He would collapse both mentally and physically and would be profoundly depressed."

"Would you expect such a person to be normal in behaviour?"

"No."

"Or rational in conversation?"

"No."

"Would you expect him to sleep normally?"

"No, sleeplessness is a very important symptom in addiction."

"Or take his food normally?"

"No. They generally have very poor appetites."

A juror interrupted, going back to the mallet. "Would a person using this mallet in the way that has been described to us be liable to get blood upon their clothing?"

Lynch's answer likely surprised most people. "I think if one single blow were struck, there is likely not to be blood on the clothing of the assailant, but if more than one blow were struck, it would be quite likely to get on to the clothing. On the other hand, I have seen cases where blows of this sort had been struck where no blood got on the clothing."

Croom-Johnson was ready for this. "I have spoken to my learned friend [referring to O'Connor] and what I am saying I am saying with his approval, and I expect with the approval of my learned friend, Mr. Casswell. Of course, both the accused persons in this case helped Mr. Rattenbury to his bedroom when there was any amount of blood about, and it has not occurred to the prosecution accordingly that any deduction can possibly be drawn adversely to any of the accused on the question of blood being on their clothes."

"I entirely agree," O'Connor said. Then he added on Alma's behalf, "There is evidence that there was no blood on the lady's pyjamas. One would expect to find some but, in fact, there was none."

Croom-Johnson next called on Dr. Hugh Arrowsmith Grierson to testify. As Brixton Prison's chief medical officer, Grierson had kept a log on George's health during the two weeks the teenager was there from May 14 to 28. "Under your care how has his behaviour been?"

"He has been normal in behaviour, rational in conversation, and he has taken his food and slept normally."

"The last day upon which he could have the dose would have been the day of his arrest, 28 March," Casswell said to Grierson. "Do you really say that you would expect to see distinct symptoms then?"

"If he was a drug addict, a cocaine addict, I should certainly expect to find some signs and some desire for the drug. The prisoners are under constant watch day and night. All night there is a special officer watching these men and noting the exact amount of sleep that each man has."

"Did he tell you that he had been taking cocaine between slices of bread and butter?"

"Slices of bread, not bread and butter."

"And did he tell you that he took a double dose at about 4:30 p.m. on 24 March?"

"He said he took two eggspoonfuls."

"It has been suggested by Dr. Lynch that two eggspoonfuls would be more than a fatal dose? You would agree with that, I suppose?"

"If it were undiluted," Grierson said. "Stoner told me that cocaine is a brownish powder with black specks, whereas, in fact, it is whitish, and if the dope pedlars had diluted it, they would certainly have done so with some substance of the same colour."

Dr. Edward Waller Mann, medical officer at Dorchester Prison where George had been from March 29 until his transfer to Brixton on May 14, echoed Grierson. "During that time, I did not notice any sign that he was a drug addict, or cocaine addict, and had been deprived of his drug. His behaviour was very good while he was at Dorchester. I did not notice anything abnormal in it. He seemed rational in conversation, and he slept well. I have no report as to his having returned any food. During the time he was at Dorchester Prison, he was healthy and normal."

The prosecution had placed on the exhibits table everything Alma had bought for George during their London excursion — suits, shirts, ties, underwear, socks, shoes, shoe trees, silk handkerchiefs, silk pyjamas, gloves, all-weather coat, and diamond engagement ring — plus the receipts. It also had put on display the Royal Palace Hotel guest register open at where Alma had signed as Mrs. Rattenbury and brother. All the sales clerks verified the purchases.

There was a pause. Humphreys broke it with a question to the Clerk of the Court, "Have you got the original statements made by the accused?"

The spectators became extra-alert.

"In answer to the usual caution, the accused Alma Rattenbury said, 'I am not guilty, and I wish to reserve my right to cross-examine and reserve my defence.' And the accused Stoner said, 'I plead not guilty and reserve my defence.'"

"Then, My Lord, that is the case for the prosecution," Croom-Johnson said.

"My Lord, I call Mrs. Rattenbury," her defence lawyer, T.J. O'Connor, said.

Dressed in the same blue coat, matching dress, scarf, wide-brimmed hat, and gloves accented by the fox fur stole she had worn Monday, Alma, on high heels, walked the short distance from the prisoners' dock to the witness box. *News of the World* reported:

> When she left the dock, the atmosphere became electrical. Every eye followed the woman who had written songs under the name of "Lozanne" as she moved slowly through the well of the court to the witness box with a wardress behind her. She took the oath in a voice that could scarcely be heard, and her counsel urged her to speak up. Her voice then became firm and at times charged with feeling. Although pale she came through the three-hours ordeal with complete composure.

The *Daily Mirror* informed the public:

> She walked slowly across the well of the court followed by a wardress and took the oath in a low voice. The moment she entered the witness box a sudden tension swept over everybody. Mrs. Rattenbury held the stage.

The *Daily Express* recounted:

> One had the same kind of exhilaration as when at Lord's in a test match, some great player goes in to bat. [Lord's is a cricket field in northwest London.]
>
> Emotion was plain to see in the hollow eyes of a woman no longer young and in the full red moist lips continually pouting and twitching.

Sitting in the spectator section beside F. Tennyson Jesse was Canadian-born actor Raymond Massey, then on the London stage. He and one other boy had attended kindergarten at Havergal College in Toronto, otherwise an all-girls school, during the time Alma, who was four years older, was a student. In his 1977 memoir *When I Was Young*, Massey wrote, "I looked back to the blurred mass of little girls, seeing one of them again in clear and tragic focus, thirty-two years later," referring to Alma.[2]

Alma was sworn in. "I swear by Almighty God that the evidence I shall give shall be the truth, the whole truth, and nothing but the truth."

Her voice was soft, almost inaudible. O'Connor requested, "Mrs. Rattenbury, will you try and help us all by speaking up and speaking slowly so that we can all hear?" From then on, she spoke clearly.

O'Connor's first question was, "Were you married to the late Mr. Rattenbury seven or eight years ago?"

"Yes."

"I think you had been married twice before?"

"Yes."

"Your first husband was killed in the war?"

"Yes."

"You had no children by that marriage?"

"No."

"You divorced your second husband?"

"Yes."

"And by him you had a boy, Christopher?"

"Yes."

"There is also a child of your marriage to Mr. Rattenbury. Since the birth of that child, did you and Mr. Rattenbury live together as man and wife?"

"No."

"Did you occupy separate rooms?"

"Yes."

"On what terms were you with your husband?"

"Quite friendly."

"No marital intimacy but were you cordial?"

"Absolutely."

"Was your married life happy?"

"Like that," Alma replied, making a so-so gesture with her hands.

O'Connor moved on to finances. "What were the relations between you and your husband as regards money? Was he free with money?"

"Very close — well, not very generous."

"Did you have to say things of which you are ashamed in order to get money from him?"

"All my married life, yes."

"Tell him lies?"

"Yes, it saved rows."

"When did you hire Stoner?"

"September 1934."

"What were his wages?"

"One pound per week."

"Did you become Stoner's mistress?"

"In November."

"Just taking it quite generally, from that time until your husband's death did relations take place between you and Stoner regularly?"

"Yes."

"In his room, or in yours, or in both?"

"Yes."

"One or the other. What attitude did your husband take toward this if he knew it?"

"None whatsoever."

"Did he know of it?"

"He must have known because he told me to live my own life quite a few years ago."

"As I understand it, there was no occasion on which you told him about Stoner, but your husband knew about it?"

"No. I told him I had taken him at his word and was living my own life."

"Oh, you told him that, did you? Can you tell me when that was?"

"I would say it was somewhere about Christmas."

"Stoner almost choked you during an argument between you in February?"

Alma downplayed the incident. "He lost his temper, but it was not very serious."

"Had Stoner ever threatened your life?"

"Well, yes, but I did not take it seriously."

O'Connor moved on. "Now, about this occasion when you went to London. I think, as your banking account shows, you were overdrawn about 10 days before your husband died and he gave you £250, which went into your banking account to make it solvent?"

"Yes."

"How did you get that money from him?"

"Like I always had. I always got extra money from Mr. Rattenbury about twice a year when I was overdrawn and I always had to, what I call, make up a different story each time to get it. I asked for, I think, more money that time than I had before, but I always got about £100 or £150 a year extra, at Christmas and in June, say."

"What was the pretext on which you got more than you usually got?"

"Having been ill. I still used that as an excuse."

Humphreys interjected, "What was the lie you told him?"

"I said I was going to London to have an operation."

O'Connor devoted only a few brief questions to the trip.

"Did you go off with Stoner to London?"

"Yes."

"You stayed at the Royal Palace in rooms quite close to one another, describing yourselves as brother and sister?"

"Yes."

"Were you during that weekend living as man and wife, in fact?"

"Yes."

"When you got back to Manor Road on Friday the 22nd, did your husband ask anything about what had been happening?"

"No, he was always jolly late at night."

"When you say he was 'jolly,' I think he used to drink a little whisky at night?"

"Yes, always."

"About how much?"

"Well, he drank quite a lot then."

"And I think from time to time you have yourself given way to drink?"

"Yes."

O'Connor had her recite the events on Sunday, March 24, culminating in Stoner telling her he had "hurt Mr. Rattenbury," her finding her husband covered in blood, and her accidentally stepping on his false teeth, which were lying on the carpet. She concluded, "That made me hysterical. I took a drink of whisky neat and I was sick and then I remember pouring out another. I tried to become insensible to block out the picture."

She said she couldn't remember anything that happened afterward: O'Donnell, the police, her arrest, her statements.

"Mrs. Rattenbury, did you yourself murder your husband?" O'Connor finally asked.

"Oh, no."

"Did you know a thing about it till Stoner spoke to you in your bed?"

"I would have prevented it if I'd known half ... a quarter of a minute before, naturally."

That ended O'Connor's questioning.

Humphreys instructed that Alma be returned to the prisoners' dock because of the arrival of New Scotland Yard Superintendent Harry Baddeley in charge of its fingerprint branch, called in by the prosecution to answer a juror's question earlier in the day as to whether there were telltale fingerprints on the mallet. Baddeley said, "I was not able to detect any fingerprints on the surface of that mallet anywhere. That includes the handle. It is not a suitable medium for retaining finger impressions. The surface is not entirely smooth. It is grained. As a matter of fact, I attempted to impress my own fingers on the surface of the handle gently and I failed to develop anything at all."

"Is there a difficulty, in your experience, in detecting fingerprints on wooden surfaces as compared with others?" Crown prosecutor Croom-Johnson asked.

"Yes, the surface must be entirely smooth. That is not so in this case."

Neither O'Connor nor Casswell had questions for Baddeley, but a juror did. "I understand there is a method of reviving old fingerprints. Was this done in this case?"

"There are many methods. They were carefully tested on the whole of the surface."

Then Humphreys announced a lunch break.

Tennyson Jesse thought Alma had done well in her responses to O'Connor. "She was an excellent witness. Her voice was low and rich. She gave a great impression of truthfulness, and she was astonishingly self-controlled. Only a nervous tic in the side of her face, which jerked perpetually, betrayed the tension of her mind."[3]

Casswell, writing in his memoir *A Lance for Liberty*, had a mixed reaction:

> To me she appeared vague and unconvincing, at times almost inarticulate; to some questions she replied merely with a gesture of her hands. She made so profound an impression on me that at one time I thought — almost certainly mistakenly — that she was under the influence of a drug.
>
> Yet, however vague and unsatisfactory the manner in which she gave her evidence, there was no doubt that its content was bitterly damning to my client's interests.[4]

During the adjournment, word spread swiftly outside the courtroom and into the crowd massed in the street that Alma was testifying. The disparate mix of clergy, lawyers, fashionably dressed women with fur stoles wrapped around their necks despite the warm weather, and others from lower social strata vied with one another to get in.

The intermission over, Alma returned to the witness box, her face shaded by her wide-brimmed dark-blue straw hat. She appeared to tremble slightly and clasped and unclasped the box's edge with her gloved hands, while George rested his chin on his hand as he listened.

Casswell later wrote in his memoir *A Lance for Liberty*:

> I did not believe at all her saying that she had no recollection of what had happened for so many hours, nor did I accept that she was innocent, but I felt myself to be at a disadvantage because of Stoner's wish to take all the blame.

His loyalty may have been a moving demonstration of the bonds of romantic passion, but it made the task of defending counsel extraordinarily difficult. It also meant that I was unable to cross-examine Mrs. Rattenbury at all strongly. If I had done so, Stoner was quite capable of interrupting me from the dock with a cry that I had got it all wrong — he was the murderer.[5]

Therefore, when the trial resumed, Casswell began with a disclaimer. "Mrs. Rattenbury, I want you to understand from the start that I am not suggesting that you had anything whatever to do with what happened on 24 March, or that you ever incited Stoner, or knew that he was going to do it." He asked her about the stay at the Randolph Hotel in Oxford in November 1934. "Was it there you first had connection with Stoner?"

"No."

"Was it before that or after?"

"After. Twenty-second November."

"How long after that visit to Oxford?"

"I do not know."

"Was it you who suggested it, Mrs. Rattenbury?"

"What — going to Oxford?"

"No, living with Stoner?"

"No, I think it was mutual."

"Mutual?" said Casswell, probably in a tone of disbelief. "Because you see he was in the position of a servant, was he not?"

"Yes."

"And quite a young man?"

"Yes."

"Did you think it might have a very deleterious effect on him?"

"No, I never would have started it if I had."

"But you made things easy by having him in the house, did you not?"

At this point, Humphreys said to Alma, "If you want to sit down, you can do so."

"I think I would sooner stand."

"You can do so if you please. You will probably be there some time and if any time you want to sit down there is a chair available."

"Thank you so much."

Casswell resumed. "I suppose you told him that you and your husband had not been living as husband and wife?"

"It was obvious to anyone living there."

"It was just an infatuation, was it not?"

"I think it was more than that."

"You fell in love with him?"

"Absolutely."

Casswell asked her about her drinking.

"I used to take too many cocktails to liven up one's spirits, taken them to excess, say, or wine. Not spirits, not like that night [March 24], not hard liquor."

"Did Stoner take them also?"

"No. He was very much upset. He did not like me taking them. In fact, I stopped taking them after he came."

"Did people get to know that you seemed to be a little bit too intimate with Stoner, do you think? Did anyone talk to you about it?"

"No."

"Do you remember Mrs. Price [the landlady] saying something to you about it?"

"She sort of referred to it, but I considered it was none of her business to interfere with my private domestic affairs. I politely told her to mind her own business."

"Did you say on that occasion, 'I told you I would make him love me and I have'?"

"Absolutely not. Absolutely a falsehood."

Casswell proceeded to ask about the London trip. "Why did you take him to London and spend all this money on him?"

"Because having said to Mr. Rattenbury I was going away, I had to go and I took that for an opportunity to get him some clothes which he very much needed."

"Why was it necessary to go to London?"

"Well, I could not think of any other place to go. I might have gone to Devon."

"Would it not have been better if you had found a room for your chauffeur somewhere else when you went up there?"

"Yes. I wish I had since."

Casswell had her recount her request to O'Donnell to ask Stoner if he was taking drugs and, if so, to warn him that it was dangerous. He next asked her about the gun Stoner had brandished at her on the night of March 24 with Francis nearby.

"I could hardly get up and say, 'Give me that gun,' in front of Mr. Rattenbury, could I?"

"Have you ever seen — I am not accusing you of anything — had you ever seen this mallet in the house before?"

"No, never."

"Had you suggested somebody should get a mallet?"

"Oh, no."

"Had you not?"

"No, absolutely no."

Casswell asked no further questions. He was succeeded by Crown prosecutor Croom-Johnson. Throughout his cross-examination questioning, he kept jabbing his pencil toward her for emphasis. His first question indicated that Alma was in for a grilling.

"Mrs. Rattenbury, you appreciate, do you, that there is only one person alive who can check your story of what went on in this house from the time that Irene Riggs went out until Irene Riggs came back on that Sunday evening?"

"Yes."

"That person is Stoner?"

"Yes."

"Tell me this. You have been asked already what the point was in the journey to London with this boy whose mistress you were. What was the point of the journey to London with this boy if, in fact, you and he had been living together practically as man and wife since 22 November 1934?"

"I tried to explain that just now. It was all for Mr. Rattenbury's benefit."

"Mr. Rattenbury's benefit?" (Probably said incredulously with a thrust of his pencil for dramatic effect.)

"Because I said I was going to London to have an operation and I had to leave home."

"What was the point of going on the journey at all?"

"Because I could not stay in that house when he had given me the money for the operation. As I say, I might have gone to Cornwall or anywhere." Only a few moments earlier, she had said Devon. The county of Devon is bordered on its west side by the county of Cornwall.

"I want to be fair with you. Before you asked for the money from your husband, had you made up your mind to go to London?"

"No."

"You got the money on the same day?"

"Oh, if —"

"The same day. Then before you went to your husband for money you had made up your mind to go to London?"

"To go to London, yes, because you would naturally say London for an operation, you see."

"With Stoner?"

"Yes."

"Am I putting it fairly when I suggest that you were in the habit of deceiving your husband in order to get what you regarded as sufficient money for your needs?"

"Absolutely."

"Did you know that your husband's securities had fallen very considerably in value?"

"No. He was always talking like that, so it was a case of the lamb calling wolf. If it was so, one would not have believed him."

"Did he tell you that it would be a considerable sacrifice if he gave it to you?"

"Yes, but he always all his life talked like that, so that no one ever took him seriously on the point of money."

"Madam, please do not tell me 'no one.' Let us confine our attention to yourself and your husband. [Probably said sharply.] When you say that you did not take him seriously —"

"No, absolutely not."

"Were you fond of your husband?"

"I did not love him, no. I was more of a companion than anything."

"If he had wanted his rights as a husband, would you have been ready to grant them to him?"

"If he had wanted what — oh, no, I do not think so."

"In March of 1935?"

"Oh, no, I do not think so — decidedly not."

"Were you fond of this boy?"

"I loved him."

"Did it occur to you that if you went to Bridport with your husband you might possibly sleep together in the same room?"

"Naturally not, or I would not have suggested going."

"Tell me one other thing about the visit to Bridport. You knew, according to your evidence that you have given here, that Stoner had refused to drive you to Bridport?"

"Yes, but I thought that he would change his mind."

"Do you mean you thought you could persuade him to change it?"

"Yes."

Croom-Johnson next asked about the London trip. "These clothes you bought for Stoner, did you regard them as necessary? You used the words this morning, I observed, that he required clothes?"

"Yes, I considered so."

"Silk pyjamas at sixty shillings a suit?" (Probably said sarcastically.)

"That might seem absurd, but that is my disposition."

"During the time that you were in London were you on what had become ordinary intimate terms with Stoner?"

"The same as at home, yes."

"You have told us that on the Sunday night Stoner came into your bedroom and got into bed with you?"

"Yes."

"Was that something which happened frequently?"

"Oh, always."

"Always? Were you fond of your little boy, John?"

"I love both my children."

"Were you fond of John?"

"Naturally."

"Did John sleep in the same room?"

"Yes, but in another bed at the other side of the room."

"It is not a very large room?"

"No, but Little John was always asleep."

Croom-Johnson, probably thundering at her, asked, "Are you suggesting to the members of the jury that you, a mother fond of her little boy of six, were permitting this man to come into your bedroom with you, in the same room where your little innocent child was asleep?"

"I did not consider that was dreadful. I did not consider it an intrigue with Stoner."

This passage probably harmed Alma the most in the trial. People were shocked and appalled.

Alma said she remembered "placing a wet towel round Mr. Rattenbury's head and rubbing his hands; they were so cold. I wanted to get his teeth in. I thought he could talk and tell me what happened." From then on, she testified, she couldn't remember anything.

"I don't remember," "I can't recall" are frequently said by evasive witnesses. Lawyers deal with this by asking leading questions.

Croom-Johnson fired a series at Alma, starting with "Do you recollect?" which provided the jury with information despite Alma saying she didn't.

"Tell me the things you recollect on that night," he said.

"Nothing on that night."

"Do you recollect Dr. O'Donnell coming?"

"I cannot."

"Dr. O'Donnell was a friend of yours and your medical attendant, as a rule, a person calculated to soothe rather than excite you?"

"Yes."

"You recollect nothing of Dr. O'Donnell that night?"

"No. As I say, I have tried in the last two months very, very hard to remember with piecing together and still I cannot."

"Do you recollect a succession of police officers coming in?"

"No."

"Do you recollect arriving at the police station?"

"No, completely nothing."

"Do you recollect being charged at the police station?"

"No, my mind is gone."

"What is the last you recollect of Stoner that night?"

"I remember Stoner kissing me good night in my bedroom and I cannot remember going downstairs to the [police] car, but I remember Little John at the door, and those are the only two things at the Villa Madeira I remember after that night."

"About conversations, your mind is a complete blank?"

"Absolutely."

"About incidents?"

"Yes. It might be somebody else you are talking about."

"About people?"

"Oh, yes."

"Is your mind a complete blank about making a statement to Detective Inspector Carter which he wrote down in this little book, Exhibit 39? Look at it. Do you see the words 'Alma Rattenbury'?"

"Yes. It is all absolute double Dutch to me."

"It has been sworn to that you said to Riggs and Stoner as you left the house, 'Do not make fools of yourselves.' Have you no recollection of that?"

"Absolutely none."

"Do you recollect the last thing that your lover said to you before you went off to prison? The sort of thing that a woman might remember?"

"He never said anything when he kissed me upstairs."

"Do you swear that you do not recollect his saying, 'You have got yourself into this mess by talking too much'?"

"No. I swear I do not remember any of that."

Croom-Johnson wound up by asking, "Do you wish the members of the jury to believe that your mind is a complete blank with the exception of the one or two trifling things you have told us?"

"But that is the truth."

Despite his skill and experience, Croom-Johnson couldn't shake her insistent "I can't recall."

Justice Humphreys wanted more information. As was his prerogative, he took over the questioning. "According to what you are presenting to the jury, do you say that you have a perfectly clear recollection of what Stoner said to you when you were in bed?"

"I think so."

"Well, have you any doubt about it?"

"No."

"You say no?"

"Absolutely."

"You remember even the trivial detail that he mentioned to you, that he had hidden the mallet?"

"Yes."

"And you are sure that is when you learned that he had hidden the mallet?"

"Absolutely. I never spoke to Stoner again."

"Well, then, the next morning we have evidence that you said to Irene Riggs, 'Tell Stoner that he must give me the mallet.' Did you say that?"

"I presume I did."

"Do you mean you do not remember?"

"Absolutely not."

"You must have remembered at that time all about it, must you not, or you could not have said that?"

"I wish I —"

"Do you really mean that you have no recollection of any conversation you had with anybody?"

"No."

"The whole of the time?"

"No. I felt as if I were the one who had been hit over the head."

"But you remember quite well what was said to you, and every word that was said to you by Stoner just before?"

"Oh, yes."

"In bed?"

"Naturally."

"You say naturally?"

"Well, I had not had that dreadful shock then. We were quite happy. I was quite happy then. Life was different."

"When Stoner told you he had done this thing, did you believe him?"

"No."

"When you found your husband, did you believe him?"

"Well, I had to believe him then."

"You did?"

"I hardly knew what to think."

"Had you any doubt at all when Stoner told you that he had hit your husband on the head with the mallet and you went downstairs and found your husband had been hit on the head, that what Stoner had said was true?"

"Well, one would naturally think so, would you not?"

"I do not know. You are here to answer my questions. I would like to have a plain answer from you — had you any doubt that what Stoner said to you was true?"

"I did think it was."

"When did you first tell that to anybody?"

"My solicitor."

O'Connor tried to do damage control for Alma. "With regard to that last question of My Lord as to whether you told anybody, I suppose you have no recollection of saying between two and half past three that very morning, 'My lover did it'?"

"Oh, no, naturally not."

"What was the thought uppermost in your mind when you heard the news from Stoner?"

"To protect him. I thought he was frightened at what he had done because he had hurt Mr. Rattenbury. I think he just sort of thought he hurt him bad enough to stop him going to Bridport, and when I said, 'I will go and see him,' then he said, 'No, you must not.' He said, 'The sight will upset you,' and I thought all I had to do was to fix Ratz up and that would make him all right."

"When you saw your husband, did you make any decision as to what you were going to do regarding Stoner?"

"No, he was worse than what I anticipated."

"Did you decide to do anything as regards Stoner?"

"No, my mind went — awful, dreadful."

O'Connor then went over her statement at the police station at 8:15 a.m. the next day. "You said, 'I picked up the mallet.' Do you have mallets lying about in the drawing room? Are mallets part of your drawing-room furniture? Have you ever seen that mallet before?"

"I could not have picked it up. It would be an impossibility to pick up a mallet that was not there. I have never seen that mallet before in my life."

"You said in your statement, 'I hit him with the mallet. I hid the mallet outside the house.' Except from what Stoner told you, had you any idea where the mallet was?"

"No, I did not know where it was, because he said 'outside' and I did not know where."

O'Connor tried to wipe away the revulsion over Alma's saying that Little John was in her bedroom when she and Stoner had sex. "Now, my learned friend seems a little surprised about Little John's sleeping capacity. Was he a good sleeper?"

"Oh, a splendid sleeper. Nothing would waken him."

O'Connor wound up with a flourish, reading from a supportive report on Alma by Dr. Morton, the governor of Holloway Prison, who believed she was innocent. Morton was unable to attend the trial because he was seriously ill. He died shortly afterward.

"This is what Dr. Morton, the governor of Holloway, has written about you — 'She was received into my custody on the evening of March 25, and I saw her early next morning for the first time. She was very depressed and seemed confused and kept repeating the same sentence over and over again. On the 28th, she was somewhat better and appeared to have forgotten what she had said and how she had behaved the previous days since her reception.' Mrs. Rattenbury, does that correspond with what you recollect about your own mental condition during that time?"

"Absolutely."

"You have told My Lord and the jury all that you know about the tragedy on the 24 March?"

"Absolutely all."

And that was it. Alma stepped from the witness box and the court was adjourned for the day. She had testified for three and a half hours, the same length of time Irene Riggs had.

Casswell thought Alma had withstood the onslaught well, never budging from her assertion "I can't recall," as he recalled in his memoir *A Lance for Liberty*:

> Both to Croom-Johnson in cross-examination and the judge in his questionings, she preserved this impenetrable barrier of loss of memory. When each of her various incriminating statements was put to her the answer was the same: "Did I say that? I can give no explanation. I cannot have known what I was saying." And the hands would wave forlornly.
>
> O'Connor's reading from Morton's report in the final moments of Alma's time in the witness box was a clever stroke. The Prison Governor was ill and could not be called so by adopting this tactic he was able to get before the jury something that was not really evidence. If the Governor had been present in court one would have wanted to cross-examine him closely as to whether a temporary loss of memory could last from approximately 10:30 p.m. on Sunday until the following Wednesday. Even though she had received an extreme shock and been injected with a considerable amount of morphia, surely the effect would have worn off long before then?[6]

Newspaper headlines had this to say about Alma:

> MRS. RATTENBURY'S LONG ORDEAL IN THE BOX
> MORE THAN INFATUATED
> MRS. RATTENBURY SAYS "I FELL IN LOVE"
> STONER'S VISITS TO HER BEDROOM
> HAIRS ON THE MALLET
> MRS. RATTENBURY AND "THAT AWFUL NIGHT"

News of the World wrote:

> During this whole trial this boy of eighteen has been like a graven image. In his neat grey suit, with his fair hair bushed back, his long fair eyelashes and his frank open face he looked what his counsel had described him as "an English boy."
>
> Throughout the long days he sat with his elbow on the corner of the dock with eyes half closed, watching counsel and the judge as they asked questions, but with apparently no interest in the witnesses, and least of all in the woman in the dock with him.
>
> Only once did he show any emotion and that was when Mrs. Rattenbury, in her deep musical voice, tense with anguish, fighting often for words that would not come and with her mobile mouth twitching with nervous strain, was laying bare her soul from the witness box.
>
> As she told intimate details of their illicit passion he fidgeted and became restless, and when, leaning over the box with hands outstretched, she barely breathed the words, "I loved him," he showed the only signs of emotion he gave throughout.

The *Daily Express* assigned James Agate, its literary critic, to comment on the trial:

> Over and over again she knocked two questions into one, like a skilful golfer with his approach shots. Asked when she became Stoner's mistress, she replied, "In November." Invited to say whether her banking account was overdrawn, she made the succinct answer, "Always." The facts of this case might be material for a great novelist.

Agate later elaborated with literary allusions:

The way in which the woman debauched the boy so that he slept with her every night with her six-year-old son in the room, and the husband who had his own bedroom remaining cynically indifferent — this was pure Balzac. In the box, Mrs. Rattenbury looked and talked exactly as I have always imagined Emma Bovary looked and talked. Pure Flaubert. And last there was that part of her evidence in which she described how, trying to bring her husband round, she first accidentally trod on his false teeth and then tried to put them back into his mouth so that he could speak to her. That was pure Zola.

The sordidness of the whole thing was relieved by one thing and one thing only. This was when Counsel asked Mrs. Rattenbury what her first thought was when her lover got into bed and told her what he had done. She replied, "My first thought was to protect him." This is the kind of thing which Balzac would have called sublime, and it is odd, so far as I saw, not a single newspaper reported it.

COCAINE?

People waited all night outside the Old Bailey, hoping to grab a seat on Thursday, May 30, for the testimony about George Stoner to be followed by the lawyers' closing arguments.[1] The judge's summing-up and instructions to the jury and the jury's deliberations were to occur the next day, Friday, May 31.

As George's defence counsel, Joshua Casswell got to go first. Instead of right away calling defence witnesses, which he could have if he wished, he delivered a preamble on why he thought extenuating circumstances should be taken into consideration for George. The legal definition of extenuating circumstances is: "Facts surrounding the commission of a crime that work to mitigate or lessen it, render it less evil or reprehensible. They do not lower the degree of an offence but can reduce the punishment imposed."

> I accept and endorse the whole of Mrs. Rattenbury's explanation of the facts and matters which happened leading up to the day of 24 March and what happened after than day. It

necessarily follows that she, in my submission, did not commit this act and had nothing to do with it and the accused does not deny, in fact, admits, that it was his hand that struck the blow.

Although the onus is on the prosecution to show you that it was his hand that struck the blow, you will probably have no difficulty in coming to that conclusion. The onus therefore remains upon the defence to show you that when he struck the blow he was, by reason, as I shall submit to you, of his addiction to cocaine, incapable of forming that necessary intent, that is, the intent to kill or the intent to commit grievous bodily harm.

You may find, if you are satisfied on my evidence that he was under the influence of this drug at the time, that he did not know what he was doing, in which case a correct verdict would be guilty but insane or, alternatively, that although he knew he was doing the deed and knew what he was doing, he was so confused in mind, as the result of the operation of this drug and its after-effects that he did not form the intent either to kill or to do grievous bodily harm but the intent merely to prevent the trip to Bridport.

After this preamble, Casswell then said, "I call Mr. Stoner."

George was well on his way to the witness box before the warden accompanying him realized Casswell actually wanted Stoner's father. "Wait!" he said, took Stoner by the arm, led him back to the dock, and shut its door.

George Senior painted a picture of his son as "not very bright but an upstanding human being" until he came under Alma's spell. Pre-Alma, he said, "One could not wish for a better boy. He had an excellent character, and I never had any trouble with him. He was a champion boy for boys younger than himself who were oppressed. That was his character right up until unfortunately he went to work for the Rattenburys. My wife and I spoke about the difference in his appearance and demeanour. We used to say that he was sunken in the eyes, had become pale, and was rather drawn."

"It has been suggested by some witnesses that your son said he found cocaine in your house and that that first started him," Casswell said. [O'Donnell had said that.] "Have you ever had cocaine yourself?"

"No, never."

"As far as you know, has there ever been any in your house?"

"There has been no cocaine or morphia or any drug of any description in my house."

In cross-examination, prosecutor Croom-Johnson asked, "You said the boy got to look very pale. Can you say you noticed any particular time when that commenced?"

"Toward the latter part of November and the beginning of December I noticed he was getting pale, but I first noticed his drawn appearance around Christmas."

"You did not know that this boy of 18 was living on terms of sexual intimacy with a woman twice his age?"

"He would not have remained there if I had known it."

George's mother, Olive, was only in the witness box a few minutes. "I saw my son on Sunday, March 24, in the afternoon. I was lying down when he came in. I think it would be somewhere about three or soon after. I do not know how long he stayed. I should say it was just before half past four when he left."

"Was he talking to you during that time?" Casswell asked.

"Well, a little. I cannot remember what he said."

"Did you notice anything peculiar about him?"

"No, nothing more than he usually is when he comes in."

"I have no questions," Croom-Johnson said.

The newspaper headlines reported:

TIRED MOTHER IN THE BOX
FATHER SMILES TO LOZANNE'S BOY LOVER
THE MOTHER'S BOWED HEAD, HER TEARS

The *Daily Mirror*'s Barbara Back wrote,

The man, tall, soldierly; the woman, frail, in tears.

When the father left the witness box and passed the dock, he smiled. His smile bore a message of affection and encouragement to his son.

Then the mother. Only for a little time was she in the box, her faltering sentences almost inaudible.

To every mother her son remains a baby all his life, and what must that poor woman have felt like! I had a lump in my throat, and my heart ached as she answered the few questions that were put to her.

She was crying when she stepped from the witness box. With lowered head she walked past the dock without a glance at her accused boy.

The *Daily Express* reported:

Mr. George Stoner, Bournemouth bricklayer, a spare little man with greying hair, passed within a yard of his son, smiled through his tortoise-shell glasses to the boy in the dock, who never looked in his direction, and told the story of the respectable household in in which the only child was born a war baby when the father was on service in the Machine Gun Corps.

Next came the mother, while a kindly policeman placed the father where he could watch his wife. The mother, worn and tired, clutched a moist handkerchief.

The mother passed within a yard of the son to join the father. Just two respectable parents passing and repassing in the grim chamber of the Old Bailey while their son did not look at them but gazed steadfastly at the sword of justice suspended over the judge's head.

Next, Casswell called Dr. Lionel Weatherly to the stand. Weatherly had examined George on April 8 at Dorchester Prison and concluded that the teenager was a cocaine addict. The press described Weatherly as "an unimposing elderly little man with spectacles who told the judge he was very deaf." He had brought an "ear trumpet," a trumpet-shaped device invented in the 17th century, considered the first device used to help the hearing impaired and still in wide use in the 1930s. They came in a number of shapes and sizes and were made of a wide variety of materials, including sheet iron and animal horns. The lower part amplified sound waves and sent them up a tube that fitted into the ear, strengthening the sound energy impact on the eardrum and improving hearing. The modern miniaturized electric signal hearing aid didn't come into use until the late 1940s.

Despite his ear trumpet, Weatherly kept saying, "I cannot hear you," "I cannot hear that." He was hard to hear because he spoke softly. Time after time he was asked to repeat. Weatherly testified:

> I noticed a very definite dilation of both of his pupils. I tested them with the ordinary normal light and also with electric light with the result that the pupils did not react at all to either. That is undoubtedly consistent with the taking of cocaine and it is a very important symptom. I examined him with a view to finding out whether he was what can be called mentally deficient, and the result of my examination was that he was not but he was backward because his education had been interrupted. As regards his physical condition, the boy was anemic and had a poor circulation. I came to a very definite conclusion that he was a cocaine addict.
>
> Stoner described very fairly, feasibly, and accurately the hallucination of touch associated with cocaine addiction — a rash moving about under his skin, insects crawling over his clothes and bedclothes.
>
> I understand that Stoner carried a dagger about with him for a time. That is one of the common symptoms of cocainism. A cocaine drug addict has besides the hallucinations of which I have spoken, very definite delusions of persecution and they often carry weapons about with them either to protect themselves or otherwise.

I have followed the evidence which has been given in this case. I have heard the evidence given by Mrs. Rattenbury of the occurrences from 4:40 onward in the Villa Madeira. Her description of what Stoner did on that occasion, his sudden turn of violence and threats when she was telephoning, are consistent with his having taken a dose of cocaine that afternoon.

"Are they also consistent with his not having taken a dose of cocaine but being very angry and very jealous of his mistress?" Justice Humphreys asked Weatherly.

"I doubt it."

"We have heard from Mrs. Rattenbury that he accused her of having connection with her husband when the door was closed, although the young son, John, was there in the afternoon," Casswell said to Weatherly.

"I consider that entirely a hallucination of hearing arising out of cocainism and this insane and unreasonable jealousy."

"You have heard that the blow struck in this case was struck by that big mallet and you have heard the other evidence about where the mallet was put. Is that consistent or not with the effects of a dose of cocaine?"

Visibly irritated, Humphreys interrupted. "What on earth does that question mean? I do not know."

Weatherly responded, "I think any assault would be consistent with the after-effects of cocaine if those effects had created an abnormal and unreasonable and insane jealousy."

Alma's counsel, T.J. O'Connor, had no questions, but prosecutor Croom-Johnson did, going on the attack and asking Weatherly, "Have you known people to get very, very jealous who were not drug addicts?"

"I have had only my experience that I have told you of cases of definite cocaine addiction. I told you of one case with the hallucination of sight. May I tell you of another case that I have had?"

"No," snapped Humphreys. "Try and answer the question. I am sure you can answer it. Do you know, after 62 years as a medical man, that some people get very jealous without cocaine or drink having to do with it?"

"Of course."

There was some spectator laughter, which Humphreys scolded.

Croom-Johnson queried Weatherly on his contention that George had been anemic when he saw him on April 8. "People suffering from anemia, commonly called 'very rundown,' do you sometimes find that their pupils fail to react to light?"

"Yes."

Casswell's next witness was Louise Maud Price, the owner of Villa Madeira. She testified for a few minutes only. "I keep a tobacconist's shop. Stoner has from time to time come into my shop to make purchases. I remember an occasion when I noticed something peculiar about him. I should think it would be in February. I noticed that he was very pale and looking very sleepy."

"Did it seem exceptional to you?" Casswell asked.

"It did, indeed."

Neither O'Connor nor Croom-Johnson had questions for her, so Casswell moved on to his next witness, Dr. Robert Gillespie. A specialist in psychosomatic medicine at London's world-famous Guy Hospital, Gillespie evaluated how mental health affected physical health. He had seen Stoner on May 25, the Saturday before the trial began on May 27.

"It isn't easy to discover whether a person is a cocaine addict," Gillespie said. "I usually find it very difficult. Stoner was very tense and anxious when I saw him. That is what you would expect."

"What is the effect of cocaine on the sexual male?" Casswell asked.

"In the male it produces very definite morbid jealousy, rather akin to the morbid jealousy of alcoholism."

"Supposing a person to be under the domination of that morbid jealousy, is he likely to misinterpret what goes on around him?"

"Extremely likely."

Once again, Justice Humphreys intervened. "Is not that true of all jealousy?"

"Yes, but I should have thought it was more likely to happen with a diseased jealousy."

"Have you ever read the play *Othello*?" (In the play by William Shakespeare, the title character, gulled into believing his wife, Desdemona, cheated on him, kills her in a jealous rage.)

"I have, a long time ago."

"Is regular sexual intercourse with a member of the opposite sex by a boy of about 18 likely to do him good or harm?" Croom-Johnson asked.

"I should think that is a very difficult question to answer. I should not say that it did him good if you are thinking of it from a moral point of view."

"No, I am not talking from a moral point of view. I am talking to you as a doctor. Is it likely to cause him to look pale?"

"I should not think that necessarily it would."

"Would you think it likely?"

"It depends on the frequency with which it occurred."

"Do you think one would be likely to look sleepy or have the appearance —"

Humphreys leaped in again. "I think you might take it in this way. To speak quite plainly, the learned counsel means as frequently as the nature of the woman would permit. I think in that case, unless he was very worried about it, I should think it might not have any physical effect, but it would obviously depend on the condition."

Croom-Johnson continued with Gillespie. "As a medical man, do you think it is likely to induce fatigue?"

"It depends on whether the capacity of nature is exceeded or not."

Humphreys jumped in once more. "Do you know in your experience any such case as this? A cocaine addict suddenly cut off from any supply, given no drug of any sort or kind to take the place of cocaine, and from the day that the supply is cut off, for a period of two months, has been a person who can properly be described as this way — throughout rational, sleeping well, taking his food well, and been perfectly healthy?"

"I should be surprised."

"For how long after a dose of cocaine would distension of the pupils continue?" a juror asked.

"Quantities of cocaine have been found in the pupils as long as twenty-one hours after the drug has been taken but how long still after that it might in certain cases be observable, I do not know."

Even Casswell's greatest admirers could not have said it had gone well for him. As he himself said in his memoir, "The defence of George Stoner was one of exceptional difficulty."[2]

OH, NO!

The closing arguments began immediately after Robert Gillespie left the witness box.[1] An effective closing argument ties together all the pieces of a trial and tells a compelling story. It includes the following:

- a summary of the evidence;
- any reasonable inferences that can be drawn from the evidence;
- an attack on any holes or weaknesses in the other side's case;
- a summary of the law for the jury and a reminder to follow it; and
- a plea to the jury to take a specific action, such as convict, acquit, or convict only on a lesser charge.

Casswell regretted that he had to go first as a result of George's name being listed after Alma's on the indictment. It had been regarded as advantageous by George's lawyer at the time, Marshall Harvey, but can end up being disadvantageous because, at the trial, the lawyer for the person listed last is required to speak first to the jury, and what he or she says can be long forgotten by the time the jury deliberates on a verdict. Casswell wrote in his memoir *A Lance for Liberty*:

> I did not even enjoy the saving grace of having the final speech for the defence before the prosecuting counsel gave his closing speech. Because of the order of the two defendants' names on the indictment, I had to address the jury on Stoner's behalf before Croom-Johnson for the Crown and O'Connor for Mrs. Rattenbury. I did what I could, but with so preposterous a defence as that with which I was saddled, it was very difficult to make a really persuasive speech.
>
> I pinned my hopes on drumming home to the ten men and two women of the jury, that if they were so minded, they could find Stoner guilty of manslaughter instead of the ultimate crime of murder.[2]

He spoke for a considerable time, appealing for leniency:

> I think I have made it clear that the defendant Stoner does not deny that it was his hand that struck the blows. What he does deny is that his mind was in such a state at that time that he was responsible for those blows....
>
> It would not have helped you at all to have Stoner in the box. He was under the influence of a drug at the time, and what he could say, and what he would know now, would be of little assistance to you.
>
> This crime is, in my submission, almost inexplicable in a young Englishman. Is it the sort of thing one expects in a lad of seventeen or eighteen, and an English lad? Was there any reason which made this inoffensive, straightforward, honest English boy do something so inconsistent with his nature?
>
> The motive suggested by the prosecution is "They wanted to get him out of the way." Whose way was he in? Here was a lad who probably had to look at every sixpence before this first

job of his; there was nothing to keep him from what has been termed an adulterous intercourse; everything was ready for him, everything was there. As far as we know, Mr. Rattenbury knew all about it as Mrs. Rattenbury said, and he did not care, or else he was in entire ignorance....

This was an act of impulse, the act of somebody who did not plan it beforehand, who made no provision for the future, but acted under an impulse, as I suggest to you, an uncontrollable impulse....

I think you will come to the conclusion that there could not have been a worse environment for any lad of that age than the one in which he found himself. It would be very difficult to find one. It was a household where the husband and wife were not living together and had not been living together for some time. It was a household where there was a most extraordinary woman, unbalanced, hysterical, and apt to fly into fits of excitement, to send for a doctor, to be given anaesthetics and be put to bed; the very reverse in character to the lad who suddenly found himself in her house, because to use her own words, in order to get the money she required, she said she had lied all through her married life — a most unfortunate atmosphere....

Up to September this lad had an exemplary character from everybody. What changed him? Was it not addiction to cocaine? It is unfortunate that Dr. O'Donnell did not tell him to find another job, to get out of this hysterical household with people up all night, and all the rest of it; cocktails, drinking to excess, people having to be put to bed, and that sort of thing....

I say to you as reasonable men and women that the verdict which you ought to find is one of these two; either he is guilty but insane, or he was guilty of manslaughter, and of manslaughter only, and not murder....

When the evening papers went on sale at newsstands, posters were displayed announcing, STONER'S COUNSEL SAYS HE COMMITTED THE CRIME.

After a short adjournment, Croom-Johnson presented his summation on behalf of the Crown. His theme was that Alma and George were equally guilty. He started by saying, "The fact that the two persons are persons who have been guilty of immorality in circumstances which you may deplore, has nothing to do with the case." Then, in the very next sentence, he said, "But from the point of enabling you to judge the truth of the evidence of Mrs. Rattenbury, those facts may be all important." He went on, "Have you any doubts in your own mind that Stoner throughout this unhappy story was dominated by Mrs. Rattenbury? I suggest that to you as a key to the solution of the problem in which you are engaged in solving."

Croom-Johnson reminded the jurors that Alma, by her own admission on the witness stand, had a history of lying and deceit. "She is a woman who, upon her own statement and, indeed upon her own conduct, has for some years been engaged in lying to her husband about money matters and with regard to her daily life for some months past, has been engaged in a constant life of the grossest deceit of her husband. 'I did it with a mallet,' she said. 'He has lived too long. I made a muddle of it. I thought I was strong enough.'"

The *Daily Express* recounted what ensued:

> Mr. Croom-Johnson paused. He is a small man, very persuasive, very tenacious. As he pleads his case, his searching black eyes never for a moment leave the eyes of the jury. "'I thought I was strong enough,'" he quoted from the woman's statement. "Strong enough for what?" he asked.
>
> Mr. Croom-Johnson urged the jury to reject the woman's defence that her mind was a blank on all these statements.
>
> He pointed out that she made the statements before she was given morphia.

Croom-Johnson scoffed at Stoner's claim that he didn't know what he was doing because he was under the influence of cocaine:

The boy has made a statement that on the day of the assault at about four o'clock in the afternoon he took two heaped-up spoonfuls of cocaine. Assuming that is right, what sort of cocaine was it? It is said that the substance he took was a brownish substance with dark specks in it. The evidence is that this cocaine of a sort the gentleman who told us about these things had never heard of. Two heaped-up teaspoonfuls would be a very considerable quantity, you may think, of this drug, and yet at eight o'clock that night this young man who, according to this theory, had been acting under an impulse, got into his master's motor car, drove some three or four miles, borrowed a mallet, had a conversation, came back again for three or four miles with the mallet, and having come with the mallet and presumably, therefore, having arrived back at the Villa Madeira sometime after half past eight, waited two hours before he struck the blows which eventually ended fatally, somewhere about half past ten, sometime just before he got into bed with Mrs. Rattenbury.

All those things, in my submission, do suggest deliberation and do not suggest an impulse brought on by a man being reduced into some condition of excitement or overweening jealousy or the like, as the result of the evils which he suffers from being a cocaine addict....

"Don't make fools of yourselves," she tells Irene Riggs and Stoner as she is about to be taken to the police car, and Stoner says to her, "You have got yourself into this mess by too much talking."

Does it suggest to your minds that Stoner and she had a common object that night, that Stoner was the person who had gone away to fetch the mallet, and that she, thinking she was strong enough, had aimed the blow or blows at her husband's head but made a muddle of it? That Stoner was a person who was likely, to say the least of it, to be acting under her domination.

This was a crime committed by these two people helping one another with one common object.

It was late in the day when Alma's counsel, T.J. O'Connor, got his opportunity to address the jury:

You may go away from here after your duty is done feeling "We do not believe everything that Mrs. Rattenbury has said." That is not enough to entitle you to convict her. You need not believe her statement, yet if it leads to a reasonable doubt as to whether it is true, the defence is entitled to an acquittal....

There is progressive deterioration and absurdity in the statements made by her as the night wears on. There is progressive disorder of mind indicated by them. There are progressive frantic efforts to grasp the one link which will clinch her own guilt and clear her lover. That is the whereabouts of the mallet. "I did it with a mallet," she said, as though a mallet were one of the everyday pieces of furniture you might pick up in a dining room or a drawing room!

It is said these statements are this woman's confessions. Confessions! They are fragments snatched from the disordered mind of a woman sodden with drink and hysteria....

Mr. Croom-Johnson has spoken to you of motive and has suggested that Mr. Rattenbury was in the way. Is there any foundation whatsoever for this suggestion? All the evidence is to the contrary. Mr. and Mrs. Rattenbury were leading the comfortable ordinary life, not very exciting perhaps, which you would expect from the disparity of ages. Is it suggested that this designing, self-indulgent woman — as the Crown wishes to make her out to be — would exchange her comfortable middle-class surroundings with her car and villa and reasonably ample means, for life with Stoner on a pound a week? I venture to suggest that the case of motive is so impalpable and flimsy that you will desire to discard it out of hand.

The Crown says this was a premeditated crime. If this woman had the foresight and cunning, is it conceivable that she should have been so clumsy as to bring home for the weekend her child who might have remained at school? Can you conceive that she would have ordered from Harrods for her lover, to be delivered on the Monday after the crime, those fatally incriminating tokens of her affection for Stoner?

It appears to me that throughout this case the Crown have been asking you to accept the most difficult hypothesis instead of the simple one.

Is it so hard to see where the truth lies here? Perhaps the most horrible part of my task is, in the performance of my duty to Mrs. Rattenbury, to have to call your attention to the facts which clearly indicate that Stoner conceived and executed this crime. But that duty must be discharged. Let us consider for a moment the facts which incriminate him.

Stoner, as you know, is still but a lad. His upbringing was simple, he had but few friends and no girlfriends. He is flung, at the age of eighteen, into the vortex of illicit love. The evidence shows him to have been an unbalanced melodramatic boy, given to violent outbursts. The witnesses for the Crown have proved that on previous occasions he had assaulted Mrs. Rattenbury. They have also proved that he used to go about with a toy dagger and with a toy revolver. An unbalanced, hysterical, melodramatic youth.

Consider his first associations with passionate womanhood. The natural reactions of a jealous youth, possibly, I do not know, accentuated by drug taking.

He is taken away from his work as a chauffeur, stays sumptuously in a west-end hotel for a week with his mistress, dressed in silk pyjamas from a west-end store and then brought back to earth and to his drudging duties and submitting to the orders of his mistress's husband.

If you were judging of moral responsibility in this case, your task might be a light one, for you cannot resist nausea and disgust at the way in which this middle-aged woman has ensnared and degraded this hapless youth.

It likely stung Alma that her defence lawyer, of all people, harshly condemned her. It was calculated. O'Connor was well aware that the public and press sympathized with George. He may have thought his candid acknowledgement that Alma wasn't perfect would convince the jury that he was similarly telling the truth that she was innocent of murder. He went on, "Judging moral responsibility is not your task today. I will say no more about what is past in Mrs. Rattenbury's life. I would only say that if you may be tempted to feel that she has sinned, that her sin has been great and has involved others who would never otherwise have been involved, that you should ask yourselves whether you, or anybody of you, are prepared to cast a stone." He was referring to the famous biblical passage in John 8:7 in which Jesus urges clemency for an adulteress: "He that is without sin among you, let him first cast a stone at her."

Tennyson Jesse later wrote that "a hush descended upon the Court when he pleaded the deathless words of one of the greatest speeches for the defence ever heard."[3]

O'Connor concluded:

You may think of Mrs. Rattenbury as a woman, self-indulgent and wilful, who by her own acts and folly had erected in this poor young man a Frankenstein of jealousy which she could not control.

I beg you, as I began, to discount your horror at her moral failure and to remember that the worst misery which you could inflict upon this wretched youth would be to convict her of something for which he knows she is not responsible.

You may, as moral men and women, as citizens, condemn her in your souls for the part she has played in raising this position. She will bear to her grave the brand of reprobation and men and women will know how she has acted. That will be her sorrow and her disgrace so long as she lives. That is not your responsibility, that is hers. Mercifully, perhaps, you may say to yourselves: "She has been punished enough. Wherever she walks she will be a figure of shame."

That is not to say she is to be branded as a murderess, that her children are to go down as the children of a murderess; that justice is to be prostituted because of your hatred of the life she has been leading.

If you allow prejudice or moral turpitude to cloud your judgment and to blur the true crime, you will not be faithful to your oaths, but you will be debauching the law and degrading our conception of justice.

All the lawyers had spoken powerfully, and the newspaper headlines reflected that:

"MRS. RATTENBURY AIMED THE BLOW" —
   CROWN COUNSEL
K.C. SAYS WOMAN WAS SHIELDING LOVER
REMORSE AT HIS HEARTSTRINGS
"JEALOUSY CREATED BY A WOMAN'S FOLLY"
SODDEN WITH DRINK
VORTEX OF ILLICIT LOVE
STONER AS FRANKENSTEIN
WIFE'S ALLEGED STATEMENT
FRAGMENTS FROM A DISORDERED MIND

Undeterred by rain, a large crowd spent the entire night outside the Old Bailey, hoping to gain entrance on the next day, Friday, May 31, to hear the judge's summing-up and the jury's verdict.

As he had on previous days, George sat motionless in his corner of the prisoners' dock, eyes downcast. "Mrs. Rattenbury also was perfectly calm, but it was a frozen not an apathetic calm," Tennyson Jesse observed. "Her physical aspect had changed in a curious manner. By Friday she looked twenty years older than she had on Monday. On the last day even her hands had changed colour and were a livid greenish white."[4] Alma was wearing her fur coat as she had throughout the trial.

The 1980 book *Tragedy in Three Voices: The Rattenbury Murder* by Sir Michael Havers, a lawyer, with historians Peter Shankland and Anthony Barrett, said about Justice Humphreys:

> Justice Sir Travers Humphreys was a supremely self-confident judge. He believed a British jury is always right in its decision — "when properly directed" as he wrote in his 1946 autobiography *Criminal Days*. His directions to the jury were always clear and precise. He believed himself to be perfectly fair, balanced, reasonable and humane — and to a great extent he was, but he was also imbued with some of the prejudices of the age in which his character had been formed, and with some of his own. He explained in his autobiography that as a result of twenty-five years in the courts (mostly for the prosecution), his experience of women had hardened into a principle: that in a case in which the question of sex might possibly account for a woman's evidence, it should not be accepted "unless there is other evidence tending in the same direction." He thought this rule should never be relaxed "even if in the witness box she behaves like an angel and looks like a Madonna."
>
> It was obvious that Alma's magnetic influence on the opposite sex (if any of it remained after her gruelling experiences of the past four days), was not going to help her with this stern, upright, methodical and unimaginative judge.[5]

The "summing-up" by a judge has two parts. The first gives directions on the law applicable to the case; the second is a "summary of the facts." During this, the judge gives his views. This part has its critics. One, Kenneth E.L. Deale, who served as a judge on Ireland's High Court, expressed his reservations in *The Irish Jurist* in 1969. They are applicable to Alma and George's trial:

THE SUMMING-UP IN CRIMINAL TRIALS

The directions on law should be explicit and usually are. Usually, the law can be fairly explained to men who have never before heard it, and are required to apply it, though that doesn't mean that they will.

The summary of the facts is a different matter, and it is here that the cause of justice can suffer. I have often wondered why the judge has to sum up the facts. Is it to tell them to the jury for the fourth time? Hardly, since three times should be enough for anybody, and in any case, repetition is boring, as the jurors' faces often show. Is the summary intended to ensure that no vital fact is left out of the reckoning? — for the advocates' speeches tend only to stress the facts important to their clients' point of view. Again, this cannot be the reason, since typed copies of the evidence could be handed to the jury before they retire. Transcribing and typing the manuscript might take up a lot of time during a criminal trial, but if our Courts were not organized as though sound-recording had never been invented, the spoken word could be typed almost as soon as it is spoken.

So what is the purpose of the summing up of the facts? Whatever its real purpose may be, it provides a vehicle for comment on the facts, and on the witnesses, especially the accused, if the judge thinks the evidence they have given is untrue, or inaccurate, or highly improbable. Of course, the judge must refer to some of the facts when he is telling the jury the law, but need he tell them what he thinks of the case? — whether it is the prosecution's case, or defence's though it is almost always the latter. I have never heard of a judge being criticized for not presenting the prosecution's case to the jury, but many times have heard the complaint that the defence case was not put. It is a common ground of appeal.

In his instructions to the jury, Justice Humphreys verbally flayed Alma:

> Members of the jury, it is not a pleasant thing to have to say anything about that woman's moral character, but even her own counsel addressing you yesterday said things about her which must have been very painful for her to hear, if indeed, she has any moral understanding at all....
>
> Whether you believe part of her evidence or whether you reject the whole of it, that to some extent must depend upon the view that you take of the sort of woman that she is. It is also necessary that you should do that for this reason — it is the case for the prosecution, as I understand, that this woman so lost to all sense of decency, so entirely without any morals that she would stop at nothing to gain her ends, particularly her sexual gratification, and if that be true, then, say the prosecution, do you think that woman would stop at the killing of her husband, particularly if she had not to do it herself, if she were once satisfied that would enable her to live the sort of life that she was living more comfortably or with less interference or prospect of interference?
>
> And so it is that it seems to me necessary that you should for yourselves have in your minds a picture of that woman, and there is one incident in this case which you may think is sufficient to show you the sort of degradation to which this wretched woman has sunk.
>
> You will remember that she gave evidence herself that she was committing adultery — she is an adulteress, of course — regularly in bed with her husband's servant in her bedroom and in that bedroom in a little bed there was her child of six. Well, there it is. That is the woman who, having ceased, as she says, to have ordinary relations with her husband, chose as her paramour a boy of seventeen, almost young enough to be her son. [Stoner was 17 when hired in September 1934 but had just turned 18 when the affair began in November 1934.]

Humphreys called Francis "that very unpleasant character for which, I think, we have no suitable expression, but which the French call *un mari complaisant*. A man who knew that his wife was committing adultery and had no objection to it." He described Alma and Stoner's lovers' holiday as "this orgy in London." And after slinging all these arrows at Alma, he did a *volte-face* and said the jury should be impartial:

> Members of the jury, having heard her learned counsel, having regard to the facts of this case, it may be that you cannot possibly feel sympathy for that woman, you cannot have any feeling except disgust for her, but let me say this. That should not make you more ready to convict her of this crime. It should, if anything, make you less ready to accept evidence against her. If you think there can be any explanation consistent with her innocence of that crime, I know you will not let it prejudice you against her. Beware that you do not convict her of this crime of which she is accused because she is an adulteress, and an adulteress, you may think, of the most unpleasant type.

Then Humphreys turned his attention to George, his tone of voice sympathetic:

> The other person in the dock, Stoner, is a person for whom no one can fail to feel regret that at the age of eighteen he should be in the position in which he now sits. He is given a good character by all those who knew him up to the time when he came across Mrs. Rattenbury.
>
> He is said to have been at first a backward boy but I do not think there is much in that because his father said that he improved very much after he left school and became an apparently strong and healthy boy — a quiet and reserved boy, one not given to going about with girls — a quiet, well-behaved lad.
>
> You will remember — it is my duty to remind you — that you must try him according to the law of this country just as

you must try her according to the law of this country. You have no more right to refuse to give effect in his case from motives of pity than you have a right to refuse to give effect to evidence in her case which may be in her favour, because you thoroughly dislike her, but it is a pitiable thing that that youth should have been brought to this pass, and I do not think I am putting it unfairly against even her when I say whatever your verdict may be in this case is due to the domination of that woman. It is a pitiable thing that he should be in that position....

Can you conceive any circumstance in which a person could deliver blows of that kind without intending to kill a man or, at least, to do him serious bodily injury. If he did, then that constitutes felonious wounding and if from that felonious wounding Mr. Rattenbury died — and the doctors said he did — then I say the crime of that person is murder.

Humphreys accepted Inspector Carter's assertion that Alma was in "normal" condition when she made her statement that she was the person who had attacked Francis. "You have seen her signature. She could write perfectly well, and she appeared to be all right. I think you will agree that her signature there is quite as good as, if not better than, some of the signatures that one has seen of hers upon other documents. It is not a sort of drunken scrawl which begins here and ends down there. It is a very good signature." In closing his instructions to the jury, he said,

Members of the jury, that is the evidence in this case. You will now be good enough to go to your room and consider your verdict. I have told you, and I repeat it, your duty is to the accused separately. If the prosecution has established to your satisfaction beyond reasonable doubt in the case of either of these persons that the charge of murder is made out, having regard to the direction upon law which I have given you, it will be your duty to say so by your verdict. If in the case of either of them, the evidence of the prosecution fails to satisfy you of the guilt of the accused, do not find that person guilty merely of suspicion, or for any other reason, but say by your verdict in regard to that person that the prosecution has failed to establish the case, by returning a verdict of not guilty. I know you can be trusted to do your duty.

It was 2:48 p.m. when the jury members retired to the deliberations room. They returned 47 minutes later at 3:35 p.m. Lawyers and members of the public who had been loitering in the corridors, thinking the jury would take hours to reach a decision, rushed quickly to their places.

Five minutes elapsed, then a *rat-tat* on the outer door hushed the court. Four aldermen, bearing bouquets of anemones and carnations, bowed Justice Humphreys in. He returned their greeting, then strode to his chair, his white gloves on the arm of his crimson robe. Beneath the gloves, there was a neatly folded square of cloth — the Black Cap of Death.

Alma was assisted to the prisoners' dock by a wardress on both sides, each firmly grasping an elbow, while George took his place.

"Members of the jury," the Clerk of the Court asked, "are you agreed upon your verdict?"

"Yes, sir," the jury's foreman replied.

"Do you find the prisoner, Alma Victoria Rattenbury, guilty or not guilty?"

"Not guilty."

"Do you find the prisoner, George Percy Stoner, guilty or not guilty of murder?"

"Guilty —"

Alma cried out, "Oh, no! Oh, oh, no!" The wardresses hurried her from the prisoners' dock to downstairs by the linking stairway.

The foreman continued. "But we should like to add a rider to that. We recommend him to mercy."

"Then you find Alma Victoria Rattenbury not guilty, and you find George Percy Stoner guilty of murder," the Clerk of the Court said. "And that is the verdict of you all?"

"Yes."

The *Daily Express* wrote:

> For a full minute Stoner stood there while the judge bowed his
> head over the court records, entering the sentence in a silence
> so still that the scratching of his pen could be heard.
>
> Women wept in the public gallery. The two jurywomen,
> set and serious in their countenance, averted their eyes as the
> judge's clerk spread open the square foot of black cloth, "the
> death cap," and placed it evenly over the white wig.

Humphreys said, "You have been found guilty and the only sentence
which this court knows in such a case is death. Have you anything to say as
to why that sentence should not be passed upon you?"

"Nothing at all, sir."

Humphreys pronounced the death sentence, which at that time in the
United Kingdom was worded: "The sentence of this court is that you will
be taken from here to the place from whence you came and there be kept in
close confinement until the date of execution and upon that that day that
you be taken to the place of execution and there hanged by the neck until
you are dead. May God have mercy upon your soul."

The *Daily Mail* wrote:

> Brave as the boy had been throughout the trial, so uncannily
> brave that it had been scarcely possible to guess what resolu-
> tions lay behind that outwardly calm face, he couldn't quite
> control his emotion at hearing the fatal words. His eyes dilat-
> ed, staring at the judge in a last supreme effort of self-control,
> he swallowed painfully two or three times, and the knuckles
> of one hand began to tap with gentle monotony against the
> edge of the dock until the judge's voice ceased. Then he turned
> abruptly toward the stairway to the cells and was gone.

Casswell asked permission from Humphreys for George's father to
see his son before the teenager left. "Certainly," Humphreys said. They

met in a "visiting box," a converted cell, but weren't allowed to touch each other.

"I am content," George told his father. "They have set her free. What happens to me doesn't matter."

Alma was brought back to court to plead on her second indictment that she was an "accessory after the fact" to murder, someone "who assists a person after he/she committed a crime with the knowledge that the person committed it and with the intent to help the person avoid arrest or punishment." The maximum sentence was life; minimum, three years.

"There is another indictment against this woman," Humphreys said to the prosecution.

"What do you propose?" assistant prosecutor Tony Hawke responded.

"My Lord, perhaps in view of the jury's verdict, Your Lordship would think it would be undesirable to proceed upon the second indictment in this case. If Your Lordship approves, I should propose to offer no evidence."

"Alma Victoria Rattenbury," the Clerk of the Court said, "you are charged with being an accessory after the fact, knowing that George Percy Stoner had wounded Francis Mawson Rattenbury with intent to murder him. Are you guilty or not guilty?"

"Not guilty, My Lord." (The press said she spoke "weakly.")

"Members of the jury," Humphreys said, "you can only return a verdict of guilty in any criminal case upon evidence. No evidence is offered upon this charge against the woman and therefore the only verdict you can return, and one which I direct you to return, is one of not guilty."

The Clerk of the Court asked, "Members of the jury, do you find the prisoner, Alma Victoria Rattenbury, not guilty upon this indictment?"

"Yes," replied the foreman.

"That is the verdict of you all?"

"Yes."

"Let her be discharged," Humphreys ordered.

Alma began to weep.

The *Daily Mail* reported:

Her self-control gone, her eyes shadowed with exhaustion, and her white face smudged with tears, this woman whom the judge had described in his summing up as a "woman so lost to all decency, so entirely without any moral sense that she would stop at nothing to gain her ends" hung limp and weeping in the strong grasp of the two wardresses who supported her. On their strength only — for her own had broken utterly — was she able to leave the dock and pass, what is ironically called a "free woman," for the last time down the steps of the Old Bailey.

Going along the downstairs corridor, Alma and George met by chance. His arms were held tightly to his sides by two burly warders. She tried to speak to him but was unable to utter a sound. He smiled at her and nodded as his escort hurried him away. For a quarter of an hour, she stayed in one of the rooms beneath the courtroom in a state of collapse. A doctor treated her, followed by the ever-loyal Irene Riggs with a gift of a beautiful bouquet of flowers.

While the trial was over, the three-ring circus surrounding it wasn't. Thousands of people had gathered outside in the street, hoping to get a glimpse of the convicted George and acquitted Alma.

George, manacled, with guards, left first, transported in a police van with dark blinds to shield him from view. Dozens of police officers prevented the crowd from swarming the van. George was taken to Pentonville Prison in north London, an all-men's prison where those awaiting execution were kept, and put in a condemned prisoner's cell.

The Old Bailey's main hall was cleared of people, after which Alma, in her fur coat and supported from time to time by two wardresses, was taken out a back door. A small crowd booed, and a woman attempted to strike Alma with her umbrella. A policeman opened the door for her of a taxi in which Pinkie Kingham was waiting, and they drove away.

Newspaper headlines summed it all up:

DRAMA OF VERDICT ON STONER
MRS. RATTENBURY CRIES "OH, NO!"

REELED IN DOCK, COLLAPSED AFTER
  ACQUITTAL
SMUGGLED FROM OLD BAILEY
CROWDS SEE STONER LEAVE
"I AM CONTENT" AFTER SENTENCE OF DEATH
"THEY HAVE SET HER FREE. I DO NOT MATTER"
TAXICAB FOR ONE: BLACK MARIA FOR THE
  OTHER

In 1953, two years after his retirement at age 84 from the Court of Criminal Appeals to which he had been promoted, Travers Humphreys wrote *A Book of Trials* about memorable cases in his career. He said about Alma:

> The woman was acquitted, as I believe, because the jury felt that in her contradictory statements to different persons at different times there was so much confusion and uncertainty about the occurrences of the fateful night of March 24th as to render it unsafe to convict her.
>
> The man did not give evidence. Mr. Rattenbury was dead and, as a result, the wife was the one person who knew or ought to have known the facts. It was on her own confession that she had been charged in the first place, but in the opinion of Dr. O'Donnell, the family doctor, she was strongly under the influence of drink on that occasion and he had been obliged to give her half a grain of morphia to quieten her. As a result, he considered she was not in a fit condition to make a statement.
>
> The man subsequently made a full confession in writing in which he exonerated the woman, who was, as he said, upstairs in bed when he assaulted her husband.
>
> After that confession, it became clear that the only case against Mrs. Rattenbury was one of being an accessory before the fact. The strongest evidence in support of that view, as it

seemed to me, was to be found in the circumstances of a visit to London paid by the pair a few days before the murder — Mrs. Rattenbury in the witness box professed to remember nothing of the events following that visit. While it is permissible to doubt whether that was true, yet anything like clear evidence of counselling or procuring her lover to commit the crime was wanting, as the jury thought, and they acquitted her. On the whole I agreed with the verdict.[6]

In 1936, a year after the trial, Alma's lawyer, Terence J. O'Connor, was appointed solicitor general of England and Wales; he held the position until his death in 1940. Crown prosecutor Reginald Croom-Johnson was appointed a High Court justice in 1938. By the end of his career, George Stoner's lawyer, Joshua Casswell, had defended 40 people accused of murder, saving all but five from execution.

PEACE

The cab took Alma and Pinkie to Keith and Katherine Miller-Jones's Belgravia home where tea was served. But Alma hadn't escaped the press or angry public; she had been followed. Outside, reporters clustered while a crowd shouted jeers. Alma could hear it all. She became so distraught that Keith was alarmed that she was on the verge of hysteria. He phoned Dr. Lullum Wood Bathurst, a specialist in the treatment of depression whose practice was in London's pricey Harley Street medical district. Keith asked Bathurst to make an emergency house call, which he did.

The doctor arranged for Alma's admission to the nearby Cleveland Nursing Home in Bayswater. Keith and Alma hurried out of his flat for his car in the courtyard where they were swarmed by yelling reporters.

"Where are you going?"

"Sell us your story!"

"If you take her to Bournemouth, we'll follow you there!"

Keith and Alma remained silent.

Like Belgravia, Bayswater is an affluent district. The Cleveland Nursing Home was on Cleveland Gardens, a tree-lined street of white-stuccoed, pillared townhouses built in the 1850s by real estate developer William Frederick Cleveland. While the home did have nurses, it was more like a spa getaway, a relaxing way to give the mind and body a chance to repair the stresses of daily life. Clients were pampered with perfumed baths, manicures, and fine meals, with morning coffee brought to their rooms, making it a favourite respite for the rich, famous, and well connected.

"Mrs. Rattenbury was in a very delicate state of health mentally," the nursing home's matron said later. To relax her, Alma was given a perfumed bath, something to eat, and at Dr. Bathurst's instruction, a sedative. He thought that would be enough. "Though clearly in a highly emotional state, she doesn't need to be under a 24-hour watch," he said.

The home sought to give patients privacy from the outside world, but the press followed Alma to it. Newspaper headlines blared: BAYSWATER NURSING HOME: "A RATHER POOR NIGHT," or simply, MRS. RATTENBURY'S POOR NIGHT.

"She was charming to everyone, as nice as anyone could expect," the matron later said. "She was a woman who had been through a terrible lot. You could see it in her eyes."

When Irene, Pinkie, and Keith and Katherine came to see Alma, she said, "I was shocked and deeply hurt at what Justice Humphreys said about me." She had hoped she might be able to return to writing songs but realized her notoriety would make it impossible to sell them.

Alma kept looking at George's photograph. She wrote her solicitor, Robert Lewis-Manning: "I see by tonight's papers immediate steps are being taken for Stoner's reprieve — also an appeal. Nothing must be left undone. I will get all the money that can possibly be raised for this end."

She sobbed to the nursing home matron, "If I could have just one word with him, if I had just one look at his face again, he would understand. I must see him once again. Can't anything be done?"

Alma pressed the matron to telephone Pentonville's governor, Reginald Tabuteau, to arrange for her to visit George. Tabuteau said no, so Alma wrote Stoner: "Darling — I wasn't allowed to see you. God Bless you — keep your courage up — Please write me I pray, and anything and everything will be done for your reprieve — sweet one — I love you always and always."

She became more and more despondent and decided that since George was going to die she would, too. Alma talked of suicide, apparently not choosing to remember her annoyance when Francis had kept saying he wanted to kill himself. She wrote a morbid verse:

> We have lived together
> We two
> We have loved together
> I and you
> We'll together die
> You and I —
> We'll swing together.

Alma asked Irene to make certain there were pink flowers at her funeral, that her body was dressed in pink, and that a pink silk nightdress be bought to serve as a shroud. Pink had always been Alma's favourite colour. Irene reported all of this to the matron, who stationed a nurse at Alma's room in case its occupant tried to commit suicide.

On Monday morning, June 3, Alma was still talking about killing herself. Hoping to divert her thoughts to something pleasant, the matron arranged for her to have a facial massage, manicure, shampoo, and permanent wave. "She looked beautiful again and seemed cheerful," the matron commented later.

As Alma puffed on cigarettes, she read newspaper coverage of the trial. "It was wrong what I answered. I should have said ..." she would murmur, her voice trailing off.

She didn't get any privacy. The newspapers let everybody know she was at the nursing home, which caused large crowds to gather there. "I can't put my nose outside the door without being stared at," she told the matron. Her mind was made up: she had to go elsewhere.

"One look at her face showed me that nothing I or anyone else could say would prevent her from going if she wanted to," the matron recounted later.

"She was that kind of woman." The matron had no authority to prevent her from leaving.

Alma telephoned Katherine and asked that she pick her up between 9:00 and 10:00 p.m. that night and take her to another nursing home, where she would register under an assumed name. Katherine drove her to the Elizabeth Fulcher Nursing Home, a short distance away, where she registered as "Mrs. Martin."

The Elizabeth Fulcher Nursing Home, like the Cleveland Nursing Home, was for the wealthy. Its Neo-Georgian architecture made it look like an elegant house. Patients had their own bedroom-bathroom suites with private telephones, and there was an elevator, three operating theatres, and a roof garden.

Alma continued to want to kill herself. On Tuesday morning, June 4, as she sat in bed sipping coffee, she wrote a lengthy suicide letter on stationery she had taken from the Cleveland Nursing Home. Throughout the missive, she wrote "Stoner," never "George." As before, spelling and punctuation weren't her strong points, nor was cohesion:

> Tuesday Morning, June 4th:
> I am afraid force of circumstances have made it imperative I get off quickly. Reporters calamering for one's "life storey" & my mind on nothing but Stoner, Stoner, Stoner. And that boy's face on the stairway looking up — with his sweet smile — & then standing there on that awful Friday. They wouldn't let me stand whilst he was sentenced — I was pulled below — down those awful stairs again, & I clung to the bars — pleading to just see him for only one second — oh! Just one more look — just one more look. Would someone be kind enough to tell Stoner or get the message through to him — that I would never have given evidence against him, had I known. I had made up my mind to say everything was blotted from 9 o'clock that Saturday night — & THEN — let the Judge and Jury fight it out amongst themselves as to who did kill Ratz.

But my lawyer informed me at our last interview that if I spoke the truth, it would clear Stoner. I went into that box feeling confident and strong — that the evidence I was giving would clear the boy.

However —

This woman — that woman that appallingly degraded woman who is now free — has wished a million times since — I had stuck to my first stories that night — that I did kill Ratz — for I remember quite well what I was doing until I drank too much — but only after 3 in the morning.

I went downstairs twice that night — after Stoner told me. And always — "oh! God, oh! God, how can I help this boy?" That was the only thought in my bewildered mind, and the whole of England knows the muddle I made of it! This woman — so low — so degraded (I can still hear the Judge's words) really loved Stoner, we both loved each other — make [of] the difference in age what you will. And lies have been told — lies & more lies — & mud slung to right & left — but our love was not a filthy thing – it was beautiful — and we loved each other from the moment we met, we just came together because it was fate.

I was not looking for a man to sleep with, that would have made matters simple if it were so — & God knows Ratz suspected dozens of times — to make up to his men friends for money — To cheer him up & pull his leg (the contempt I felt one would have thought EVEN he could have seen) I agreed to make myself attractive to his various friends that Sunday afternoon. "A kind man — a charming man" — & always agreeing to everything with a smile, "Yes, darling, no, darling etc." — always trying to cheer him up — so that the atmosphere would be pleasant at home. I don't think I ever spoke one word of truth to Ratz. He knew as much about me as I know about Timbucktoo. All he saw was a smile, all he heard was the "yes, darling — no, darling" — a mask that agreed with his every mood. And heaven help one if they did otherwise!

Am writing this in bed — having coffee. Slept last night — thank God for sleeping draughts — & my beloved had been up two hrs. I wonder whether he was allowed the 2 letters I wrote. So many Regulations to prison life. This is the only reason I thanked God [I] was not back in Holloway — I am at least free — free to a sense — that is I hope so — when I take (I hope) my last walk this morning.

Had it been possible to have made a home for my beloved children I would have stuck it — but what help to boys — having a mother who would always be pointed at as — "That woman." Never to go to a cricket match again to see Christopher play or Little John when he grows up. Never to have any of their friends at the house — I had looked forward — just to see their dear little faces again — but as this would be too unkind for them — to rekindle memories of the mother they loved and were proud of. It is better I just fade from the picture. Kinder for them. The pain in my heart is so intense, it is almost not a pain. I can't look back on memories, I have no future. And the present is Hell.

God Bless Stoner — God bless my children. When we meet again, may it be under happier circumstances. Stoner used to say, "I feel I have not earned this love; it has dropped into my hands too easily & I must surely have to pay the price for it someday, somehow." I tried to think that perhaps the price I had paid for life — the unhappiness — the previous marriages that I wished to heaven had never happened — might atone for him & spare him unhappiness — but oh, it didn't. When we are born again, surely our love will be happy then. How many times we have talked of this. We didn't row — "quarrel" as it was said. We were too happy for that. Stoner used to ask me to write a "love song" to us. I said that was the one song I would never really write. "How write a love song whilst one was living it?"

Stoner would never say "goodbye." He said that was one word he couldn't say. I have thought of that thousands of times. So we have not said goodbye. And will never say goodbye.
Alma Rattenbury

> By some mistake, by some divine mistake,
> I dreamed awhile, but now I wake! I wake!

Alma placed the letter in her snakeskin leather purse, put on her fur coat (although the weather was now warm since it was June), and a light-beige hat. She asked the matron, "May I please borrow £2 to buy toys for my children?"

The statement that she was going toy shopping was a subterfuge. Instead, she walked the 10- to 15-minute distance from the nursing home to the Oxford Circus Underground station, one of the busiest in the system. Her intention was to kill herself by throwing herself under an incoming train. She was about to jump when she changed her mind because she thought with so many other people there someone might prevent her. She considered hurling herself under a bus but realized the situation would be the same.

Oxford Circus has many stores. At one of the ladies' clothing shops, Alma bought a pink silk nightgown in accordance with her telling Irene that she wanted to be buried in pink. Next, she went into a hardware store and purchased a sheathed knife with a sharp eight-inch blade, which the sales clerk put in a paper bag for her.

It was now around noon. Alma walked back to the nursing home, ate lunch, then wrote a short supplement to her long suicide letter:

June 4th
I want to make it perfectly clear that no one is responsible for what actions I may take regarding my life — I quite made up my mind at Holloway to finish things — should Stoner be sentenced — & it would only be a matter of time — & opportunity — And every day night & minute is only prolonging the

appalling agony of my mind. They say I dominated Stoner — am afraid I have never met the person who could dominate that boy. He had colossal strength. Never have I known any one with so much determination & strength of opinion, & character. "Weakness & Stoner" could never be associated in the same breath. He should make a wonderful man — if he uses that strength the right way.

Alma Rattenbury

Between 2:30 and 3:30 p.m., she left the nursing home in her fur coat and hat, carrying her snakeskin purse and a brown umbrella. As she departed, she told the matron, "Don't be worried if I am later than nine o'clock." Then she went to Waterloo Railway Station and, remembering how George tossed a coin to reach a decision, threw one up to help her choose between Bournemouth and Christchurch, the stop before. Bournemouth and Christchurch are close to each other, 4.5 miles/seven minutes apart by train.

The Christchurch side won, so she bought a one-way ticket to there. George and she had one time driven to Christchurch and strolled through water meadows lining the River Avon, which flows by to Three Arches Bend, a remote spot where train track went over a three-arch railway bridge. Once, he had told her, he'd almost jumped out of a train as it crossed the bridge.

Her train left around 4:30 p.m. As it moved along, she wrote a third suicide note, using a pencil rather than her fountain pen. Perhaps the pen was out of ink by now. Again, she said "Stoner" rather than "George."

Diary

Please do not bury me near R(atz).

Surely my death can wipe out a little — the appalling things said — its so awful — those two children thinking through their lives — Their mother was worse than Mary Magdalen. To know all — is to understand and forgive all. I did think that by my saying "I did it" & being arrested, it would help Stoner, but oh God I made such a muddle of everything — & never helped him at all. If only my lawyer had not told me to speak the truth, at our last interview, that boy might be free now.

Alma wanted to write more but had run out of paper, so she searched in her purse for an empty envelope. She took out one she had addressed to the governor of Pentonville Prison and wrote, "If I only thought it would help Stoner, I'd stay on but it has been pointed out to me too vividly I cannot help him and that is my death sentence."

Next, she pulled out an envelope addressed to her and wrote on the back: "It must be easier to be hanged than to have to do the job oneself, especially in these circumstances of being watched all the while. Pray God nothing stops me tonight. Am within five minutes of Christchurch now. God bless my children and look after them."

From Christchurch's train station, she walked through the water meadows alongside the River Avon, ending up at Three Arches Bend. She sat in the long grass by the water's edge, lit a cigarette from her large cigarette box, and took a letter from her purse that Christopher had written to her when she was in prison. On the back, she scribbled: "One has to be so blastedly careful — it's awful having to wait until dark — I do hope it gets dark soon — the smell of the grass is marvellous. I wonder how deep the water is. I pray God it's deep enough."

On the back of one of the envelopes she had written on in the afternoon, she wrote:

> 8 o'clock. And after so much walking, I have got here — and oh! To see the swans and spring flowers — to just smell them. And how singular I should have chosen the spot where Stoner said he nearly jumped out of the train once as it crossed the bridge. It was not intentional, my coming here. I tossed a coin, like Stoner always did, and it came down "Christchurch."
>
> It is beautiful here. What a lovely world really. It must be easier to be hanged than to do the job oneself, especially under these circumstances of being watched all the time. Pray God nothing stops me tonight. God bless my children and look after them.

She pulled another envelope from her purse, addressed to her, and wrote, "I tried this morning to throw myself under a train at Ox. Cir. Too many people about. Then a bus — still too many people about. One must be bold to do a thing like this. It is beautiful here, and I am alone. Thank God for peace at last."

Alma put all the notes in her purse, laid it on the ground beside her, and stood. Then, after placing her umbrella, fur coat, and hat alongside the purse, she knelt at the water's edge.

By chance, a local cowman, an elderly fellow named William Mitchell, was just about to cross the bridge to reach a nearby field where his heifers were. Turning his head, he spotted Alma, first thinking she was bending over to pick flowers. Then, to his horror, he saw her raise a long knife in her right hand and plunge it into her left breast multiple times. She then toppled into the water.

Mitchell rushed to the spot. "I was afraid to go in the water because I can't swim, so I lowered myself at the edge of the riverbank and tried to reach her with my foot, but she was just too far for me to touch her," he later said. "All this time she was staring fixedly at me with a terrible look in her eyes. I saw her coat lying on the bank and snatched it up and threw it into the water toward her, yelling out, 'Catch hold of this!' As I said the words, her head moved farther back as though trying to go into midstream, and as she did, blood oozed up to the surface from a wound in her chest. She turned her head and looked at me and uttered one long cry which sounded like 'Oh!'"

The cowman ran to a nearby house for help. The person who answered his pounding on the door was named James Penny. Grabbing a long pole, Penny joined Mitchell to race back to the river. When they got there, Penny stretched the pole across the water and caught hold of Alma's body, pulling it into the riverbank. Then he and the cowman lifted it out and laid it on the ground. Word had spread, and people came to gawk as Alma's body was driven away. It was taken to the Fairmile Public Assistance Institution, a hospital in Christchurch. The police went to Irene Riggs in Bournemouth, told her the news, said they needed her to identify the body, and drove her, accompanied by her father, to Fairmile. Irene wept so much she could barely speak.

Three Arches Bend, the isolated spot where Alma killed herself.

Newspaper headlines in Britain cried:

> MRS. RATTENBURY STABBED AND DROWNED
> ACQUITTED BUT SELF-CONDEMNED
> DRAMATIC SEQUEL TO MURDER TRIAL
> MYSTERY OF LAST HOURS
> WHY ALMA RATTENBURY DIED
> HOW SHE PREPARED
> PERMANENT WAVE, PERFUMED BATH
> LAST CIGARETTE IN FIELD OF BUTTERCUPS
> MRS. RATTENBURY'S TRAGIC END

In Canada, the *Winnipeg Evening Tribune*'s front-page headline was MRS. RATTENBURY ENDS LIFE AFTER ACQUITTAL. The *Vancouver Sun*'s was

MRS. RATTENBURY STABS AND DROWNS HERSELF IN ENGLISH RIVER. Inside, the story continued with the heading "EVERY MINUTE ONLY PROLONGS MY AGONY." The *Saskatoon Star-Phoenix*'s front-page headline was MRS. RATTENBURY ENDS LIFE IN RIVER.

Katherine Miller-Jones, on a casual stroll in London, stopped in horror at a newsstand when she saw the huge headlines. She collapsed from the shock and had to be taken by an ambulance to a nursing home. Her brother, Keith, said later, "I had no idea she would leave the nursing home as she did. It has all been a great shock."[1]

Robert Lewis-Manning, Alma's solicitor, maintained:

> All her statements had been directed toward exonerating Stoner from any participation in the murder of her husband. She was convinced that Stoner would never be convicted of murder and thought that the worst that could happen would be a verdict of manslaughter.
>
> Every time I or my partner visited her in prison, Mrs. Rattenbury asked anxiously about her two boys. In many ways indeed Mrs. Rattenbury was a noble woman. I think she would have been a far finer woman had it not been for the series of tragedies that had marred her life.[2]

After her suicide, some newspaper stories were sympathetic. The *Bournemouth Times and Directory* wrote: "The last tragic moments of the life of Mrs. Alma Rattenbury have done something to mitigate, if not condone, her guilt in a human drama the terrible consequences of which could never conceivably been foreseen. It is a reasonable assumption that she had found an escape from self-condemnation impossible. In this desperate plight, Mrs. Rattenbury is an object for the pity of the least forgiving." The *Sunday Graphic* commented: "The public conscience may have passed a harsh judgement upon Mrs. Rattenbury, but the tragic circumstances of her death have softened the condemnation." The *Daily Sketch*, which had written, "It does not seem right that the woman who is morally the more guilty should go free and a morally less guilty boy lie under sentence of death," did a *volte-face*:

"The sense of honour was certainly not dead in her for it seems to have been the point of honour and moral justice that pricked her conscience and so severely that she sought death. It was a Roman or Japanese suicide to save honour, and though it is not countenanced by the ethics of Christianity, it is one that human nature everywhere can at least respect. Suicide can be the most cowardly and contemptible of crimes; this suicide was not."

The *Sunday Post* was quite unsympathetic toward Alma: "What she felt impelled to do she would do — and neither convention nor the moral code would stand in her way. Unlike her more conventional friends and neighbours, she permitted the primitive to control the rational."

The inquest was conducted in the boardroom of the Public Assistance Institution in Christchurch, presided over by South Hampshire County Coroner Percy Ingoldby on his own without a jury. There were few chairs for the public, forcing many people to sit on tables. A policeman carried in Alma's umbrella, purse, hat, and box of cigarettes, plus a paper bag with the sheath that had contained the knife — the knife itself was never found — and her suicide notes. Ingoldby read aloud extracts. The pathologist, Dr. Jones, who conducted the post-mortem said,

> There were six stab wounds in her chest: five in the upper part of her left breast, all passed downwards and inwards. The left lung had been punctured in four places and there were three wounds in the heart, one where the knife passed more than once, another where it had entered once and a third which was a slight scratch. She must have died almost instantaneously and was certainly dead before she entered the water.

Ingoldby brought the proceedings to a rapid close: "The deceased, not being of sound mind, did kill herself." The inquest lasted only 29 minutes.

Concerning the inquest, the newspapers said:

CHOSE DEATH BECAUSE SHE COULD NOT SAVE
LOVER
THREE WOUNDS IN HEART

MRS. RATTENBURY'S LAST LETTERS OF DESPAIR
"MY DEATH SENTENCE"
"APPALLING AGONY"
ANGUISHED CRY OF "I CANNOT HELP STONER"

The *Daily Mirror* invited readers to send in their reactions to Alma's suicide. They were mixed. There was sympathy: "If ever a human being has been hounded to death by merciless condemnation, she has." And there were those who were unsympathetic: "I cannot agree with your correspondents who seem to want to make a martyr of Mrs. Rattenbury. She was not hounded to death except by her own rightly distressed conscience. Mrs. Rattenbury's death cannot be deplored. It was best even for her own sake."

Alma's funeral was scheduled for Saturday, June 8, at Wimborne Road Cemetery on the outskirts of Bournemouth, one day before what would have been her 43rd birthday and eight days after her acquittal. The public and press turned it into a three-ring circus. Three thousand people, mostly women according to newspaper stories, turned up and stampeded for a good vantage point, trampling over graves in their eagerness. Mingling with the tremendous crowd was a man asking people to sign a petition calling for George Stoner to be reprieved. Hundreds signed. A few spectators had brought flowers and wreaths with supportive inscriptions. Others, however, proclaimed they didn't feel charitably toward Alma and argued with anyone who differed.

The throng was so thick that it was difficult for the funeral cortège to get through. Irene had dressed Alma all in pink, her mistress's favourite colour, just as she had wished. The coffin was made of polished oak and bore her name as well as "Widow of Francis Mawson Rattenbury." Pink rhododendrons were heaped on top.

A short, private service, to which only the chief mourners were admitted, was held in the cemetery chapel, with the doors locked to keep out the huge crowd that tried to burst in. Irene had arranged for pink flowers inside the chapel.

Alma hadn't wanted to be buried "near" Rattenbury. They are twenty feet apart.

The newspaper headlines about the funeral were:

QUARRELS OVER MRS. RATTENBURY
AMAZING DAY AT HER GRAVESIDE
POLICE CALLED TO CONTROL CROWDS AT
   FUNERAL
3,000 BESIEGE CEMETERY AT MRS. RATTEN-
   BURY'S FUNERAL
WOMEN CLAMBER OVER TOMBSTONES
FUNERAL OF MRS. RATTENBURY — EXTRAORDIN-
   ARY SCENES

After the crowd was gone, Irene returned and left a card on the cushion wreath of pink carnations she had placed: "All my love, darling — Irene." She agreed to be interviewed by the *Bournemouth Daily Echo*:

> I would have stayed by her no matter what happened. I spent a long time with Mrs. Rattenbury after the trial and her distress was pitiful. In her more hopeful moments Mrs. Rattenbury was determined to live the scandal down. We had planned to go somewhere far away until people had begun to forget. But she was always thinking of Stoner and all the terrible things people were saying about herself. She was so sensitive to criticism.
>
> When I took her to the nursing home after the trial she told me that as long as she lived she would remember what the judge at the Old Bailey had said about her. I think his words hurt her more than anything else. I did think, now that Mrs. Rattenbury is dead, people who did not know her — how kind and generous and good to others she was — would be more charitable. Their evil tongues are pursuing her to the grave. It was shocking to hear some of the things that were said by the crowds at the graveside today. They say the most scandalous and untrue things about Mrs. Rattenbury and now about me as well.

I simply cannot bear it any longer. I am going away where no one knows me so that I can get rest and peace.

I am sorry now that I was not able to stay with Mrs. Rattenbury in the nursing home. Perhaps I might have been able to save her life, but I was too ill. My nerves have gone.

I had no idea when Mrs. Rattenbury told me what she would like to have done when she died that she had any thought of suicide in her mind. I am happy now to think that I have been able to carry out her last wishes. I dressed her all in pink — the colour she loved — before she was buried and I saw that there were plenty of pink flowers at the funeral. She had a horror of white.

I say, in spite of everything and everybody, that Mrs. Rattenbury was a wonderful woman. No one knows what an agony it was for her to give the evidence she did at the trial. Few other women would have had such supreme courage.

The words with which Alma concluded her initial suicide letter — "By some mistake, by some divine mistake / I dreamed awhile, but now I wake! I wake!" — were from the last verse of a song she'd written in prison. London's *Sunday Graphic* published it the day after her funeral, Sunday, June 9, with this introduction:

MRS. RATTENBURY'S PRISON SONG "TO KEEP MY MIND SANE"

The public conscience may have passed a harsh judgement upon Mrs. Rattenbury, but the tragic circumstances of her death have softened the condemnation.

The *Sunday Graphic* therefore publishes the words and music of the prison song of "Lozanne" (Mrs. Rattenbury). From the prison she wrote that she "kept repeating the extraordinary words over and over again to help keep my mind sane."

The unhappy woman wrote this song from the fullness of her heart; the words convey her love for the tragic boy Stoner. She blames Fate for their meeting — "By some mistake you filled my empty days." But so long as she lived she knew that never could she put him out of her mind, try as she would.

This is one of the most poignant documents ever published. It appears in the *Sunday Graphic* exclusively:

By Some Mistake

By some mistake my spirit held you dear,
But now I wake to agony and fear
To fading hope and thought distressed and grey
With outstretched hands I put your face away
With outstretched hands I put your face away.

By some mistake you filled my empty days
But now I wake to face the parting ways
I see you smile; I hear the words you say
With no reply I hush your voice away.

By some mistake, by some Divine mistake
I dreamed awhile, but now I wake, I wake,
Yet, dying, dream you keep my vision true,
I seemed to climb to Heav'n in loving you.

The song was recorded by Frank Titterton and can be found at the British Library.

After the funeral, Villa Madeira was ransacked by souvenir hunters. Most stole plants or flowers from the garden. But some broke into the house and pilfered possessions: a little wooden house that Francis had made for John, letters, two of Francis's pipes, a black fox fur, Frank Titterton's autographed photograph, kitchen knives, ornaments, even a packet of tea. People picnicked in the garden. On one occasion, Villa Madeira's owner, Louise

Price, found a group of four men, six women, and numerous children sitting in the garden and eating ice cream. They said they had come especially from London to visit the scene of the crime.

Finally, Mrs. Price and her husband had enough. They moved into the house and announced that legal action would be taken against trespassers. Except for books, the remaining contents were taken to the home of Irene's parents to whom she had moved back. The books were sold to a dealer who got a good price for them, particularly those with bloodstains on them.

Irene moved to London and became a bookkeeper. She never married and died in 1964 at age 55 of breast cancer.

Tennyson Jesse had this to say in her introduction to the trial transcript, published later in 1935.

> Her life had been given back to her, but the whole world was too small a place, too bare of any sheltering rock, for her to find a refuge.
>
> Blind and muddled humanity had been even more blind and muddled than usual, and everyone concerned had paid a terrible price for the sin of lack of intelligence.[3]

Justice Humphreys tersely only write this in his 1953 *A Book of Trials*: "Shortly after her release Mrs. Rattenbury committed suicide. After writing some pathetic notes, she stabbed herself and fell into the river — dead."

ONE OF US

mmediately after George Stoner was convicted and sentenced to death, residents in Ensbury Park, where his family lived, formed a committee to collect signatures for a petition for clemency. George's father attended the inaugural meeting. The petition said the sentence should be repealed because

- "he is a boy";
- he "was subjected to undue influence";
- he was " a victim of drugs";
- he was "probably under their influence when the crime was committed";
- he "showed by his behaviour at the trial that he was capable of better things";
- he "might, if reprieved, turn out to be a respectable member of society and an asset to the state"; and
- he "was temporarily insane when the crime was committed, though not legally so."

It ended: "He might have been the son of any one of us."

Committee members wearing placards saying STONER PETITION, PLEASE SIGN UP stationed themselves at street corners, hotels, boarding houses, stores, public gardens, outdoor band concerts, and amusement places throughout Bournemouth and nearby communities. Members also drove around with petition posters under their windshield wipers, stopping to distribute them. Bournemouth's mayor, Henry George Harris, was one of the first to sign the petition. Similar campaigns were undertaken all over the country.

George's execution was to be on June 18. Since 1907, condemned prisoners had the right of appeal against their murder convictions. On June 8, the same day as Alma's funeral, Joshua Casswell, George's lawyer, filed a notice of appeal. The filing automatically put Stoner's execution on hold. Wrapped in four huge brown paper parcels, the petitions for George to be reprieved, bearing more than 320,000 signatures, were personally handed to Home Secretary Sir John Simon by Members of Parliament Sir Henry Page of Bournemouth and Gordon Hall Caine of the nearby East Dorset constituency. Simon said it would be "improper" for him to consider a reprieve while an appeal was pending. When informed of Alma's suicide, George wept.

John Bickford, the managing clerk to Marshall Harvey, George's solicitor, delivered a copy of the notice of appeal to Stoner and told him that if he was finally prepared to make a statement it must be by Monday, two days later. Stoner spent the weekend writing it. He had been a poor student, and there were many spelling, punctuation, and grammatical errors:

> Dear Sir,
>
> I sincerely hope that my writing to you will be of great use. In the first place I wish to say that you have been mislead in my case. My reasons for this of course was to be the greates benfit to Mrs. Rattenbury to whom I'm in love. I may state that you would not have had the real story, had it been that Mrs. Rattenbury was still alive.
>
> I will start of by saying that I am perfectly inncent of this crime. On Sunday evening the day of the crime, I fetch the mallet for a perfectly inncent reason, that was to erect a tent

on the following Monday. I did this because Mr. Rattenbury said, he would be using the car on Monday, by this I knew I would not be able to get home so quick and back again on the Monday. When I came back with the mallet I put it in the coal seller and, went up to my bedroom. I undressed and got into bed. I also went to sleep, this is the front bedroom.

When I awoke I had been asleep just over an hour. I judge by this time that Mrs. Rattenbury was in bed, so I got out of my bed, came out of my bedroom on to the landing. I stopped for a second and lean over the bannister, at this moment Mis Riggs appeared at her door and she ask me what was the matter. I replied. Just looking to see if the lights were out. Which was perfectly trues because sometimes they are out when I go into other bedroom. She appeared to be satisfied and withdrue in her room.

I continued on my way into Mrs. Rattenbury's bedroom. There I found her in bed, she seem to be in the most terrified state, she said two words, "hear him" at that moment I heard a loud grown. At this she got out of bed and ran down stairs. I immediately redressed excpting for my coat and waistcoat, because I gain the impression that something was wrong down stairs. I came down stairs into the drawing room, there I found Mr. Rattenbury in the arm chair with severe head injuris, quit by axident I found my mallet beside the settee. Apparently Mis Riggs had not notice it, so when she went to telephone, I hid the mallet out side the house. When Mis Riggs came back from the phone, we, that is all three of us, carried Mr. Rattenbury into the bedroom and laid him on his bed.

I then went out and got the car out and went round for D.c. O.Donald, who had left before I got there, he had arrived back on the premises before me. When the ambulance arrived back on the scenes Mr. Rattenbury was taken to the nursing home. Under the direction of Mrs. Rattenbury I follow the ambulance so as to bring D. c. O.Donald back. When we arrived back the police were there. Mrs. Rattenbury was under the influence of drink. D.c.O.Donald seeing her in this condition gave her morphine and put her to bed but when he had gon she came down stairs, this time I carried her up stairs and put her to bed.

In the morning inspector carter asked for a statement, had I known Mrs. Rattenbury had made any statements, I would have placed myself in her position there and then. When Mrs. Rattenbury was arrested I was terribly upset. I did everything I thought would get sufficient evidence against me. I showed Mis Riggs were I fetch the mallet because I knew she would have to give evidence.
Yours Faithfully
George Percy Stoner

Casswell commented in his memoir *A Lance for Liberty* that he didn't know which of them to believe, Alma or Stoner, and he supposed the murder would continue to be a mystery to the end.[1]

Years later, British lawyer Sir David Napley in his 1988 book *Murder at the Villa Madeira* contended that Alma was the killer, not Stoner:

> The likelihood is if Stoner's was the hand which wielded the mallet, each of the three blows would have been of equally devastating force. But the second and third blows were much more consistent with frenzy than with any attempt to kill. Is it not more likely that Alma's strength may have been partially dissipated after the first vicious blow?
>
> If Alma had struck the blows, Stoner may well have been both horrified at what she had done and desperate in his anxiety to protect her from it.[2]

Criminal appeal cases are held at the Royal Courts of Justice located on Fleet Street in central London. It has soaring arches, stained-glass windows, and a mosaic marble lobby. It somewhat resembles a cathedral.

Stoner's appeal was heard on June 24, a sweltering hot day. A few people walked back and forth in front of the building, wearing signs saying STONER MUST BE REPRIEVED. STOP THE LAW KILLING THIS BOY. END CAPITAL PUNISHMENT.

Appeals are heard by a three-judge panel to provide a "fair view of the decision of the single trial court judge." It also prevents a tie vote. Decisions are by majority. George's appeal was heard by Lord Chief Justice (Gordon) Hewart, with Justices Swift and Lawrence. Casswell appeared for Stoner; Croom-Johnson once again for the Crown.

The courtroom was packed with spectators. George was brought in wearing the same grey suit he had worn at the trial. The weeks in jail in the expectation of being executed had taken their toll. His face looked strained and had lost its healthy tan.

Casswell repeated his argument from the trial that Alma and Stoner should have been tried separately, then asked that Stoner be allowed to testify.

"There is no need to reiterate the evidence in this squalid case," Hewart said. "It is a mere waste of time."

The justices conferred and reached their unanimous decision in three minutes. "There is nothing wrong with there having been a joint trial," Hewart said on behalf of the panel. "The fact, if it be a fact, that a lad of good character has been corrupted by an abandoned woman old enough to be his mother raises no point of law nor can it be employed as a ground of appeal in this court. We have no power, nor have we the inclination, to alter the law relating to the murder in this respect. The appeal is dismissed."

Newspaper headlines included:

STONER DAZED BY HIS FATE
SCATHING JUDGMENT BY LORD CHIEF JUSTICE
DEMONSTRATION OUTSIDE LAW COURTS

George seemed to be doomed, but the next day Home Secretary Sir John Simon gave a reprieve, commuting George's death sentence to life. The home secretary isn't called upon to give reasons for his or her decisions.

The last-minute pardon received by George Stoner.

The reprieve came three weeks after Alma's suicide. In their 1980 book *Tragedy in Three Voices*, lawyer Sir Michael Havers, with Peter Shankland and Anthony Barrett, wrote, "He probably felt the tragedy had gone far enough, so perhaps Alma had helped Stoner with her death." Or perhaps Simon was influenced by the huge outpouring of public support for Stoner. Also, the jury and Justice Humphreys had recommended mercy.

The governor of Pentonville Prison, Reginald Tabuteau, went to Stoner's condemned man's cell to personally deliver the good news. Stoner listened almost unbelieving as Tabuteau told him, then put his face in his hands, which were trembling, and wept. "Thank you, sir," he said. Tabuteau handed over the love letter Alma had sent him at Pentonville — "Sweet one — I love you always and always."

George's mother told a reporter: "I wish I had some wine to offer you. This news is so good, so great, after all we have been through. I am very grateful for all that has been done to save my boy."

His father said, "Let us be glad, at least, that he will not hang and that he is spared to us. Who knows that we may live to welcome him home one day."

As the news spread throughout Bournemouth, large numbers of people went to the Stoners' home to extend congratulations.

Stoner was sent to Maidstone Prison, 47 miles southeast of London. It was one of Britain's oldest prisons, dating back more than 200 years. Originally serving as a county jail, it was converted to a prison during the 1740s. At first it was for both men and women, becoming men only in the 1800s.

Worried that the good-looking, young Stoner might be sexually assaulted by older prisoners, prison authorities placed him with young offenders in the hope he would be safe with them.

In July 1941, the sixth year of George's term, Casswell wrote to the home secretary proposing that the young man be released. In August, the department's secretary of state, the person responsible for paperwork, said George would be freed after he served seven years, subject to good behaviour. George was sent to Camp Hill Prison on the Isle of Wight, a minimum security men's prison close to Bournemouth and Ensbury Park, where his parents lived. Visitors were allowed; there was a ferry to the island.

On May 27, 1942, exactly seven years after the start date of his trial, George was released "on licence for life," meaning that though free he would be under the supervision of a parole officer for the rest of his life.

He found work as a mechanic and tractor driver. In November 1943, as the Second World War continued, he enlisted in the British Army and was stationed in England as a transportation driver for heavy equipment. After the war ended, he married. He and his wife had a daughter and moved into his parents' home after the death of his mother in 1945. George's father died in 1949, leaving the house to his son. Some people in Bournemouth were hostile to George, but most weren't.

In 1975, British playwright Terence Rattigan (*Separate Tables*, *The Winslow Boy*) wrote *Cause Célèbre*, a radio play about the deadly triangle, in which he used the real names of everyone except George, who had objected. All the other main people were dead. Rattigan substituted "Wood" for "Stoner" but retained "George." In 1977, Rattigan turned the work into a stage play. By the 1970s, the women's rights movement had been under way for some time, and *Cause Célèbre*, which was sympathetic to Alma, was hailed for its point of view. It became a theatrical staple and is still performed.

In the late 1980s, George developed dementia. In 1990, at the age of 74, he was convicted and placed on probation for "indecently assaulting" a 12-year-old boy at a public toilet. When arrested, he was naked except for his socks, shoes, and hat. He died on March 24, 2000, at age 83, from a brain tumour. The date was 65 years to the day that he had struck Francis three times on the head with deadly results.

In August 2015, long-time Bournemouth resident Vera Head told *Bournemouth Daily Echo* reporter Darren Slade: "I was 15 and working for solicitor Marshall Harvey [George's initial lawyer] in Fir Vale Road when the murder happened. We didn't have so many murders as we do today. It was quite an event. Everybody in the country knew about it." She was among those who petitioned to save Stoner from the gallows. "I got quite a lot of signatures," she recalled. "I used to knock on people's doors." She added, "It made me laugh that he said he'd take the secret to his grave of who did it because we all knew it was him."[3]

THE BOYS

ecause Christopher, fourteen, and John, six, had lost both parents and were minors, they became "wards of the court." The boys had little money. They were Alma's sole heirs, but her outstanding debts of $1,975 — $225 for funeral expenses, $1,750 fees owed her lawyers — exceeded her assets of $1,602, so there was no money for them to inherit. Francis's December 18, 1929, will had designated her his sole heir with the residue to go to the boys upon her death. Since Alma had died soon after Francis, all the money remaining in Francis's estate should have gone straight to the boys. At the peak of his career, Francis had earned $100,000 per year. His wealth had been whittled away over the years, and at the time of his death, the net value of his estate was $28,124, including personal effects.

Francis's children by his marriage to Florrie, Frank and Mary, appealed to the British Columbia Supreme Court to "vary" Francis's will on the grounds that they were entitled to "adequate provision" as his children.

Mary was married to the president of a car dealership turned realtor. Frank had never been able to hold a job for long. He was unemployed at the time of the appeal.

The court ruled that Frank should receive $125 per month and Mary $25 per month for a year. Since there wasn't a lot of money at stake, it would seem that Frank and Mary were punishing Christopher and John as surrogates for their unrelenting hatred for their father and Alma, although both were now dead.

Christopher and John were separated. Christopher's aunt, Daphne "Pinkie" Kingham, let him live with her and her family. Keith, John's godfather, sent John to boarding school. Christopher left the Kinghams in 1937 when he was 16 and went to Vancouver to live with Grandmother Frances, Alma's mother. He was deeply scarred emotionally from the double trauma of Francis's and Alma's close-together deaths. "My parents' tragedy had a deep effect on me, but by the age of thirty or so I had got over it," he told Anthony Barrett when Barrett interviewed him for the 1980 book *Tragedy in Three Voices*.[1] That was 16 years later.

Thomas Compton "Compy" Pakenham, Christopher's father, did nothing to help. He had disappeared permanently from Christopher's life after Alma divorced him in 1923 a few months before Christopher's second birthday. Compy had gone on to marry for a third time, and he and this wife had two children, a boy and a girl. He is credited with helping to start *Newsweek* magazine in 1933.

Christopher's turmoil was manifested in his inability to stay in one place long. He left Vancouver and became a vagabond, drifting across the United States with no fixed address, telling Barrett that he had been "drawn to delinquency." While he had gone by "Rattenbury," Francis hadn't adopted him, and he reverted to his birth name Compton Christopher Pakenham.

He had dual nationality, since he had been born in the United States. Circa 1940, he received a U.S. Army draft card under the name "Compton Christopher Pakenham." It listed him as a student at Newark High School in Newark, New Jersey. Joe Hoffman, also a student there, was named next of kin, indicating how cut off Christopher was from family.[2]

On April 1, 1942, he enlisted in the army. His enlistment record says:

> Marital status: Single, without dependents
> Citizenship: United States
> Residence: U.S. at large
> Education: 2 years of college
> Civil Occupation: Unskilled sailor and deckhand, except U.S. Navy[3]

Christopher served with the 133rd and 34th Infantry Divisions and was awarded Bronze and Silver Stars.[4] After he was discharged, he returned to Newark and became a commercial artist; he had been good at drawing since childhood. In 1947, he married and had three daughters. His wife died in 1984, he in 1995 at age 74.

It wasn't until a year after Francis's and Alma's deaths that John found out the truth:

> I was too young to know and everybody was afraid to tell me. How do you break that kind of news to a six-year-old? Then one day a boy at my school rather cruelly told me that my father had been murdered and my mother had killed herself. It was such a shock. I'd been told they were on vacation.
>
> The years after my parents' deaths were a difficult period for me. I'd sit in class and suddenly burst into tears for no apparent reason. Some of the teachers used to give me hell. In a way, though, I think my immaturity helped shield me from some of the emotional fallout. On one level it was very painful. But at that age you're pretty resilient. And I threw myself into my studies and into sport — I played rugger and cricket — in an attempt to block out my parents' deaths.[5]

In the summer of 1940, with the Battle of Britain above England, threats of a German land invasion from across the England Channel, and signs of the impending Blitz, nighttime bombings across England, the British government began a program of evacuating children to countries in its empire that were safe, including Canada. Keith decided to send John, 11 years old, to Canada to live with Grandmother Frances in Vancouver.

The ship he was on landed in Montreal, 2,287 miles east of Vancouver. John had a train ticket to Vancouver, but it was for two days later. In the meantime, he had to fend for himself. He didn't know anybody in Montreal. Not knowing what to do, he sat on his trunk, probably very frightened. Many hours passed until a kind couple offered to look after him until his train journey. Grandmother Frances died six months after his arrival, and her youngest sister took him in.

Since his parents' death, John, like Christopher, had had to deal with a lot of upheaval in his life. He had a lot of grit. At 16, he got a job as a logger on the Queen Charlotte Islands (now called Haida Gwaii) off British Columbia's northwest coast to earn money to study architecture. "It must have been in my genes," he later said. Between 1946 and 1949, he attended the University of British Columbia for architecture courses, followed by Oregon State College until 1950. During this time, he read a 1948 issue of *Architecture Forum* featuring Frank Lloyd Wright's architecture. Wright was an icon, regarded as the "father of American modernism" in architecture because he blended the many houses he designed with the surrounding environment through low roofs, natural stonework and woodwork, curved lines, huge windows, and an easy indoor-outdoor flow. He called his style "organic architecture."

In 1932, Wright established his own school of architecture, Taliesin West, in the Arizona desert near Phoenix. He called it "Taliesin" because he was of Welsh descent, and in that culture's mythology Taliesin is the "god of the bards." Enrolment was kept small to enable personal attention and hands-on learning.

John applied to Taliesin in the fall of 1950 and was accepted. Students lived in tents in the desert. They were taught desert masonry construction, electrical and lighting work, Wright's style and methods — and to cook breakfast. "We developed a strong mutual affection," John later said of Wright. "It's funny. Frank had the same Christian name as my father, he was born in the same year as my father, and he, too, had a wife about 30 years younger."

They also had in common that someone they loved was murdered. In 1903, Wright, while living in a Chicago suburb, had abandoned his first wife and their children to hook up with Mariah Cheney, a married Chicago woman with two children whom he'd met through her husband, Edwin, a client. Wright and Cheney made no secret of their affair, just as Francis and Alma hadn't. Mariah got a divorce, but Wright's wife refused to give him one. He and Mariah with her children moved to Wisconsin where Wright set up a combination home and workplace compound. In August 1914, when Wright was in Chicago on business, a servant set fire to the living quarters, killing Mariah, her children, and four others with an axe as the fire burned.

John became a vital part of the Taliesin West community, volunteering to organize Wright's architectural drawings. When Wright died in 1959, John helped co-found Taliesin Architects, headquartered at Taliesin West. The 14 main architects had worked under Wright. They completed Wright's unbuilt designs and did projects of their own. John was "principal architect and planner" and was hailed as "one of America's most eminent architects." In 1968, at age 40, he married Kay Davison, who had been Wright's personal assistant, and became stepfather to her daughter from a previous marriage.

From Alma, he inherited a love for music. He had a good voice and would break into song in the firm's dining room.

In early 1997, widely read *Life* magazine asked John to develop plans for its recurring "Dream House" feature that had famous architects design blueprints for a beautiful home that people on a moderate income could afford — a dream house. John's design was in the May 1997 issue. John not only designed a model house, he also "built the dream to make it a reality." Over 500 sets of his plans were sold in the United States.

He was invited to be the guest of honour at celebrations on February 10, 1998, marking to the exact day the centennial of the opening of British Columbia's Parliament Buildings in Victoria, his father's masterpiece and colloquially known as "The House That Rattenbury Built." It was a big event. Carillon bells were rung from a nearby tower, and the lieutenant governor and his wife arrived in a horse-drawn carriage, greeted by a marching band, a military regiment, and an antique gun salute. Choirs sang in the rotunda, and birthday cake was served to the public.

"I think it's a wonderful building, it's an inspiring design," John told reporter Jim Beatty of the *Vancouver Sun*. "It's a building for the people and it's beautiful. In today's architecture, that's becoming more and more rare. You simply can't do this today. To find the craftsmen capable of doing this is impossible. There was really a lot of love that went into this building."

John, however, told reporter Patrick Murphy of Victoria's *Times-Colonist*: "My father would be appalled at some of the buildings that clutter the harbour entrance. He had a vision when he designed the buildings. If he were here today and had an opportunity to wipe his hand across, we would see a lot of things go away."

In 2007, John Motherwell, a Victoria surveyor and engineer and admirer of Francis's architecture and his Klondike Gold Rush paddleboat venture, generously laid out $3,200 for a headstone at Francis's plot in Wimborne Road Cemetery, Bournemouth. It has an engraving of his Parliament Buildings and the inscription "B.C. Architect," Francis's description of himself in his winning submission.

In conjunction, John agreed for the first time to speak to a reporter about Francis's murder and Alma's trial and suicide, granting an interview to York Membrey of the *Times* of London. He dismissed Sir David Napley's claim that Alma had murdered Francis and that George had covered up for her:

> I don't believe that for a moment. She was too naïve and innocent to do anything like that.
>
> Very few people mentioned my parents' good qualities — my father's architecture and my mother's musicianship. That's how I prefer to remember them. And whatever anyone says, I know my mother was a good woman.
>
> I've had a wonderful life. I think that my mother and father would have been proud of me.

John expressed no bitterness at having his parents snatched away from him, saying he thought some good might have come out of the tragedy. "It gave me an understanding from a very early age of other people's pain and sorrow, and that's a quality I possibly wouldn't otherwise have possessed."

He said he bore no ill will toward George Stoner. "I've always thought it was such a sad business. I was driven to school by Stoner, but I didn't know he'd murdered my father until some years later. He was so young, so impressionable, and he had this older, beautiful woman doting on him. I've never felt any animosity toward him. I just felt he was a terrible victim of circumstance. And then of course he went to prison. I'm sure he suffered great guilt over what happened. It must have been a terrible life."

John died in 2021 at age 92 of cancer.

There is no headstone, no identification whatsoever, at Alma's plot in Wimborne Road Cemetery.

GHOST

There are claims, primarily by tour guides and from time to time by the media, of sightings of Francis's ghost perambulating around his famous Parliament Buildings and nearby Empress Hotel in Victoria, British Columbia.

Mike Smyth, a columnist for the *Province* newspaper, looked into the matter in his October 25, 2014, column, headed "Is the B.C. Legislature Haunted? A Lot of People Sure Think So." He was prompted to write the article because Halloween was approaching and "spirits and spectres gather in B.C.'s most haunted city, Victoria, as Halloween draws near."

He interviewed Craig James, clerk of the legislature. "Many of the staff around here have seen things and heard things — things they can't explain," James said. As an example, he talked about "the committee clerk who was working alone in her office a few years back. She looked out her door, just down the corridor from the legislative chamber. All of a sudden she saw a figure in a black cloak floating along the hall. It went along the speaker's corridor, past the entrance to the chamber, and then turned left into the library. She was terrified and phoned security. They told her, 'Don't worry. It was probably just Rattenbury.'"

Smyth also spoke to John Adams, a Victoria "ghostly walks" guide, historian, and researcher into the paranormal, as to why he thought Rattenbury's ghost was flitting around. Adams said, "Rattenbury was egotistical and arrogant and full of himself. But in England he was completely unknown. That's why his ghost returned to haunt the legislature and The Empress — to gratify his insatiable ego and craving for attention."

Adams cited a story told to him, he said, by a couple who had honeymooned at The Empress. "They were talking in the lower lobby and the newlywed wife noticed a man in an old-fashioned suit peeking around a corner at them. Then, as they walked up a staircase, she looked over her shoulder and the man was suddenly at the bottom of the stairs. She whispered to her husband, 'There he is again.' Now they both looked back — and the figure instantly disappeared before their eyes."

Adams also recounted to Smyth that an actor portraying Rattenbury in a historical pageant at the legislature had told him that he "was waiting for his fellow performers in the upper rotunda. They arrived and said, 'How did you get up here so quickly?' He said, 'What are you talking about? I've been standing here waiting for you.' They said, 'No, you haven't! We saw you downstairs and you came up in the elevator with us!' They realized Rattenbury's ghost must have been in the elevator with them."

Smyth wrapped up his article: "Things real. Or things imagined. Decide for yourself. But in British Columbia's cryptic capital, many believe there is more than political hot air swirling through the halls of the people's haunted house."

On October 28, 2020, as that year's Halloween approached, Bridgette Wilson of CBC (Canadian Broadcasting Corporation) News talked about "haunted stories of B.C. Parliament Buildings" being told online for free until October 30, giving this summary:

> Architect Francis Rattenbury, who built not only the parliament buildings, but the Empress Hotel as well, has been allegedly spotted wandering the legislature and hotel lawns in

his ghostly form, likely lamenting the days when he was kind of a big deal. Before, that is, his name became synonymous in some social circles with extra-marital affairs and murder. As the story goes, after being feted for his architectural accomplishments, Rattenbury started a relationship with a woman 30 years his junior.

It is safe to say the affair did not go over well with the prim and proper Victorian society set — let alone Rattenbury's wife. So, while still very much a living, breathing human, he ghosted Victoria. In other words, he split town.

Rattenbury married his new love. His young bride became cozy with a chauffeur. So cozy, in fact, that her jealous teenage lover would eventually sneak up behind Rattenbury and club him to death with a mallet.

◈   ◈   ◈

As in crime novels, true crimes are more than a murderous act; they are also studies of the whys and wherefores of human behaviour. In *Crime and Punishment* by Fyodor Dostoevsky, published in 1866 and generally regarded as one of the greatest crime novels of all time, there are themes aplenty, many of which also occurred in the deadly triangle of Francis, Alma, and George and are universal and timeless, although events differ. Online analyses by *Encyclopaedia Britannica*, *Spark Notes*, and litcharts.com say *Crime and Punishment*'s themes are love, violence, morality, guilt, free will, money, family, drugs, alcohol, alienation, suffering, judgment of the characters, and the characters judgment of one another. Was there fairness, was there justice? The perpetrator of the crime may not always have been bad.

Circa 260 BCE, *Aesop's Fables* gave this wise advice, well known and relevant down through the ages: "Be careful what you wish for, lest it come true." Francis wanted Alma, Alma wanted George, George wanted Alma. Result: Deadly Triangle.

ACKNOWLEDGEMENTS

Many, many thanks to the gracious, diligent librarians and archivists who, despite the Covid-19 lockdown, kindly and speedily answered my emails. Canada: Toronto Reference Library; University of Toronto Library; Provincial Archives of Saskatchewan; Greater Victoria Public Library; City of Victoria Archives; Royal BC Museum and Archives; Vancouver Public Library; Kamloops, British Columbia, Public Library; Penticton, British Columbia, Public Library; Library and Archives Canada; St. Ann's, Kamloops; St. Ann's, Victoria; and Havergal College, Toronto. Also: Office of the Clerk, Legislative Assembly of British Columbia. United Kingdom: British Library; British Newspaper Archive; National Archives; Dorset History Centre; Bournemouth Library; Ensbury Park Library; Hampshire Archives; Reach Licensing; Bodleian Library, University of Oxford.

My appreciation also to Professor Anthony A. Barrett, University of British Columbia and University of Heidelberg; Kass McGann, "Reconstructing History Patterns," reconstructinghistory.com; and crime author Delvin Chatterson for his incisive suggestions about the back cover wording.

A big thank-you to the talented, hard-working team at Dundurn Press, and to the book's editor, Michael Carroll — a first-rate pro and gentleman.

And a very special thank-you to Mr. John D. McKellar for his advice over the years.

NOTES

Chapter 1: Francis

1 Patrick Watson (host), *The Canadians: Faces of History — Francis Rattenbury*, television series, Historica Canada and Great North Productions, 1998.

2 Rhodri Windsor-Liscombe, "Rattenbury, Francis Mawson," *Dictionary of Canadian Biography*, vol. 16, biographi.ca/en/bio/rattenbury_francis_mawson_16E.html.

3 R.B.D., "Note & Comment," *Daily Colonist* (Victoria), February 19, 1932, 4. R.B.D. were the initials of Robert Broadfoot Dunn. He wrote the "Note & Comment" column for the *Daily Colonist* from the First World War until a few months before his death in 1938.

4 Michael Gates, "The Klondike Gold Rush," *The Canadian Encyclopedia*, July 19, 2009, thecanadianencyclopedia.ca/en/article/klondike-gold-rush.

5 In 1999, the Canadian Pacific Railway spun off Canadian Pacific Hotels into a separate company called Fairmont Hotels and Resorts. It ordered that the prefix "Fairmont" be added to the hotels' names, including the Empress. This led to protests by Victoria's newspapers and citizenry who viewed this as sacrilege. In response, Fairmont made no changes to the hotel's original exterior signage.

6 Philip Jensen, "The Architect and the Lady," *The Beaver* 79, no. 3 (June–July 1999): 22–27.

Chapter 2: Alma

1 Birth registration certificate #92-09-009883. Alma's father didn't do the registration until 1897, which may partly explain why she got away with saying she was younger than she was and newspapers were mistaken. It is also

inaccurate, as some past accounts have said, that she was born in Kamloops, British Columbia; others, Prince Rupert, British Columbia.

2   Some past accounts say that Alma attended Sisters of St. Ann's Academy, Victoria. Others say St. Ann's Kamloops. Incorrect. Carey Pallister, province archivist, Sisters of St. Ann Archives, Victoria, October 28, 2020, email to author: "I have checked the student records for St. Ann's Academy, Victoria, and Alma Victoria Clarke did not attend the school." Stephanie Baird, office administrator, St. Ann's Kamloops, October 27, 2020, email to author: "We have no record of Alma."

3   No byline, "Purely Personal," *Daily Colonist* (Victoria), September 4, 1899, 2, and September 6, 1899, 2.

4   Debra Latcham, archivist, Dr. Catherine Steele 1928 Archives, Havergal College, October 29, 2020, email to author: "Alma is listed as a graduate of 1912 in our alumnae directory. I have no other records."

5   *Daily Colonist*, May 1, 1907, 6.

6   *Daily Colonist*, May 10, 1907, 6.

7   *The Globe*, May 27, 1909, 14.

8   *Westward Ho!*, February 1910, 89.

9   *Daily Colonist*, April 30, 1911, 16.

10 Sir Michael Havers, Peter Shankland, and Anthony Barrett, *Tragedy in Three Voices: The Rattenbury Murder* (London: William Kimber, 1980), 21.

11 "The Cost of Canada's War," *Canadian War Museum*, warmuseum.ca/ firstworldwar/history/after-the-war/legacy/the-cost-of-canadas-war.

12 *Tragedy in Three Voices*, 22.

13 Full citation: "In Memory of Captain C.R.J.R. Dolling, 2nd Bn, Royal Welch Fusiliers, who died on August 20, 1916. Remembered with Honour. Flatiron Copse Cemetery, Mametz. I.D. 39, Commonwealth War Graves. Commemorated in perpetuity by the Commonwealth War Graves Commission."

14 By the end of the First World War, they had provided 12 hospitals — in France, Belgium, Serbia, Russia, Corsica, and Salonika.

15 *Tragedy in Three Voices*, 23.

16 The Croix de Guerre was created in 1915 by the French government to honour heroism. There were four degrees indicated by pins on the ribbon, such as a star and a palm leaf.

17 Pakenham married twice more for a total of four marriages. He helped start *Newsweek* magazine in 1933 and later became its Pacific Bureau chief, based in Tokyo. He died in 1957 at the age of 64.

18 *Daily Colonist*, December 6, 1923, 8.

Chapter 3: Alma and Francis

1   "Samuel Maclure: West Coast Architect," *Canada's Historic Places*, historic-places.ca/en/pages/7_samuel_maclure.aspx.

2 "Divorces," General Statistics Branch, Dominion Bureau of Statistics, Department of Trade and Commerce, 1926, publications.gc.ca/collections/collection_2016/statcan/84-D-20/CS84-D-20-1926-eng.pdf.
3 *Daily Colonist*, July 30, 1924, 2.
4 Washington State Board of Health, Bureau of Vital Statistics, Certificate of Marriage, License No. 7325, April 8, 1925. On the line where the certificate asked "number of marriages," Francis said two (the first being to Florrie). Alma also said two, although this was her third; maybe she meant two previously.
5 *Daily Colonist*, June 12, 1926, 8.
6 Washington State Board of Health, Bureau of Vital Statistics, Certificate of Marriage, License No. 8135, July 19, 1926.
7 *Tragedy in Three Voices*, 39.

Chapter 4: Villa Madeira

1 Reprinted in the *Globe and Mail*, January 12, 2008, F8.
2 F. Tennyson Jesse, ed., *Trial of Alma Victoria Rattenbury and George Percy Stoner* (London: William Hodge, 1935), 83.
3 *Tragedy in Three Voices*, 40–41.
4 His birth surname was Teschemacher. He was English, but because of anti-German sentiment in England during the First World War, he changed his German-sounding name to Lockton. He wrote the lyrics for 2,300 songs.
5 *Daily Express* (London, England), June 1, 1935.
6 Jozef Sterkens, "'Dark Haired Marie' Frank Titterton and Alma Rattenbury at the Piano 1932," (June 3, 1932, Keith Prowse Music), April 28, 2014, YouTube video, 2:36, youtu.be/Or3b02NhLU4.
7 Chris Iliades, "Why Boozing Can Be Bad for Your Sex Life," *Everyday Health*, January 4, 2012, everydayhealth.com/erectile-dysfunction/why-boozing-can-be-bad-for-your-sex-life.aspx.
8 *Globe and Mail*, January 12, 2008, F8.
9 "Bipolar Disorder," *Mayo Clinic*, mayoclinic.org/diseases-conditions/bipolar-disorder/symptoms-causes/syc-20355955.
10 Jesse, ed., *Trial*, 184.

Chapter 5: George

1 The primary source for this chapter is Jesse, ed., *Trial*.
2 Terry Reksten, *Rattenbury* (Vancouver: Douglas & McIntyre, 1978), 145, 196, note 4, chapter 11.
3 H. Charnock, "A Million Little Bonds: Infidelity, Divorce and the Emotional Worlds of Marriage in British Women's Magazines of the 1930s," *Cultural and Social History* 14, no. 3: 363–79.
4 Leonora Eyles, *Women's Own*, August 18, 1934, 565.
5 Jesse, ed., *Trial*, 5.
6 Jesse, ed., 19.

7   Jesse, ed., 36.

Chapter 6: Poor Ratz
1   The primary source for this chapter is Jesse, ed. *Trial*.
2   The term *mallet* originates from France in the late 14th to early 15th century. "'Le Maillet' — a hammer with a large, usually wooden head, used especially for hitting a chisel. The tool dates back to ancient Rome and Egypt, made from branches and roots. Mallets have been used by most types of craftsmen throughout history from furniture makers and boatbuilders to stonemasons and craftsmen. Today, mallets are also made of metal, plastic, or rubber." "The Wooden Mallet," Handsome & Co., handsomeandco.com.
3   Sean O'Connor, *The Fatal Passion of Alma Rattenbury* (London: Simon & Schuster, 2019), 439, note 16.

Chapter 7: Not Obliged
1   The primary source for this chapter is Jesse, ed., *Trial*.
2   The station no longer exists. The current one is across from where it was.

Chapter 8: Ghastly Nightmare
1   Phrase used by Alma in letter from prison to George, March 26, 1935.
2   Ronald Richenburg, Bodleian Reader Services, Bodleian Library, University of Oxford, March 18, 2022, email to author: "I have consulted the 1934 editions of both *The Solicitor's Diary* and *The Law List*. In both publications, the name of the firm is given as Other, Manning & Boileau-Tredinnick. I was unable to find any information about the unusual (and interesting) name 'Other.'"
3   Jesse, ed., *Trial*, 64–65.
4   *Tragedy in Three Voices*, 52.

Chapter 9: Who Comes First?
1   Published in 1935, text in "Four Love Songs" by Alma Clarke "Lozanne," Cambridge, 1992, SJ Music.
2   *Daily Express*, June 1, 1935.
3   *Bournemouth Daily Echo*, April 11, 1935, 1.
4   The newspaper headlines in this chapter and the following chapters are from the British Library, online newspapers; *Tragedy in Three Voices*; and Canadian newspapers.
5   *Tragedy in Three Voices*, 58–61.
6   *Tragedy in Three Voices*, 58–61.
7   *Tragedy in Three Voices*, 58–61.

Chapter 10: Adulterous Intercourse
1   The primary source for this chapter is Jesse, ed., *Trial*.

2   Michael Cross, "Star Solicitor Helped VIP Avoid Paedophilia Prosecution," *Law Society Gazette*, February 26, 2020, lawgazette.co.uk/law/star-solicitor-helped-vip-avoid-paedophilia-prosecution/5103226.article.

3   Sir David Napley, *Murder at the Villa Madeira: The Rattenbury Affair* (London: Weidenfeld & Nicolson, 1988), 76.

4   Jesse, ed., *Trial*, 33.

Chapter 11: Can't Recall

1   The primary source for this chapter is Jesse, ed., *Trial*.

2   Raymond Massey, *When I Was Young* (Toronto: McClelland & Stewart, 1976), 22; *Tragedy in Three Voices*, 117.

3   Jesse, ed., *Trial*, 33.

4   J.D. Casswell, *A Lance for Liberty* (London: George G. Harrap, 1961), 111.

5   Casswell, 111.

6   Casswell, 113.

Chapter 12: Cocaine?

1   The primary source for this chapter is Jesse, ed., *Trial*.

2   Casswell, *A Lance for Liberty*, 114.

Chapter 13: Oh, No!

1   The primary source for this chapter is Jesse, ed., *Trial*.

2   Casswell, *A Lance for Liberty*, 114.

3   Jesse, ed., *Trial*, 35.

4   Jesse, ed., 33.

5   *Tragedy in Three Voices*, 180.

6   Sir Travers Humphreys, *A Book of Trials* (London: Pan Books, 1953), 132.

Chapter 14: Peace

1   *Daily Express*, June 1, 1935.

2   *Daily Express*, June 1, 1935.

3   Jesse, ed., *Trial*, 40.

Chapter 15: One of Us

1   Casswell, *A Lance for Liberty*, 116.

2   Napley, *Murder at the Villa Madeira*, 222–23.

3   Darren Slade, "Rattenbury Murder: 'We All Knew It Was Him,'" *Bournemouth Daily Echo*, August 7, 2015.

Chapter 16: The Boys

1   *Tragedy in Three Voices*, 234.

2   Compton Christopher Pakenham in the U.S. World War II Draft Cards

Young Men, 1940–1947, National Archives and Records Administration (U.S.), World War II Selective Service Draft Cards, Fourth Registration, 1942, M1986 for the State of New Jersey.

3   Compton Christopher Pakenham in the U.S. World War II Army Enlistment Records, 1938–1946, National Archives and Records Administration (U.S.), Electronic Army Serial Number Merged File, Record Group 64, Box No. 00551, Reel 48.

4   *Courier News* (New Jersey), November 1, 1995.

5   York Membrey, reprinted in *Globe and Mail*, January 12, 2008, F8.

BIBLIOGRAPHY

BOOKS

Barrett, Anthony A., and Rhodri Windsor-Liscombe. *Francis Rattenbury and British Columbia Architecture in the Imperial Age*. Vancouver: University of British Columbia Press, 1983.

Havers, Sir Michael, Peter Shankland, and Anthony Barrett. *Tragedy in Three Voices: The Rattenbury Murder*. London: William Kimber, 1980.

Humphreys, Sir Travers. *A Book of Trials*. London: Pan Books, 1953.

Jesse, F. Tennyson, ed. *Trial of Alma Victoria Rattenbury and George Percy Stoner*. London: William Hodge, 1935.

Napley, Sir David. *Murder at the Villa Madeira: The Rattenbury Affair*. London: Weidenfield & Nicolson, 1988.

O'Connor, Sean. *The Fatal Passion of Alma Rattenbury*. London: Simon & Schuster, 2019.

Rattigan, Terence. *Cause Célèbre*. London: Hamish Hamilton, 1978.

Reksten, Terry. *The Fairmont Empress: The First Hundred Years*. Vancouver: Douglas & McIntyre, 1997.

———. *Rattenbury*. Vancouver: Douglas & McIntyre, 1978.

Windsor-Liscombe, Rhodri. "Rattenbury, Francis Mawson." *Dictionary of Canadian Biography*, vol. 16. Toronto: University of Toronto Press. biographi .ca/en/bio/rattenbury_francis_mawson_16E.html.

JOURNALS
"Divorces," General Statistics Branch, Dominion Bureau of Statistics, Department of Trade and Commerce, 1926, CS84-D-20-1926.

MAGAZINES
Jensen, Philip. "The Architect & the Lady." *Canada's History*, February 14, 2017. canadashistory.ca/explore/politics-law/the-architect-the-lady.

NEWSPAPERS
Canada
Daily Colonist (Victoria)
Globe (Toronto)
Globe and Mail (Toronto)
Province (Vancouver)

United Kingdom
Bournemouth Echo
Daily Express (London)
Daily Mail (London)
Daily Mirror (London)

VIDEOS
Wyntersea Productions. "Francis Rattenbury — The Architect." January 16, 2013. YouTube video, 2:21. youtu.be/vEBJUHxKHXo.

WEBSITES
"Capt Caledon Robert John Radclyffe Dolling." Find a Grave. findagrave.com/ memorial/56520862/caledon-robert_john_radclyffe-dolling.
"Captain C.R.J.R. Dolling." Commonwealth War Graves. cwgc.org/find-records/ find-war-dead/casualty-details/556482/c-r-j-r-dolling/.

"Compton Pakenham." MyHeritage. myheritage.com/names/compton_pakenham.

"In Memory of Captain Caledon Robert John Radclyffe Dolling, MC." *Yumpu*. yumpu.com/en/document/read/4235297/c-r-dolling-the-royal-canadian-legion-west-vancouver.

"Kamloops." Encyclopedia Britannica, September 19, 2013. britannica.com/place/Kamloops.

"100-Year-Old Newspaper Front Page Brings News of Peace to Kamloops." Kamloops This Week, November 10, 2018. kamloopsthisweek.com/local-news/100-year-old-newspaper-front-page-brings-news-of-peace-to-kamloops-4374430.

IMAGE CREDITS

INDEX

ABOUT THE AUTHOR

Deadly Triangle is Susan Goldenberg's tenth book and second true crime book. Her first one, *Snatched! The Peculiar Kidnapping of Beer Tycoon John Labatt* also was published by Dundurn. Her other books have been non-fiction business sagas on a wide variety of subjects. Susan won a Canadian Authors Award for her book *The Thomson Empire*, an unvarnished account of the business empire built by Canadian father and son Roy and Kenneth Thomson. She also writes for *Canada's History* magazine and does a monthly heritage column about the district of Toronto where she lives. Before writing books, Susan wrote for Canadian and American newspapers and won a Canadian Business Editors' Award. She has a B.A. in history and economics from the University of Toronto and an M.Sc. in journalism from Northwestern University, Chicago. She volunteers at a Toronto hospital and is on the board of a local historical society.